Marjorie Garber

SEX AND REAL ESTATE

Marjorie Garber is William R. Kenan, Jr., Professor of English and the director of the Humanities Center at Harvard University. She is the author of, among other books, *Vested Interests: Cross-Dressing and Cultural Anxiety*, *Symptoms of Culture*, and *Dog Love*. She lives in Cambridge, Massachusetts.

SEX AND REAL ESTATE

Sex
AND
REAL ESTATE

Why We Love Houses

MARJORIE GARBER

Anchor Books
A Division of Random House, Inc.
New York

Grateful acknowledgment is made to Pantheon Books, a division of Random House,
Inc., for permission to reprint an excerpt from *Memories, Dreams, Reflections* by C. G.
Jung. Copyright © 1961, 1962, 1963 by Random House, Inc.

The Library of Congress has cataloged the Pantheon edition as follows:
Garber, Marjorie
Sex and real estate : why we love houses / Marjorie Garber.
p. cm.
ISBN 0-375-42054-1
1. Home—United States—Psychological aspects.
2. Dwellings—United States—Psychological aspects.
3. Homeowners—United States—Psychology.
4. Home in popular culture—United States. I. Title.
HQ536.G349 2000
307.3'36— dc21   99-059107

Anchor ISBN: 0-385-72039-4

Book design by M. Kristen Bearse

www.anchorbooks.com

Printed in the United States of America

BVG 01

For Barbara

Contents

SEX AND REAL ESTATE

SEX AND REAL ESTATE

What do college students talk about with their roommates? Sex. Twenty years later, what do they talk about with their friends and associates? Real estate. And with the same gleam in their eyes.

Real estate today has become a form of yuppie pornography. The most intense discussions at office parties or dinner parties seem to revolve around house-hunting, outbidding, remodeling, and rent control. Upwardly mobile middle-aged professionals scan real estate ads with the same vague prurience with which they scan personal ads, not with the intention of pursuing anything, exactly, but for the pleasure of enjoying the fantasy such ads represent. And when they meet up with those old college roommates, the true confessions swapped over lunch are more likely to be about the hot housing market than the hot affair—stories of the dream, the stunner, the charmer, the oh-so-desirable one that got away.

Sex and real estate are two of the most erotic terms in the language. Especially when you put them together. "Real estate is to New York what the after-dinner orgy was to Rome," observes columnist Russell Baker with gloomy relish. "Nothing makes the New Yorker roar with pleasure more surely than a ghoulish tale of competing apartment hunters racing the undertaker over a threshold where the lone occupant of a decent apartment has just breathed his last." Baker deplores the fact that—as his own newspaper had reported a few days earlier—modern-day "tycoons" are paying in the high five figures a month for *rentals.* That's the high six figures (say, half a million dollars) a year.[1]

In Manhattan "no one can stop talking, incessantly and inanely, about real estate," reports a woman who travels back and forth between New York and Washington. The gossip at cocktail parties in the nation's capital may center on politics, but it's property values and twelve-foot ceilings that catch the eye and quicken the pulse in New York.

And not only in New York.

"We're not writing our offers in the back seats of cars," said one broker, commenting on the fast-moving sellers' market in New England. "But in fact, you don't have much time to act."[2] The same boomers who once fooled around in the back seat are now feverishly scribbling proposals of a different kind. Counseled to bring their checkbooks to open houses and to be prepared to make an offer on the spot, buyers are entering the housing market with more celerity (and more salaciousness?) than they once entered the marriage market, and outbidding one another for "unique properties." As an artist who has owned and restored six houses since 1982 remarked, "I never move to a house that I don't mean to grow old in, but when it comes to real estate, I'm slightly promiscuous."[3] In Britain, reports an acquaintance who is a journalist there, this phenomenon is referred to as "decor-porn."

When *House & Garden* magazine resumed publication in 1996 after a three-year hiatus, editor Dominique Browning set the tone of seduction, declaring that the magazine "ought to be a place where the reader can indulge in a kind of design promiscuity, falling in love at the turn of a page with completely different kinds of rooms, not knowing whether the affair will last a day or a lifetime."[4] The fact that promiscuity of this kind is not only permissible but encouraged and indeed "indulged" may say something, not only about the culture that we live in, but about why sex and real estate are such a hot couple today.

Unlike the "sex, drugs, and rock 'n' roll" of their adolescence and young adulthood, today's boomers have found that an interest in real estate can be both legitimate and legitimating: it's not immoral, illegal, or fattening. Mom and Dad will not only approve but boast of your accomplishments. (They'll also come visit.) The bumper sticker of a few years back, "He who has the most toys when he dies, wins," spoke vernacular boomer philosophy, but in this case the "toys" are also investments, bragging rights, lifestyles, and legacies.

Rich, poor, or middle-class, Americans have long equated owning a home with the American dream, and these days the dream merchants of real estate are everywhere, from the Internet to the cable networks to the ubiquitous, and ever more lavish, shelter magazines.

What most people lack today, perhaps even more than money, is time. And the quest for the perfect dream house—or houses, for in real estate monogamy is not a necessary virtue—allows us to substitute space for time. We build exercise rooms instead of exercising, furnish libraries instead of reading, install professional kitchens instead of cooking. And our fantasy spaces include not only houses themselves but house plans, house magazines, "home" stores, the movies, and the Web.

Dating Services

When you stop to think about it, buying and selling a house is a lot like dating. The same emotional overinvestment; the same daydreaming; the same quickening of the pulse; the lingering around the phone, willing it to ring; the surreptitious visit to the place where you know the desired one will be, just to catch another glimpse ("it won't hurt just to drive by—it's only a little bit out of the way"). And, of course, all too often, the same broken heart.

Check the real estate pages in your local paper. What you'll find are "singles" ads. Literally. "Smashing single." "Fabulous

renovated single w/custom euro kit." "Very handsome & oversized 2BR." "Exclusive, adorable, customized." "Cute as a But-
ton." "Enjoy this Charmer." "Cute & cozy." "Bright and cheerful
3 BR Colonial in super loc." Bright and cheerful, handsome and
oversized, adorable: these are the siren songs of houses with personality, fabulous, available "singles" waiting for mates.

The vocabulary of real estate is flirty, seductive, a come-on.
"Classic Beauty, Sutton Area," "Light & Lovely on West End
Avenue," "Prewar Beauty"—this is the language of New York
real estate. Compare these invitations to those for "Gorgeous,
statuesque brunette," "Classic Mediterranean good looks," "Soul
soothing, attractive, trim," or "Wonderful, professional SWF 41,
beautiful inside and out," all from the Meet Your Match personal
line of my local newspaper (or "Lakefront Lady," "Bachelor by
the Beach," and "Recyclable Antique," from the Dateline pages
of the *Chicago Tribune*). Whether for singles, beauties, or ser-
viceable antiques with elegant bones, these advertisements often
deliberately blur and cross the line between animate and inani-
mate, descriptive and seductive. What they promise is not just
a place but a relationship. Sunday real estate listings proclaim
the availability of "sophisticated," "striking, gracious," "exciting,"
"stunning yet authentic & charming" properties and invite you to
"call today."

The comparison between sex and real estate cuts both ways.
I've heard a woman describe a man as a "fixer-upper," raw material that needs some work but might be a good investment for
the future—what used to be called, in an era with slightly different benchmarks for value, a diamond in the rough. (Some
houses, like some spouses, fall into the dangerous category of "I
can change him—or her—after marriage.") On the other hand,
realty synonyms for "fixer-upper" include not only "handyman
special" but also "just needs love."[5]

And there is also this, from the classified real estate ads of
Harvard Magazine: "Looking for a match? Find one in our Vacation Rentals!"

Dazzling tropical oceanfront cottage, breath-taking scenery, hideaway location seeks kind, considerate renter who appreciates walks on the beach, snorkeling, sailing, or simply relaxing under the stars.

Here the distinction between cottage and owner has wittily collapsed altogether, and it's the cottage that seeks a perfect (kind and considerate) match.

Many buyers these days are like fraternity boys ogling a freshman face book, looking for the babes. Are looks really everything? What about character issues, beauty that is more than skin deep: the plumbing, the wiring, the basement, all that unglamorous stuff that is meant to last? Alas, sometimes it seems that no one cares. A coat of paint or a new carpet, a newly sodded lawn for the open house, freshly washed windows (squeaky clean now, but wait till the first rainstorm).

"There's a saying in the real estate business," a New York City broker confided to me. "Buyers are liars."

"*Buyers* are liars?"

"Yes," he said, with a nice mixture of sheepishness and bravado. "Buyers are liars."

But what did it mean? What could a buyer possibly lie about? From a home buyer's point of view, it would seem more likely that sellers, or indeed realtors, were liars, boasting of a property's "antique features" (read: falling-down condition), "waterside prospect" (read: confluence of the area's drainage), or "convenient location" (read: opposite the trolley stop, with attendant round-the-clock clamor).

But why should a *buyer* lie?

The saying, it turned out, was not unique to the New York market. A realtor in Madison, Wisconsin, confirmed that "buyers are liars" is a cliché in the industry. Buyers, it seems, lie about their financial situation, about the sum they are willing to spend, about their desires, and even about their preferences in location. They will say they are only interested in houses or apartments on the east side of town, and then call up weeks later to report that they have bought—through another broker—a property on the west side. They will insist on keeping to a strict dollar limit and then buy a house (from someone else) for a hundred thousand dollars more.

"This is one of the few businesses where the principals on both sides are complete amateurs," said the New York broker. As a result, he finds that he is often acting as a counselor as well as a salesman. "It's a crisis in your life," he says of his clients, both buyers and sellers. "This is a big change for both of them. So there is this emotional rawness which people bring to the table which I as a broker enjoy dealing with. I'm trying to be like the eye of the hurricane—the calm of the storm." When the crisis of selling is exacerbated by another personal crisis, like a divorce or even a move from one city to another, things can get out of control. "Dealing with the vagueness of a divorcing couple is difficult," he said. "That's a real wild card situation and it can go either way—any way."

"Everyone lies about sex," Jerry Seinfeld once observed. "People lie during sex. If it weren't for lies, there'd be no sex."[6] So lying, it turns out, is something else that sex and real estate have in common.

Blaming the Matchmaker

Sometimes house-buying (and house-selling) is like going on a blind date. You get matched with a likely prospect, but things can go wrong from the start. As in the wishful world of romance, both sides then often blame the matchmaker.

The house we were trying to sell was on a busy street. A very busy street. Our realtor estimated that of all the potential buyers she and her colleagues brought to look at it fully 70 percent wouldn't go inside. They sat in the car and said, "Forget it." On one occasion we were still at home when the doorbell rang and the realtor's key grated in the lock, setting up the face-to-face confrontation every seller (and buyer) tries to avoid. There on the doorstep stood three reluctant candidates (it would be exaggerating to call them "suitors"). They looked everywhere but at us—or at the house. (This is a difficult thing to do when you are actually *in* a house.) Staring at the floor, they couldn't help seeing the floor. Carelessly staring off into space, they had to encounter walls, windows, stairways, fireplaces. They couldn't look *away,* because every way they looked was—our house. In short, the combination of mulish indifference and aloof politeness that one adopts on the subway or the supermarket line failed completely to mask the fact that they had come to a house—*our* house—to look it over and see if they found it attractive. Attractive enough to "want to see it again." Even enough to make an offer, a proposal (you see how marital, or at least prenuptial, this language becomes). They didn't, and beat a hasty retreat, dragging the poor realtor with them.

Not that I blame them for not wanting to meet us. When we were house-hunting we had a similar experience: our realtor had called to tell the sellers we would arrive at a certain hour, expecting them to vacate the premises and thus allow us, in the universal manner of real estate browsers, to imagine ourselves in residence ("the couch will go against this wall"; "that corner would be perfect for the breakfront"; "what if we combine these two rooms to make a bigger kitchen?"). This space of fantasy—grown-ups literally "playing house"—is crucial to the process. So we were all disconcerted to find that the owner, a regal older woman, was not only at home but at dinner, eating something or other that wafted its cooking smells through every room in the house. The broker, securing her permission, led us doggedly from room to room, but it was clear the magic opportunity was lost. We couldn't wait to get out of there. There's nothing that's more inhibiting to a feeling of heady romance than finding the lawful spouse unexpectedly at home. Falling in love with a house can be like starting an affair. You don't want to be reminded that the loved one has an ordinary (and boring) life of his or her own.

On the other hand, as in love, so in real estate—a rival suitor's desire sometimes acts as a spur to one's own infatuation. "In the heat of passion, people promise anything," said Barbara Corcoran, the owner of a Manhattan brokerage, about the "over-heated" co-op market in New York City. After choosing impulsively or promising more than they can deliver under the pressure of competition, buyers sometimes suffer morning-after remorse. Said the executive director of the Real Estate Board of New York, "It's like choosing a spouse. You don't do it because somebody is pressing you to or because you hear somebody else is engaged to the same person."[7] Oh yeah? Remember the "popular girls" and "popular boys" in high school? What made them so desirable? Was it just the fact that they were already desired? Competition makes the heart grow fonder—and sometimes creates a bidding war.

When a Manhattan couple lost out in two bidding wars for West Side apartments, the sensation was, the wife recalled, like going out on a first date and "sort of falling in love; like you want to spend the rest of your life with him—and he doesn't call you back."[8] (To add insult to injury, a newspaper photo caption of the pair, picking up on the theme of disappointed love, declared them "Two Time Losers.") Fear of "rejection" haunts those who try to buy into the New York co-op market, where more and more applicants with sufficient funding are turned down by selective (or snobbish) co-op boards. "If the buyers—whether young or old, gay or straight, single or a family with children—do not meet some undisclosed profile, then they are rejected without any explanation, leaving buyers, seller and agents frustrated and guessing."[9]

Philosopher Robert Nozick has criticized governments that "forbid capitalist acts between consenting adults," arguing (in a book published in 1974) that the state that regulates least is the most just. But ten years later he went to court to force his then-landlord, novelist Erich Segal, to roll back an increase on a rent-controlled apartment overlooking the Charles River. Nozick had rented Segal's condominium for $1,900 a month. Instead of the desired $500 increase Segal wound up lowering the rent to $1,300, then paying Nozick $21,000 in "overcharges" and an additional $10,000 to vacate the apartment so it could be sold.[10] The spectacle of the sentimental author of *Love Story* ("Love means never having to say you're sorry") locked in battle with the libertarian author of *Anarchy, State and Utopia* may have offered wry amusement to those who already wonder whether academics practice what they preach. Certainly, whatever else it demonstrated, this multi-year court battle suggests that when it comes to real estate, "capitalist acts between consenting adults" are being performed at the participants' risk. In real estate transactions there's no such thing as free love.

Mixing and Cruising

In general buyers tend to imagine themselves as besting other buyers, winning the hand of the most popular house on the block. But there's a kind of "rescue fantasy" that also sometimes enters the picture. ("You poor house, downtrodden and afflicted by the present owner's terrible taste. I'll take you away from all this, give you a new coat of paint, get rid of those awful drapes . . .") The Cinderella house—or the Beast that becomes a beauty when looked upon with the eye of love—is one of the great dreams of the house hunter. It's no accident that so many stories of "house love" begin with the discovery of a neglected, falling-down property that needs to be nursed back to health and beauty—to be, in short, Understood.

The open-house experience seems oddly reminiscent of the mixers of my college days. You primp and preen, trying to make things look as good as possible. You vacuum and dust and bake bread and put out fresh flowers. Then everybody stands around and sizes up the goods. If you're a prospective buyer, you get to check out the scenery—and the competition. Is that couple caucusing in the corner about to make an offer? If you're a seller, you've absented yourself from the open house, and indeed from any showing. But that doesn't keep you from identifying with your house, and resenting reported slights confided by your realtor. (The hallway is *not* pink! It's a subtle shade of adobe or terra cotta. What do they mean, "not funky enough"?) As confident as you may feel, or think you feel, coming up empty at the mixer level may lead to the desire for a makeover. After being told several times that our bedroom was "peach," a color I associate with the worst of the Doris Day fifties, we called in the painter and had it redone in nineties ochre.

Some people cruise open houses to get decorating tips, or as a way of spending a lazy Sunday afternoon. They may not really be in the market at all. Others are just trying to figure out how to "solve the impossible demands of space" in their own houses or apartments, or are stirred by yet baser motives: "prurience, reassurance, the gratifying condescension of seeing how other people decorate" (my informant here is a battle-weary Manhattanite). And the experience can be complicated, as reported in a *New Yorker* short story called "Real Estate."

At first looking at other houses on Sunday afternoons—wandering across other people's floors and carpets, opening closets to look at other people's shoes—gave Ruth a thrill. The tacky photos on the potter's piano. The dean with no doorknobs. The orthodontist with thirty built-in cubbyholes for his thirty tennis shoes. Wallpaper peeling like birch skin. . . . But soon she backed off. "I could never buy a house that had that magazine on the coffee table," she said once.[11]

Open houses don't always work, any more than mixers do—a 1991 survey by the National Association of Realtors suggested that "just three percent of people who had bought existing homes found them through an open house"[12]—but they sometimes get realtors and buyers together, which can lead to a future sale (of a different house).

Perhaps most evocative of the dating game is the agonizing experience of the seller waiting for the phone to ring. The forced passivity of the post-house-showing period when there's nothing to do but wait will evoke familiar memories in any woman brought up in the fifties and sixties. It's so easy to get your hopes up, and then see them dashed. (Pop music fans may recall the sensations feelingly recorded in Vikki Carr's "It Must Be Him.") Your palms can go sweaty with the tension of the moment. ("They came for a second visit, so that must mean they're interested. Will they call? *Please* let them call . . .")

Meantime the buyers are asking themselves: Did I seem too eager? Was the offer I made too low—or embarrassingly, uncoolly high? Is there a Rival Purchaser with an inside track? Maybe a lowball offer will carry the day. Nothing ventured, nothing gained, you think. But then there's the dread fear of insulting the seller with a too-low figure. Will he or she ever speak to you again? If properties in New York City are "trading" (NYC jargon for what much of the rest of the country calls "selling") at "within 5 percent of the asking price"—up from the 75 percent of only a few years ago—you can outsmart yourself in trying for a smart buy. In a market where people identify so closely with their houses and apartments, flattery, especially with a price tag to match, can get you everywhere.

But what about when your house lingers on the market and doesn't sell? This happened to us for fifteen long (and nail-biting) months, and the narcissistic wound was amazingly painful. We felt rejected, even humiliated. Our walls had become wallflowers.

There's a technical term for this in real estate jargon. We were the unhappy possessors of a "stale house"—one that had been on the market too long, had grown old and familiar to prospective buyers, and was being passed over for fresher faces, newer entrants into the market. In a curious twist of fate and language, it's the stale house that "will get a bad reputation."[13] It's just too—available. Not hard enough to get.

There are some houses that are "family," and some that are *liaisons dangereuses.*

After a while, we began to think that the house we were selling was the kind of house that you have an affair with and decide not to marry. It had elements of glamour and style (bleached floors, granite kitchen counters, marble fireplace surround) but its location on that busy street meant it wouldn't be easy to resell. And some of the "designer" elements that struck us as most pleasing (the round window, the mirror in the hallway that cleverly created the illusion of a double-sized space) seemed to make purchasers nervous. Was it "homey" enough for them? Domestic, cozy, reliable? Or was its beauty off-putting? Was it, in short, the kind of house you could take home to Mother? Things weren't helped when the realtor—actually the Big Boss Realtor, arriving in his tinted sunglasses and breast-pocket handkerchief to explain to us why our house was still on the market after all those months—leaned forward and confessed that ours was the "kind of house that helped sell other houses." *Ouch.* Good enough to flirt with and put prospectives in the mood to settle down—elsewhere.

Face Books

Though looking *for* real estate may be stressful, looking *at* it can be incredibly alluring. High-end real estate circulars arriving daily in the mail are like *Playboy* (or, indeed, like the aptly named *Penthouse*), with opulent, expensively produced centerfolds. Where the Playmate of the Month is always airbrushed to perfection, the Playhouse of the Month poses, pertly, on an impossibly green lawn against an eternally blue sky in a four-color, glossy, heavyweight, fancy, magazinelike catalogue. New York's Douglas Elliman mails its "Treasury of Fine Homes" to over a hundred thousand people, including "the heads of Fortune 500 companies, all the heavy-hitters nationwide." Individual brochures, still in full color but featuring a single property, flood the market, conferring publicity if not always producing sales. "It's about ego," says one upscale broker. "It's a feel-good for the seller." For me, too, though I don't intend to purchase any of these pinups. I like to have them around. "Display advertising is more impressive than classified. Photos are more upscale than straight copy. And four-color is more impressive than black and white," explains the head of a major agency. "Selling houses is showbiz," said one Florida developer who specializes in gated communities. "You go after the emotions. We don't go out and show a gate in the ad. But we try to imply and do it subtly. In our ad, we don't even show houses. We show a yacht. We show an emotion."[14]

Once on a visit to Boca Raton I saw an ad for a new restaurant announcing optimistically that it was "Soon to be famous in South Florida." This is the logic of the cart-before-the-horse, what's called *hysteron proteron*, the fallacy of assuming as a premise something that's yet to be proved. It's a technique that works very well in real estate, where what you are buying is prestige, "a good address," and—above all—desire.

"Postcard views from floor-to-ceiling windows," proclaimed one invitation to purchase. The property in question was the penthouse at the Trump International Hotel and Tower on Central Park West, but don't let that piece of glamour distract you. What's really fascinating here is the way, in such real estate come-ons, life is advertised as imitating art. Even, or especially, commercial or popular art. What is desirable is the recognizable, the already seen, the virtually experienced, the framed.

"Just published in a renowned national magazine," read an ad for an expensive residence in Boston's Back Bay, "this incredible Penthse offers some of the most beaut. rms in the city." Here again, what art critics might call an "inset"—a play-within-a-play, for example, or a painting or mirror within a painting—raises the old question of appearance and reality. Which is more "true"? Will we find the Back Bay penthouse especially alluring because it's already become "famous"? Is what we "recognize" as beauty something that has been certified by an aesthetic expert—in this instance the editors of the "renowned national magazine"? Are we paying (the price tag for this listing was a cool $2.6 million) for its celebrity, for the fact that it's already been discovered by a talent agent?

The point may be even clearer in the case of the "magazine-quality kitchen" featured in an advertisement for a suburban house. What makes the kitchen desirable is that it resembles not a kitchen, but a kitchen-in-a-magazine. It's easy to imagine what this might mean (slate or granite counters, under-mount sinks, cherry cabinets, central work island with bar sink, miniature halogen lighting, and so forth), and, in fact, when you're trying to save space in a real estate ad "magazine-quality" may be very effective shorthand. But the allure of this house's kitchen is a kind of Zelig allure: the prospective buyer imagines herself or himself magically transported to the pages of *Architectural Digest* or *Elle Décor*. "Celebrity-style" kitchens is what another article calls them—but is the celebrity in question the supposed owner, the kitchen itself, or (most probably) an imagined occupant, like Julia Child or the Galloping Gourmet, as seen on TV?

Known in the trade as shelter magazines, those glossy, delicious-to-the-eye home and garden monthlies, from *Architectural Digest* (*AD* to its intimates) to *Elle Décor* and *Metropolitan Home,* have an appeal that is undeniable—and growing. In the expansive 1980s, "interior design magazines were almost as avidly followed in some circles as the stock market,"[15] according to the *New York Times*. What they sell is desire. "We love the voyeurism of going into somebody else's home," remarked Browning, the editor of *House & Garden.* Calling herself a " 'shelter magazine' junkie," Browning aptly identified both the addictive passion and the permission to be nosy that makes these journals the eye-candy of the boomer crowd.[16] The median age of readers for the "shelters" is the early forties; their median income is somewhere between $45,000 (*House Beautiful*) and $63,000 (*Architectural Digest*).[17]

Have you ever noticed that there are usually *no people* in the luscious layouts of these magazines? The overstuffed couch, the Persian rug, the grassy lane, the inglenook with the nautical view—all are empty, available, inviting. Though some home-decorating magazines have experimented with human beings as photo props—"hired models in real homes" in the European editions of *Elle Décor,* and household servants in uniform in *House & Garden* ("we needed a figure for scale," explained *H&G*'s editor)—the more common practice is to omit the humans and focus on the furniture, plants, and dogs. "When readers look at an interior," says *Architectural Digest*'s editor in chief Paige Rense, "part of the enjoyment is actively projecting themselves into it." Besides, adds Ingrid Sischy of *Interview,* "pictures of hubby and the wife" now look "old-fashioned," since family structures have changed.[18] Children, "less old-fashioned" as accessories, make occasional cameo appearances along with the more usual pugs and whippets, but the overwhelming majority of magazines still prefer the allure of the perfectly set table and the deliciously furnished, temptingly empty room.

It's crucial, I think, that such images are visually untenanted. It means they're waiting for *you*. To see someone else actually dwelling in these coveted spaces, even if it's the Honorable Rosina Lytton Cobbhold and her infant daughter posing "in the water gardens with spectacular Knebworth House in the background" (a typical snippet from Britain's popular lifestyles magazine *Hello!* is to foster quite a different spirit of emulation.[19] "If the people are shown too prominently, it shuts the reader out," says Paige Rense. Far better, for the shelter magazines, to keep offstage and out of camera range the Westchester couple with the magnificent French garden ("combines echoes of antiquity with a startling modernism that is rare in a private landscape" says *House & Garden*),[20] or the carefully anonymous "media executive and his wife, relocated to Los Angeles," whose Martha's Vineyard house was redesigned by Robert A. M. Stern (*Architectural Digest*).[21] As the come-on ads have it, you have only to insert "*your name* (or in this case, *your picture*) here." This is fantasy space, waiting to be entered by the wistful, prurient, or lustful reader, the 900-number of your dream house, where what awaits you is the stuff of your own desires. Two new shelter magazines of 1997, *Wallpaper* and *Nest*, took the idea of fantasy spaces in a different direction. *Wallpaper* published pictures of "glamorous pseudo-homes occupied by young models," reported the *New York Times*, while in the pages of *Nest* there were photos of Barbie's 1992 Dream House "as if it were an actual interior."[22]

Designer Mario Buatta suggested to a reporter that the shelter magazines' attraction was "like hero worship. The magazine becomes a sort of wish book. They are looking in the windows of houses where they would never be invited."[23]

I recognize the feeling. When I first moved to the place where we now live I used to take long, aimless walks in the evenings, when the lights were on in the town's many eighteenth- and nineteenth-century houses. Without precisely peering in the windows, you could still get a quick glimpse of color, shape, and form—ideas for decorating and for fantasizing about a shingled cottage of one's own. If this sounds like Browning's "voyeurism," it should. And yet it's not only acceptable to ogle other people's wallcoverings, in some circles it's absolutely de rigueur. Advertisers are delighted with the demographics. As the *New York Times* business section noted, homes—and especially gardens—have "emerged as the baby boomers' chic new playgrounds."[24]

Techniques of Seduction

House love can be addictive, producing sensations that might lead some to want to join a kind of Buyers Anonymous. One buyer told a broker that he wanted a New York apartment so lavish that when people walked into it they would gasp. She found the perfect place, with floor-to-ceiling windows and panoramic views. The problem was, someone else had just bought it a month ago. The enterprising broker invited the owner to name an impossible selling price, and they settled on $6 million, a markup of $2 million over the previous price. ("Don't tell my wife," he implored. "We've already called in a decorator.") When the broker took the buyer there, he gasped. And bought.[25]

But it's not only the very rich who fall prey to galloping house desire.

At the beginning of the 1990s the National Association of Home Builders met in Atlanta to chart strategies for the new decade. "The children of the sexual revolution are looking to put romance back in their lives and return to traditional lifestyles," said a Chicago-based designer. "We're trying to reflect that nostalgia in the area of design. People seem to be looking for touches they would have remembered from visiting their grandparents." The word "romantic" was on everyone's lips. Buyers were seeking "the romantic touches that give a classical feeling, such as fireplaces (especially in the master bedroom and master bath)," she said. "The children's bedroom is another place to really tug at the heart. It all moves back to the issue of hitting the romantic soft spot."

"You've got to push their romantic buttons," added a designer from New York. "People aren't finding romance outside the home any more—they're going out less and staying home more. What we're looking to do is to add charm, and that's not costly. We're not trying to build the Taj Mahal every time."[26] In fact the Taj Mahal, built by a Mogul emperor after the death of his wife and widely regarded as perhaps the greatest architectural love token in history, is one of the phantasmic ideals, the dream houses of culture. Only we want it built and furnished for us *now*, while we are alive to enjoy it.

Seductive galleries of homes to browse through on television or the Internet are ready to accommodate our fantasies. The virtual-reality "walk-through" has become a feature of the high-end market, whether in New York or in Hong Kong. Taken with a fish-eye lens, and allowing a 180-degree view, "left to right, floor to ceiling," such tours are not only a convenience for the busy tycoon, but also the ultimate in voyeurism. You peek, you peer, you pry—and no one but your accommodating broker knows you're there. The very word "broker," while it has always meant agent or intermediary in a general sense (*insurance broker, pawnbroker, stockbroker*), used also to be a synonym for a pander, procurer, pimp, matchmaker, marriage agent, or go-between in love affairs.

Emotion is in high supply in such transactions, and it's often sexualized. The hard-to-satisfy clients in Richard Ford's *Independence Day* are desperate to find a nice house they can "both afford and fall in love with." At one promising showing the realtor-narrator observes that the wife had "the look of 'this is the one, this is the place' written all over her flushed, puffy face."

But when her interest wanes he doesn't know how to restimulate it, how to "bring the hormonal roller coaster into the station."[27] That telltale symptom, the inadvertent flush, is a sign—in literature as well as life—of the erotics of real estate. In a recent *New Yorker* short story a philandering husband is temporarily distracted by a passion for his new "dream house." "The simplest discussion—of doorjambs or gutters—made his blood move around his face and neck like a lava lamp. Roof-shingle samples—rough, grainy squares of sepia, rose, and gray—lit his eyes up like love. He brought home doorknob catalogues and phoned a plasterer or two. After a while, however, she could see him tire and retreat, recoil even—another fling flung."[28]

"Hit the prospect at every emotional level," counsels a decorating consultant who advises home builders. Some decorators fantasize fictional characters to give a house "a lived-in look with plenty of personality"—where "personality," a term of art in the interior design business, is a deliberate contradiction in terms, the illusion of a person in residence in an empty dwelling. "We write a script just like for a movie," says a representative of a California decorating firm hired to glamorize a development in Lakewood, New Jersey.[29] Decorating fees for model houses may approach 20 to 30 percent of the house's selling price.

Professional "stagers" now advise sellers in cities like Washington, Los Angeles, Miami, and some of the New York City suburbs on how to make their houses more appealing to upscale buyers—whisking away family photos (too distracting and personal), replacing dark bedspreads with light ones, locating potted plants in front of cracked or peeling walls, even renting furniture that looks better than the owner's own. Staging is analogous to the much-disputed practice of "propping" in shelter magazine layouts, a practice that has been called the home-design magazines' "dirty little secret": bringing in museum-quality furniture, chenille throws, borrowed art, and masses of flowers to produce the illusion of a beautifully arranged "home." As one freelance stylist commented, "Interiors used to be so much more theatrical. Everyone wants it clean and natural now. But let me tell you: The authentic look is even more expensive to do."[30] The stager, whose job title proudly displays the elements of theatricality and performance essential to a successful home sale, is something between a personal trainer for your house and an old-fashioned society chaperone (the kind that makes the most of her charge's looks rather than policing her behavior). The cost for such a makeover? Sometimes as high as $50,000, if the stager remodels the rooms and overhauls the furniture. "I think it is the best money a seller can spend," says a San Francisco broker. "If a homeowner is going to retire and this is their last big sale, then I make a very strong presentation for them to use a stager."[31]

Designers of new homes sometimes spray them with scent, aromatherapy for the buyer. One sprays Joy cologne all over his most expensive units.[32] Others use cinnamon or other "homey" scents. Realtors often urge sellers to bake bread or roast a chicken so that the smell wafts through the house. (After a while, when we were house-hunting, we got used to seeing these accoutrements to a meal set out on the kitchen counter, and we ourselves kept a special section in the freezer for "exhibition breads" that could be reheated for showing after showing.) The scent of a wood fire is another olfactory come-on, subliminally whispering "home" into the ears—or, more accurately, the nasal passages—of browsing potential buyers. "Say the Smiths are looking for a new home," said an interior designer. "When they enter a model, they should see the logs burning in the fireplace, maybe smell a pie in the oven. It makes them comfortable and that's what leads to sales."[33] It's all a matter, apparently, of emotional rapport: the "need to arouse a feeling of kinship with the house." Such tactics can backfire, too. A couple I know who have been looking for a suitable New York apartment for quite a while now viscerally recoil at the smell of bread baking when they're shown a property; to them it says "real estate hype," not "this is home."

Real estate today is theater, show business, seduction—and

fashion. Like clothing lines, new houses are sold through the seductive power of "models"—or, in the case of the luxury home market, supermodels, tricked out in fashionable and flattering outfits. The average U.S. home buyer sees up to a dozen houses before making an offer to buy (desperate city apartment seekers may see twice or three times as many), so "a well-executed model makes its subject stand out from the competition." Furnishings "can add a touch of glamour," and—as with tall, striking runway supermodels from Naomi Campbell to Linda Evangelista— "furnished models also look larger."[34]

Older houses and apartments, showing the signs of their years, are sometimes prepped by brokers for a cosmetic makeover. It's no accident that the term "face-lift" has migrated into the sphere of property. The famous "white paint and ficus number" is always popular: paint the house or apartment white, camouflage flaws with a ficus tree. But so too are tricks with mirrors and lighting, old standbys in the world of human cosmetology. Where aging humans seek the flattery of dim, atmospheric lighting, though, and glance only warily at mirrors, sellers of older homes are urged to increase the wattage of their light bulbs and install mirrors everywhere to create the illusion of spaciousness. ("Place a vertical strip of mirror beside windows that have limited views, for the same optical delusion.")[35]

As for the middle-aged owners of these "older homes," many find themselves strongly attracted to new construction after a lifetime of restoration, remodeling, and repair. Older buyers are lured by "pastels that flatter older skins and are easier on the eyes." "No one has ever bathed in that tub," I remember thinking, desirously, when I toured an elegantly furnished unit that boasted a pristine marble bath. New houses are like debutantes coming out for the season, whose unspoiled freshness and newness may recommend themselves to the jaded appetite. Is this another version of the fantasy of beginning life over again with a younger, more beautiful partner—or a younger, more beautiful self?

Houses have always occupied a central place in the imaginations of poets, writers, and philosophers, as well as in the minds of architects, real estate agents, and home dwellers. But what *is* the relationship we imagine with our houses? The chapters that follow will explore the cultural role of the house as lover, mother, body or self, fantasy, trophy, history, and escape. In all of these visions, as we will see, the imagined house is a dream house. Yet, as anyone who has ever bought—or aspired to buy—a house can testify, that has never kept people from trying to bring the dream to material life.

THE HOUSE AS BELOVED

Falling in Love with a House

Anyone who doubts the possibility of falling in love with a house—with all that implies of fast-beating heart, sweaty palms, and waiting for the phone to ring—just hasn't met the right one yet. "Your house is the other person in your life," an architectural designer once said to me. In our present-day culture the house often plays the role of lover, partner, significant other—the dream date and the dream mate—the one who will realize our desires and give a purpose to our plans and days.

The language of love and desire is so common in house-hunting stories that we tend to forget that it's a figure of speech. What Freud called "the overestimation of the object"—regarding the beloved as more beautiful, wiser, more amiable, more perfect than a more "objective" observer might report—is part and parcel of the experience of falling, and remaining, in love.

Realtors and house agents often find themselves functioning as therapists, psychologists, and marriage counselors.

- "Do you believe in love at first sight?" inquires a shelter magazine rhetorically, answering its own query with a home owner's confession: "I told the real-estate agent I wanted to live in this house before I'd even gone upstairs."[1]
- "Sometimes a buyer is infatuated with a house even before he walks through the threshold," reports a real estate columnist, who hastens to reassure her readers that "there's

nothing inherently wrong with feeling passion for a particular property." More than 50 percent of all buyers experience such overweening desire, according to an expert in the
field.

- "I've seen people fall in love with a house that wasn't right
  for them," says the former president of the National Association of Realtors.
- "If you bond emotionally to a property, you're in danger of
  making a blunder from which you cannot recover," cautions
  a broker for a national chain.[2]

Living Together

It makes sense to think of buying a house or apartment as a moment of stock-taking and self-definition. The question, Is this
where I want to spend the rest of my life? leads, all too naturally,
to a related question: Is this the person I want to spend it with?
Sometimes this can have unexpectedly positive effects, from a
romantic point of view.

A friend of mine had been dating two men with quite different sets of interests and goals. She wasn't at all sure which of
them was right for her, or whether either was, and the situation
had been going on for several months (one man was in New
York, the other in Boston) when she decided to sell her apartment in the city and move to a more spacious place in the nearby
suburbs. When the broker showed her a charming and idio-
syncratic house with a lawn sloping down to a pond she was
charmed—and so was her Boston boyfriend, who had gone with
her to look at the property. "All of a sudden I could just see our
life together," she told me later. On the spot they decided to buy
the house and move in together. The house and the ideas and
fantasies of a life that could be lived there had acted as a kind of
couples counselor or marriage broker, breaking through the wall
of indecision and offering her a vision of her future.

Here's another, perhaps more pragmatic, example, in which a

real estate purchase again precipitated a wedding. A New York City couple who wanted to buy a West End Avenue apartment were advised by the building's co-op board that they would be more "acceptable" (for purely *financial* reasons, this group of urban sophisticates hastened to explain) if they were married. The broker, doing double duty as realtor and *schadchen* (matchmaker), had a further suggestion which was also adopted: that the ceremony should be performed by the Episcopal priest who was selling the apartment.[3]

Yet with these romantic pleasures inevitably come dangers. As in the case of other kinds of love at first sight, wise heads warn you to go slow. "Even if you fall in love with a house, you ought to take your time and look at the surrounding area," recommends a real estate advisor, the cultural therapist of our times. "Bond with an agent who will steer you clear of the wrong purchase." Easy for you to advise, if you're the one who's not head-over-heels in love. But if you are? Will your one-and-only wait around?

"Is the property so attractive that you dare not wait to make your offer?" If so, something like a prenuptial agreement is recommended. "Be sure that your contract is conditional on a thorough home inspection." In short, "Try not to fall for the first pretty façade you see," since "Emotion can blind house hunters who fall in love at first sight."[4]

There is also this, from yet another real estate maven: "The home buyers most likely to regret their purchase decisions are those who fall in love with a house before finding out what they need to know about it. In that respect, buying a house is a bit like a whirlwind romance: Love at first sight (or site?) can be exhilarating, but it also can prove to be disappointing—and very expensive."[5] As one buyer confessed, "The reality is you fall in love with it (the property) first, then figure it (the price) out later."[6]

And as painful as love can be, *lack* of emotion can be a sign that there is something wrong with you. "Worry if you don't fall in love after a lengthy home search," counsels a realty column.

"Certainly there are perils that can await the love-at-first-sight home buyer who is blinded by emotion. But the prospect who can't seem to find anything that suits her tastes may also have problems."[7]

Consider the case of those perpetually unsatisfied clients in Richard Ford's novel *Independence Day*, who are trying, perhaps too hard, to fall in love. The wife is "intent on loving [a house] as much as possible" before her husband finds fault with the latest prospect, while the husband, "even in spite of loving the house" they are shown, is "inventorying his brain for something more to say, some barrier to erect." They leave without making an offer, even though the realtor thinks this may be the house they've been hoping for, "the fabled long-shot house, the one I'd never shown them."[8] Here the trajectory of desire (the perfect house is by definition ideal, unattainable, inaccessible) gets in the way of the possibility of fulfillment. Like Groucho Marx's famous attitude toward exclusive clubs ("I don't care to belong to any club that will accept me as a member"),[9] this kind of "house love" is, so to speak, self-*un*fulfilling. It is designed—as the realtor finally sees—to fail.

But is this use of a term like "love" just hype, a careless and inflated way of thinking and speaking? Is love an emotion that should be focused only on ambient and sensate beings and not on a possession, however magnificent or comforting? Is there something *wrong* with actually "loving" a house? To think so is to disavow some of the most profound and recurrent emotions bodied forth in our culture.

Films, novels, and even poems are full of love scenes—between people and their houses. "House love" is an idea that has been immortalized in literature—though often it is underestimated as merely a figure or a ploy. Falling in love with a house —what might be called love at first site—is a common phenomenon of both dinner party conversations and modern fiction. Often these encounters are highly romantic *and* highly erotic, combining elements of dream and lust, as the prospective buyer stands, mouth half-open, staring at the front door of her dream mansion, or the house hunter runs his hand lovingly down the curve of the banister. Nor are such moments only a by-product of contemporary malaise or over-the-topness; as we'll see, the passion for a house—often embodied in telltale signs like the blush or heavy breathing—has had a long, if not always honorable, history.

Love at First Site

For a fast course in this love-at-first-site emotion, nakedly and comically displayed, we might look to Eric Hodgins's wonderful little novel *Mr. Blandings Builds His Dream House* (1946), later made into a film starring Cary Grant and Myrna Loy. Shown the "old Hackett place" with its Colonial beams, dilapidated outbuildings, and splendid view, the advertising man and his wife are instantly smitten:

> Mr. and Mrs. Blandings traveled back to New York in a heavy flush; in a flush, still, they sat in the New York apartment which had been home to them until that afternoon. It was home no longer; the old Hackett place on Bald Mountain was home, now. They wanted it as once, fifteen years ago, they had wanted each other, and the symptoms were much the same: ravishing desire at one instant; at the next, a sick slump into hopelessness that the desire would ever be fulfilled.[10]

Many modern house hunters will recognize this sensation of mingled lust and shame. How could anything—anything *else*? anything at *our* age?—stir such uncomfortable passions? Even when the Blandingses' naïvely generous (and panicked) offer is accepted, they are in a fever of anticipation to be in residence.

Impatience suddenly curdled in Mrs. Blandings. It would be *weeks* before she could begin this new life to which she had dedicated herself. Her husband and Mr. Hackett had first to sign a purchase agreement; then, after an infinite hocus-pocus that would involve her husband's young friend and attorney, Bill Cole, Mr. Hackett, and heaven knew who all else, the deed would be signed in the Lansdale County Courthouse and the property "conveyed." It was tedious beyond belief.[11]

The love affair between the Blandings and their house comes as a kind of early midlife crisis or seven-year itch. The couple are seized with passionate feelings, and they fall in love, together, with a third party: the old Hackett place. A less successful remake of the film, now titled (with the directness of the 1990s) *The Money Pit*, likewise begins with an instance of love at first site as the lovers catch a glimpse of their ill-fated dream house.

We might think of these stories as morality tales about our own materialist culture, where things seem to matter as much as or more than persons. But falling in love with a house is something that happens quite a lot in older literature. And—equally to the point—it is not always easy to tell where the beloved object leaves off and the person begins. A classic case is that of *Pride and Prejudice*, where the erotic relation is filtered through two ironic voices, Jane Austen's and Elizabeth Bennet's, but emerges all the more strongly as testimony to a recognizable "real" love.

"My dearest sister, now *do* be serious," says Jane Bennet to her sister Elizabeth. She has just learned to her amazement that Elizabeth has consented to marry Mr. Darcy, a man she had previously rejected as too haughty and proud. "Will you tell me how long you have loved him?" asks Jane. "It has been coming on so gradually," Elizabeth replies, "that I hardly know when it began. But I believe I must date it from my first seeing his beautiful grounds at Pemberley."[12]

Jane takes this remark, as she is meant to, as another example of her sister's wit. But there is more than a germ of truth in the observation. Falling in love with a house is easy to do. And the next step is falling in love with its owner. Readers who regard such a view as either (1) condemning Elizabeth as a scheming materialist or (2) mistaking her "light" remark for a serious comment themselves err in underestimating Jane Austen. For few writers see so clearly how a relationship with a wonderful house changes one's life, and few have her unerring eye for the complex and contradictory paths of love.

"To be mistress of Pemberley might be something!" Elizabeth finds herself thinking, when, ascending a hilltop with her uncle and aunt, her eye is "instantly caught by Pemberley House."[13] It's love at first site, for Pemberley appears, like its master, "large, handsome," and "standing well on rising ground."

> Elizabeth was delighted. She had never seen a place for which nature had done more, or where natural had been so little counteracted by an awkward taste. They were all of them warm in their admiration; and at that moment she felt, that to be mistress of Pemberley might be something!

There is evidence within the novel that its author knew quite well what she was doing in tying these feelings together. The all-purpose word "handsome" (used by Austen to describe Darcy, his sister, and his ancestral estate in the course of two pages) nicely illustrates the conflation of Elizabeth's passions. Touring the house, she finds its interior admirable in every respect: "The rooms were lofty and handsome, and their furniture suitable to the fortunes of their proprietor." A painted miniature and a full-length portrait of Darcy reveal him, Elizabeth now acknowledges, to be likewise "very handsome." And when the man himself arrives she finds him unexpectedly agreeable. He seems "stately," her aunt observes, but not, as he has been reputed, proud. From this point on the stately home and its stately owner are clearly versions of one another. "And of this place," she

thinks, "I might have been mistress!"[14] Since the novel begins
with the news that the Bennets' home has been entailed to a
male relation (the egregious Mr. Collins, who duly proposes to
Elizabeth and offers the house as an inducement), the notion
that the house rather than its owner is the lure is in fact what sets
the marriage plot in motion.

"One of the hallmarks of Jane Austen's writing—her vivid
characterizations compiled of several fragments of real personalities—undoubtedly also applies to the houses in her novels,"
writes the author of a book on the architecture and culture of
Austen's time. "But the people are gone. It is the houses that remain." And they remain, for the most part, "as proud and beautiful as ever."[15] Falling in love with Mr. Darcy is a complicated
business for Elizabeth Bennet, but that first sight of Pemberley,
like an indrawn breath, lingers in the mind.

In our own time the dramatic appearance of the house in a
version of *Pride and Prejudice* produced for British television in
1995 has had a similar effect, making the house a movie star.
After its featured role as "Pemberley," Lyme Park in Disley,
Cheshire, became the historic house in England with the fastest-
growing number of visitors, up 178 percent in a single year.[16] It is
perhaps no accident that Emma Tennant's modern sequel to
Austen's love story, subtitled *Pride and Prejudice Continued,* is
called after the name of the house: *Pemberley.*

In *Pride and Prejudice* the house is the catalyst, the matchmaker, the transitional object. The reader's or viewer's eye is on
the human-human relation. Yet on occasion the house and the
human share equal erotic billing, with the house sometimes even
edging out the human in the end as the primary object of desire.
The most spectacular examples are, perhaps predictably, those
that involve fantasy houses, houses so enormous, so exquisite, so
unimaginably grand or costly that they may hardly seem comparable to our own. But we are speaking here of the dream house
and of love. The palace is its natural metaphor, and the model—
even the "model home"—for our patterns of idealized love.

Pleasures and Palaces

"Louis XIV fell in love with Versailles and Louise de La Vallière at the same time," writes Nancy Mitford. "Versailles was the love of his life." With these striking phrases Mitford begins her biography of the Sun King, and what she terms "the house" (Versailles itself, transformed over the course of Louis's life from a hunting lodge with twenty rooms and a men's dormitory to the greatest palace in Europe) has pride of place in the story.[17]

Virginia Woolf well understood the mingled passions of love for another person and love for a house. She clearly saw that Vita Sackville-West was more in love with Knole, the Sackville family home, than with her husband or any of her lovers. Knole, a vast estate dating from Elizabethan times, had 365 rooms, 52 staircases, and 7 courtyards, making it an architectural emblem of the calendar, a measure of time as well as space. A journalist of the time characterized it as "too homely to be called a palace, too palatial to be called a home," a glib formulation with which Vita was forced to admit she agreed. For her the house and grounds were like a beloved person. "Oh, my lovely Knole," she apostrophized it in her autobiography.

When she decided to marry, Vita wrote teasingly to her husband-to-be, Harold Nicolson, "If I leave my beautiful Knole which I adore, and my Ghirlandaio room which I adore, and my books and my garden and my freedom which I adore—it is all for you, whom I don't care two straws about." But in her private diary she lamented the need to go abroad as a diplomat's wife: "I simply can't leave Knole for Vienna!"[18] On the eve of her wedding she wrote a passionate poem to the house that began,

> I left thee in the crowds and in the light,
> And if I laughed or sorrowed none could tell.
> They could not know our true and deep farewell
> Was spoken in the long preceding night.[19]

When Sackville-West's father died, the estate, entailed to the male line, passed to her uncle rather than to her. It was the brilliant stroke of Virginia Woolf, who had been one of Vita's lovers, to transform Vita Sackville-West into a man in her novel *Orlando*, and thus to reunite her, imaginatively, with the ancestral house she had lost. Vita's son and biographer Nigel Nicolson, who described *Orlando* as "the longest and most charming love letter in literature," saw clearly that the central relationship in this fictional tour de force, which covers three centuries and chronicles Orlando's change from Elizabethan nobleman to modern woman, was that between Vita and her house. "The novel identified her with Knole for ever. Virginia by her genius had provided Vita with a unique consolation for having been born a girl, for her exclusion from her inheritance, for her father's death earlier that year."[20]

But falling in love with a house doesn't necessarily require something as grand as Knole or Versailles or Pemberley (any more than falling in love with a person requires that he or she be as grand or forbidding as Mr. Darcy). Often, like the boy or girl next door, the dream house is not exotic but local—a house like the one two women from Brooklyn passed on the street day after day, falling in love with the garden, with the windows, with everything about it—and then, miraculously, it came on the market, and it was theirs.

Once on two successive days I heard about a colleague's decision to move from Cambridge to the suburbs and a second colleague's decision to move from the suburbs to Cambridge. A few days later I found myself at lunch with a high-powered, immensely likable woman who is married to an internationally known journalist. Our business was—well, I can't even remember what had brought us together, because before the waiter had arrived with the San Pellegrino we were talking real estate. She had just put her house on the market; I was almost late for our lunch because I was looking at houses. She told me, room by room and decade by decade, the story of her Cambridge house, which was, inevitably, at once the story of an intellectual couple, an international salon, and an improvised bed-and-breakfast for hundreds of overnight guests over the years. It was, as well, the loving biography of a house.

"I am amazed at the irony that my deepest relationship is with a house," writes biographer Honor Moore about the Connecticut antique with the tilty floor she loved as a child and later bought from her father.[21] No irony, I think. Both historically and in the present day, the almost animate and often passionate relationship of house and dweller, house and owner, house and wistful admirer-from-afar has brought out deep feelings of identification, fantasy, and desire.

Listen, for example, to the language of famed society decorator Elsie De Wolfe in her book *The House in Good Taste:* "Probably when another woman would be dreaming of love affairs, I dream of the delightful houses I have lived in."[22] De Wolfe's love affairs were not with houses *instead* of persons—this is not a love-logic of substitution or emotional compensation, as is often said, quite wrongly, of the relationship between, say, people and their pets. The highly successful De Wolfe lived in her houses with a companion, Elizabeth Marbury, and led a busy, even frenetic, social life. But her deliberate juxtaposition of "love affairs" and "houses" declares another kind of real love, a primary relationship between a human being and a house.

Portrait of the Artist as an Old House

There is something both irresistibly attractive and romantically melancholy about the doomed relationships between aristocratic families and their ancestral estates. Within this genre Evelyn Waugh's *Brideshead Revisited* is a particularly complex and sophisticated example of falling in love with both a family and a house. The narrator, Charles Ryder, is traveling with his Oxford friend Sebastian Flyte, with whom he is, at the moment, very much in love. (Much later he will have an affair with Sebastian's sister Julia, and the novel's plot is structured as a series of substitutions, in which Sebastian, Julia, and the house itself all jockey for position as Charles's real, and ultimately lost, love.)

After a delicious morning of motoring, strawberries, and wine, he writes,

> In the early afternoon [we] came to our destination: wrought-iron gates and twin, classical lodges on a village green, an avenue, more gates, open parkland, a turn in the drive, and suddenly a new and secret landscape opened before us. We were at the head of a valley and below us, half a mile distant, prone in the sunlight, grey and gold amid a screen of boskage, shone the dome and columns of an old house.

"What a place to live in!" Charles exclaims, enraptured. But he is instantly disconcerted by Sebastian's cool reply: "It's where my family live."[23]

The tug-of-war between Sebastian and his aristocratic family for Charles Ryder's affection and loyalty will form the core of the "fierce little human tragedy" that is Waugh's novel.[24] For a while Charles will make his own home at Brideshead in a ménage à trois with Julia and her vulgar, successful politician husband, and he will later characterize himself, self-mockingly, as "homeless, childless, middle-aged, loveless." But what is so striking, both in the novel's title and in its shapely plot, is the return to the lost beloved.

The story of Charles Ryder's several "revisits" to Brideshead—from his first sight of the place as a jejune Oxford undergraduate to his unplanned return during the war as a disillusioned army officer—offers an ironic English version of Proust's sublime search for lost time. "Brideshead" is the name of both house and householder, and its geographical etymology—the house is located at the source of a stream called the Bride—doesn't completely mask its kinship with words like "maidenhead." Certainly Ryder, who is to become a celebrated architectural painter, regards his first encounter with the house and its inhabitants as a crucial loss of innocence, an initiation into a new and seductive world.

But though the themes of family, home, and homelessness are central to the narrative, what was so striking to me in revisiting *Brideshead Revisited* is that Charles resolves his emotional situation by *painting portraits of houses.* For Charles's painting career is, even in his eyes, a displacement of his passion for the Flyte family and its variously seductive members. He finds his vocation almost by chance when the eldest son, also named Brideshead, asks him to paint a series of pictures of the family's London home, Marchmain House, which has been sold and will be demolished to make way for a block of flats.

"A picture of the front, another of the back on the park, another of the staircase, another of the big drawing-room," specifies Bridey. "That is what my father wants done for a record, to keep at Brideshead."[25] Charles has to "work against time, for the contractors were only waiting for the final signature to start their work of destruction." But "in spite, or perhaps because, of that," the paintings are a success and Ryder goes on to publish "three splendid folios—*Ryder's Country Seats, Ryder's English Homes,* and *Ryder's Village and Provincial Architecture.*" His career, as he notes wryly, is based to a certain degree on nostalgia and loss:

> The financial slump of the period, which left many painters without employment, served to enhance my success, which was, indeed, a symptom of the decline. When the water-holes were dry people sought to drink at the mirage. After my first exhibition I was called to all parts of the country to make portraits of houses that were soon to be deserted or debased; indeed, my arrival seemed often to be only a few paces ahead of the auctioneers, a presage of doom.[26]

Failing to preserve the houses, the owners, like Lord Marchmain (himself living in self-imposed exile with his mistress in Venice), preserve their images. Charles sees himself, with irony and clarity, as a kind of glorified undertaker.

A painting of a house also features crucially in Daphne du Maurier's *Rebecca*, perhaps the most celebrated piece of twentieth-century gothic fiction in the repertoire and one of the most dramatic accounts of "falling in love with a house."

As a child on holiday in the west country, never dreaming that she would live there, the heroine is struck by a picture postcard at a village shop. "It was the painting of a house, crudely done of course and highly coloured, but even those faults could not destroy the symmetry of the building, the wide stone steps before the terrace, the green lawns stretching to the sea." She asks the shopkeeper what it was meant to be, and is told, with astonishment at her ignorance, "That's Manderley."[27] This memory recurs throughout the novel—a memory of the postcard, the enchantment with a house before she even learns its name and lineage, and long before she fulfills the fantasy of marrying its owner. In fact it is the *house* that is her pinup, a postcard view of an impossible, celebrity love object that, astoundingly, becomes hers. The house has a fine-sounding name, while the heroine, destined to be (however briefly) Manderley's mistress, is symptomatically nameless. Her very anonymity invites us to put ourselves in her place.

When she marries the aristocratic Maximilian de Winter, the owner of Manderley, she reflects to herself, "I know now why I had bought that picture post-card as a child, it was a premonition, a blank step into the future." As their car approaches the driveway for the first time, she can hardly keep her mind on the landscape because she is "thinking of that self who long ago bought a picture post-card in a village shop"—and when they arrive she sees her dream before her: "Yes, there it was, the Manderley I had expected, the Manderley of my picture post-card long ago. A thing of grace and beauty, exquisite and faultless, lovelier even than I had ever dreamed." Introduced to the denizens of the household, especially the formidable house-keeper Mrs. Danvers, she keeps "trying to instil into myself some measure of confidence, some genuine realisation that I was here, at Manderley, the house of the picture post-card, the Manderley that was famous."[28]

Although house portraiture was a favored art form among the wealthy in the eighteenth and early nineteenth centuries both in England and in America—John Singer Sargent, celebrated for his portraits of human subjects, was commissioned to paint a likeness of Biltmore House, the vast Vanderbilt estate in North Carolina—the impulse to preserve the past on canvas has not been entirely superseded by new media like photography and film. And nowadays house portraiture is not confined to the upper and moneyed classes.

Boston-area sidewalk artist Alfred Mira has made a career of house portraits executed in oils, at an affordable $350–$450 per image. "He's painted my life on that canvas," said one local homeowner. "My dog, my birdhouse, my flowers . . . they're all there." Another happy client hung the portrait Mira painted over his kitchen fireplace: "I can't stop staring at it," he said.

For yet another client, Mira's portrait of her house was "not just a painting, but an extension of myself—something inti-mately my own."[29] These are probably not people who would sit for their *own* portraits, or stare with fascination at themselves captured on canvas. But they have few qualms, and much plea-sure, in contemplating "my life" and "myself" as depicted, and deflected, through the image of the house. For we live at a time when it is the house, rather than any other kind of partner, which can be readily described as "something *intimately* my own." "I had always wanted a painting of my own house," said a collector who discovered Mira's work when he came upon him painting a portrait of someone else's home. "I knew I just had to have one of those."

Commissioning a painted portrait of the beloved was, at least in the days before photography, a recognizable sign of being "in love." Thus Austen's Emma is misled by the unctuous clergyman Mr. Elton, whose fascination with the portrait she is sketching of her friend Harriet she takes to be a sure sign of his love for Harriet, and not for herself. Shakespeare's Benedict, having long dismissed love as a folly, astounds himself by realizing that he is in love with Beatrice, and immediately vows, "I will go get her picture." And so, perhaps inevitably, when I visited a flea market on Nantucket one scorching hot day and saw a woman exhibiting watercolor portraits of local houses, I was seized by a desire to have my own house "done."

The artist arrived for her appointment on schedule, to interview the subject and do some sketches. Should it be a front view or a profile? Close-up or from a distance? Besotted owner that I was, I couldn't choose between the beguiling sketch of the front door and the equally fetching side view of the deck and grounds. Without a blink I commissioned *two* portraits of this modest and unexceptional dwelling, to which the painter contributed some cosmetic flourishes of her own, "maturing" the landscape some five years or so with the stroke of a brush and erasing the cliff behind so that the house seemed to stand free of surrounding encumbrances. The resulting portraits remind me a little of the pastel likenesses of children executed by sketch artists on the Atlantic City boardwalk in my childhood—a little generic, a little airbrushed, inoffensive and bland. But hung in the hallway of a house far away from Nantucket, they give enormous pleasure, recalling to me, every time I round the stairs, the hot summer days and pond lilies and the smell of wild roses.

The House as Spouse

"Partner, spouse, wife, husband, cohabitee," writes psychoanalyst Adam Phillips. "The problem of monogamy is that we have never found the words for it."[30] "Cohabitee" is an awkward coinage, though we often use its equivalent when we say that a couple are "living together." But this is a case in which one and one often make three, for there is a third partner in the arrangement, and one that sometimes usurps the primary attention of one or another of the first two players. Sometimes the house is the spouse.

The Hollywood romantic comedy *Housesitter* (1992) is the story of a naïve young architect (Steve Martin) who believes so firmly in the power of falling in love with a house that he builds his dream dwelling, complete with "wraparound porch" and "switchback stairs that go up to a loft," as what he calls an "engagement ring" for the woman he loves. "Marry me!" he implores, when he takes her to the site and displays the house, wrapped in a huge red ribbon. "You built this house for me?" she asks incredulously. "For *us*," he replies. But though she says "this is like something out of a fairytale," she turns him down—she doesn't want to marry a "dreamer." The stage is set for the arrival of the "housesitter" of the title, Goldie Hawn, who represents herself to the community as Martin's wife because she wants to live in the house. In this case, quite literally, falling in love with a dream house leads (on the part of both Martin's architect and Hawn's sexy off-the-wall squatter) to falling in love with a person, as the make-believe marriage turns into a real one, complete with in-law cottage over the way.

It sounds cynical to say that one marries a house, but (1) on the one hand people often do marry or choose life partners because they'd like to "set up housekeeping," and (2) marriage is different from infatuation or "romantic love" in that it often does come with a set of material constraints and possibilities, from gift china to a thirty-year mortgage. The word "husband" began as a term for householder. The "husband" needed a wife, indeed a "housewife," to manage the household affairs (husbandry) and bear and rear the children. Eighteenth- and nineteenth-century novels often emphasized the "property" side of marriage, with legal settlements and dowries. Marriage for a young woman of a certain class might mean moving directly into her husband's home. For families where the house and grounds were entailed on the eldest son, his marriage might mean displacing a widowed mother, either to lesser apartments or to a "dower house." The new bride became the mistress of the house.

In these romantic and enlightened days we tend to think of such arrangements as "arrangements," and thus perhaps oppressive. But many a young person dreams of "the house I will live in when I grow up," and this house, or at least the imagined house, usually includes a live-in partner. Movies of the fifties often include a scene in which the husband carries his new bride, all tricked out in tulle and satin, over the threshold of their new home. Without thinking about it very deeply I assumed, as a child of those years, that a house and a marriage were part of the same expectation—or the same bargain. It's no surprise—and it should not be deflating—to realize that marriage, like other social and property arrangements, is a "deal" as well as a dream.

One of the things that sometimes "saves" marriages, and relationships more generally, is projecting desire outward, toward another love object, a permissible infidelity—in short, a house. Is a house then an emblem of monogamy? Or a protector and palpable endorsement of the state of single wedded bliss? Let's consider an exception that may or may not prove the rule.

What has been called "a quietly emerging American subculture: the polygamous bourgeoisie" is busy building houses for Mormon plural families. Polygamy is still a felony in Utah, but it is not generally prosecuted. Fundamentalist Mormons still practice what church founder Joseph Smith termed plural or celestial marriage, and though the custom was officially renounced as a condition of statehood for Utah, there are, it is said, some 30,000 to 35,000 practicing polygamists in the United States today. "Among the States," a 1990 Department of Commerce report observes, "the percentage of housing units with 4 or more bedrooms varied significantly. . . . Utah had the highest percentage of housing units in this category (29 percent), about double the Nation's average."[31]

Where do they live? Not only in Utah, but also in Missouri and Arizona, among other states, a vernacular polygamous architecture has developed, with a number of houses over 12,000 square feet. In the mid-nineteenth century Brigham Young built the Lion House, a Gothic Revival mansion with twenty bedrooms and a private passageway leading from his office to the room of one of his favorites. Today one Utah man lives in a former gristmill (latterly a bed-and-breakfast) with three of his eight wives and their children. His other five wives leave nearby. Another man designed a house south of Salt Lake City for himself and his three wives (in what was called "a considerate gesture" he made sure none of the master bedrooms was directly on top of, or below, another). "I believe the girls should have their own identity and place," he said; but he thought they might want to work together at times, "like when they're canning fruit." Although the arrangement was expensive (each wife has her own entrance, her own décor, her own television and refrigerator), he was upbeat: "I have really good wives. It works out."

For yet another man, who built a 35,000-square-foot house with 37 bathrooms and 31 bedrooms for his 10 wives and 28 children, cost was not an issue. A central kitchen with four refrigerators, a home theater, and a computer room were part of the compound. His own master suite boasted a four-poster bed, a Jacuzzi, and a freestanding fireplace, and his wives, housed in other wings, were free to follow their own taste in decorating. This seems like the ultimate in the romance of real estate. But lest polygamy set a new trend in luxury home construction, the husband cautioned overeager imitators: "Believe me, there are cheaper ways to have sex."[32]

In this case the "plural marriage" arrangement was mirrored (for better or for worse) in the architectural structure of the house. Instead of infidelity the husband had multiple fidelities. But as we've noted, just about *every* marriage or domestic partnership has a third party: the house. "Two's company, but three's a couple," quips Adam Phillips. Three, though, can be a difficult number. And a house can, sometimes unwittingly, be a homewrecker.

A Plague on Both Your Houses

When love goes wrong, the rose-covered cottage can become the object of a bitter custody battle. It's not that love for the *house* is lost, but rather that love between persons, itself often based on fantasy, overestimation, and wish fulfillment, is more fragile and less forgiving. When love in a cottage—or a palace—turns sour, it is often the cottage or the palace that is sundered or dismembered.

Divorce is good for the real estate business. That's a fact. Where once people may have scoured the obituaries looking for apartments in hard-to-find places, now they would be just as well advised to haunt the divorce courts, or to read the proceedings. "The good thing about a 'divorce' house," says a house agent in Britain, "is that you know, absolutely, that it is on the market to sell."[33] On the other hand, since both parties are looking to make money (and facing the possibility of a lowering of income and lifestyle as a result of the divorce), "divorce houses" are often priced too high, at least at first. One house agent told of a man who came to him for a house valuation, confiding that he was thinking of getting a divorce but hadn't yet told his wife. He accompanied the man to his home, appraised the premises, and then showed him some flats to rent. The next day the wife came in with the identical request. The agent went through the property a second time, pretending that he hadn't seen it before, and even showed the wife some of the same rental flats that he had shown her husband.

A retired Cape Cod couple splitting up after thirty-five years of marriage were going through what their real estate agent characterized as a "nasty, messy divorce" and the breakup was getting in the way of listing the house. So the realtor, with the couple's permission, had all the disputed house contents hauled away and put in storage. Two weeks afterward, the "de-cluttered" house sold for a good price. This anecdote was offered as a parable of real estate know-how, with the broker as therapist and problem solver. No word on whether the feuding couple ever resolved their legal disputes.[34]

"It can get ugly," notes a broker who manages real estate offices in Brooklyn. In a divorce, "any acrimonious feelings the spouses may have get transferred to the property."[35] Or, as the *Wall Street Journal* put it succinctly, "In a divorce, a house is not a home. It's a weapon."[36]

In the 1989 film *The War of the Roses* a marriage-gone-wrong plays itself out as a battle royal for the possession—or, failing that, the destruction—of a house. Michael Douglas and Kathleen Turner are the Roses, a yuppie couple with a house to die for. In fact, Turner found the house by "falling in love" with it when she first saw it, then leaving notes for the owner saying she wanted to buy it—a pattern of real estate chutzpah that I've seen practiced with astonishing success even in "real life." But in this out-of-control film, inadequately labeled a black comedy, the house becomes the figure, and the scapegoat, for everything that's wrong with the marriage.

Inevitably, the "War of-the-Roses-style divorce battle" became a newspaper staple in the years that followed the film's release—the more so because the kind of breakup it chronicled was already all too familiar in the press and in the divorce courts.[37] House custody virtually replaced child custody as the key factor in many marital splits, especially when the divorcing pair were wealthy people and/or celebrities with more than one "home" in their portfolio. And sometimes, when all else failed, a kind of joint custody was agreed upon—as had happened with the Roses. Neither partner wants to move out, or, perhaps, neither can afford to do so. Actor Harry Hamlin and his wife Laura Johnson both wanted to keep the $1.2 million home they shared in Lake Glen, California. The year was 1989, the same year *The War of the Roses* was released, and a Los Angeles judge decided the couple should split the house down the middle, each staying on his or her side. But Johnson charged in court that Hamlin had strayed into her part of the house—with his new girlfriend, who had gone through Johnson's closets. She also charged that Hamlin had taken the antique light switches off the walls, an accusation he hotly denied. Hamlin bought out Johnson's share, married the new girlfriend, and—when they divorced three years later—kept the Lake Glen house, ceding another house in Bel Air to her.

Donald Trump and ex-wife Ivana also wound up sharing a property, slightly more successfully. Ivana got the forty-five-room Connecticut mansion, a Trump Plaza apartment in New York, and a housing allowance of $4 million. But she wanted the former Marjorie Merriwether Post estate, Mar-a-Lago, with its 118 rooms on the Palm Beach coast in Florida. Trump wanted it too; they compromised on sharing it, with Ivana permitted to use the house for certain periods of the year.[38] And—to return to our theme of the fantasy of living and loving in a palace—there is this: When Prince Charles negotiated his divorce from Princess Diana, the settlement took away her title as Princess of Wales, but permitted her to keep her apartment in Kensington Palace.

We often hear of couples who stay together "for the sake of the children." But some in Britain are apparently staying together for the sake of the house. It seems that divorce rates go up when the property market goes up. "When you can't sell and you can't buy, it doesn't make a lot of sense to divorce," says the former chair of the Solicitors Family Law Association. "You grit your teeth and wait." After the property crash of the 1990s, couples who wanted to split up couldn't afford to do so until, and unless, the family home sold.[39] Recent developments in U.S. real estate law have made it more advantageous—or less disadvantageous—for divorcing couples to be honest about who owns, who resides in, and who sells the "family home." Now, if a separation agreement or divorce decree gives one partner exclusive use of the house, the other can continue to call it home. "The divorce penalty is gone," said one divorce lawyer. "The new law reduces the number of games we play, like who owns the house and whether a client should move out." And another added, "Even two warring parties should realize that they have a common enemy—the Commissioner of Internal Revenue."[40]

But it isn't always the practical side of things that governs the decision to keep the house even when one sheds the spouse. Sometimes it's just plain house love. "There is a strong minority of people who are very seriously attached to their house and will not budge," says a divorce lawyer in New Jersey. "There are people who say to me—and they're dead serious—do you understand my husband, or my wife, whichever, loves this house more than he loves me?"[41]

TWO

THE HOUSE AS MOTHER

The House Loves Us

How is "home" like "mother"? Let us count the ways.

- It loves you unconditionally.
- It will take you "the way you are," without dress-up or pretense.
- It is comfortable, not challenging or threatening.
- It takes care of your basic needs: food, clothing, shelter.
- It makes you feel safe.
- It contains you.
- It nurtures you.
- It prepares you for the world "outside."

"Not *my* mother," you may be saying to yourself. Or "Not *my* home." But this is precisely the point. We are speaking here of ideals, fantasies, hopes and dreams, of the "home" that is like a "mother" because it anticipates and answers all your needs before you know you have them. Both "home" and "mother" are fictions here, or composites, or idealizations.

The fantasy of home as mother is a powerful and abiding one—the more so (as is often the case with fantasies) when the reality of the situation seems to fall short of the ideal. "Home," famously declares a speaker in a poem by Robert Frost, that least sentimental of writers, "is the place where, when you have to go there, they have to take you in." That both the speaker and the narrator here are men seems symptomatic: the idealization of the home as an all-seeing, all-knowing, all-forgiving mother is a wish, not a fact, and it has little to do with "real" gender—or, for that matter, with physiological maternity.

On this model, the house, or rather the "home," is modeled after an ideal "human" relation—the affectionate and caretaking relationship between mother and child. (Notice that even the word "caretaker," now newly again in use to denote a parent— "primary caretaker," in legal jargon—is also a term we have adopted to describe someone who assumes responsibility for overseeing the physical, material house.) But it is not so much a functional as an emotional relationship that we imagine and long for: the house, we would like to think, loves us.

Perhaps it will be useful, therefore, to begin with some terms and categories that are often conflated: woman and mother; house and home. In each of these pairings the first term is physical and material, the second relational and affective, suffused with emotion (pro or con)—imagined away from the mere physicality of body and space.

Mother is certainly as "biological" as *woman*. But to imagine the house as a woman is—it will be readily seen—quite a different mental exercise from imagining the house as a mother. And conversely, to imagine a mother as a house is rather different from imagining her as a home.

A house is a space full of rooms, each with a function. Sometimes the house has been simply and directly mapped onto the female body. As Jane and Lesley Davison note, "the association between houses and women has long had snickering overtones in sex-linked colloquialisms. . . . A 'housebit' in the mid-nineteenth century referred to a paramour servant; 'house under the hill' to a woman's private parts, as did 'housewife' itself. The term for widow was 'house to let.' " The same was true in German, as Freud pointedly observed: " '*Zimmer*' ['room'] in dreams stands very frequently for '*Frauenzimmer*' [a slightly derogatory word for 'woman'; literally, 'women's apartment']. The question whether a woman is 'open' or 'shut' can naturally not be a matter of indifference. It is well known, too, what sort of 'key' effects the opening in such a case."[1]

But we might notice that when the female body is imagined this way, in parts, private or public, it is not the body of a *mother*, or at least not "*the* mother." For *mother* in this phantasmic sense, the sense of "house as mother," is by definition whole, not partial; containing, not contained. And *home*, whatever the sum of its parts (or, in the standard phrase, "be it ever so humble"), is likewise in the cultural imagination whole, perfect, and waiting for us.

House and Home

Let's admit it: If we begin to inquire too closely about mothers in particular historical and economic venues, this fantasy of home as mother quickly comes apart. For example, an aristocratic mother in the early modern period would probably have employed a wet nurse and seen her children only on relatively formal occasions. A middle-class mother in eighteenth-century England, like Jane Austen's mother, might have "fostered out" her children to a local farm family until they were trained and presentable, at which point they would re-enter the family home. A late twentieth-century mother in the United States is very likely to work "outside the home," as the saying goes.

But in a way these historical particularities are beside the point. At the turn of the twenty-first century we are dealing with a nostalgia, a memory, and a fantasy. It is not "mothers" but Mother who is imagined as the indwelling spirit, the *genius loci*, of the (virtually anthropomorphic) "loving home."

In *The Feminization of American Culture* Ann Douglas takes account of the shifting role of the home in the lives of middle-class Northern women in the middle of the nineteenth century. She calls it "feminine disestablishment," or "the end of 'Mother Power.' " "Formerly an important part of a communal productive process under her protection, [the home] had become a place where her children stayed before they began to work and where her husband rested after the strain of labor. Once her family had looked to her quite literally to clothe and feed them; now they expected a complex blend of nurture and escape from her 'voluntary' care."[2] What minister Horace Bushnell called in 1851 "The Age of Homespun" gave way to a different kind of economy. The "transition from mother and daughter power to water and steam power," he noted, was so extreme that "the very terms 'domestic manufacture' have quite lost their meaning." Married women in this economic and regional niche ran households, and helped their husbands spend their income increasingly tied to work outside the home.

As the woman in the home became less of a producer and more of a consumer, her centrality became less self-evident, and—from the point of view of a psychoanalysis of culture—more anxious and overcompensated. Etiquette books of the 1830s stress domestic piety at home for "ladies," and mercantile commerce for gentlemen. Dress and fashion were suitable preoccupations, as was the reading of novels. Advertising, as Douglas points out, played a crucial part in instilling "new needs" in consumers, and focused particular attention on women. As Nathaniel Fowler, a key figure in the development of American advertising, would claim, "woman buys, or directs the buying of . . . everything from shoes to shingles." Thus an advertisement had "not one twentieth the weight with a man that it has with a woman of equal intelligence and the same social status."[3]

Domesticity became "an aspect of leisure" for the middle-class modern woman.[4] Eva van Arsdel, the heroine of Harriet Beecher Stowe's New York novels, *My Wife and I* and *We and Our Neighbors,* has an elegant, expensive home and an elegant, expensive wardrobe; the work of the house is done by her Irish cook, Mary Scudder. "In the newly commercialized and urbanized America of the middle decades of the nineteenth century, the woman consumer," Stowe's novels seemed to argue, "is more important, more indispensable, than the woman producer; luxury items can and must function as necessities."[5] If this was true in general of women, the wives and daughters of comfortable middle-class men, it was especially true of mothers. Viewed from this economic and cultural perspective, the famous nineteenth-century "cult of motherhood" has a double significance and a double utility. It emphasized the importance of the female consumer while at the same time disavowing any crass commercial motivations. Economic concerns were displaced onto spiritual ones. Instead of "value," one could think about "values."

The 1840s and 1850s had seen a flood of books written and published on the topic of mothers and motherhood. The mothers of famous men were praised; the role of mothers as inspirers and nurturers of greatness was extolled. The importance of maternity was urged upon women for a wide variety of reasons, from keeping them at home to compensating them for their lost economic productivity to preserving the balance (or rather the imbalance) of the races in the wake of immigrant arrivals. "The American mother of the mid-nineteenth century, encouraged to breast-feed, oversee, and educate her child, was theoretically assuming, for better and worse, almost godlike prominence."[6] In 1872 Julia Ward Howe, the author of "The Battle Hymn of the Republic," proposed an observance called Mother's Day, although it was not until 1914 that President Woodrow Wilson officially proclaimed it a national holiday.

While "mother" was becoming, officially, a national treasure, the "home" was increasingly designated as her dominion. In 1869 Harriet Beecher Stowe collaborated with her sister Catherine Beecher on a book called *The American Woman's Home,* an enlarged version of Beecher's earlier, and enormously successful, *Treatise on Domestic Economy.* In it they describe the "family state," which was the "earthly illustration of the heavenly kingdom," by detailing, in the most precise and specific terms, architectural plans and instructions for furniture, heating, ventilation, lighting, the planting of gardens, and household activities from child care to financial management and waste disposal. The book was pointedly dedicated "To the Women of America, in whose hands rest the real destinies of the republic." Rather than a self-absorbed, private space, the "home" is here imagined, through the vehicle of an intensely and deliberately practical guide, as (in critic Jane Tompkins's phrase) "a blueprint for colonizing the world in the name of the 'family state' under the leadership of Christian women."[7]

The revolutionary nature of this work, Tompkins goes on to note, lies in its very conservatism. "By resting her case, absolutely, on the saving power of Christian love and on the sanctity of motherhood and the family, Stowe relocates the center of power in American life, placing it not in the government, nor in the courts of law, nor in the factories, nor in the marketplace, but in the kitchen." Women—which is to say, mothers, or women playing "mothers'" roles—dominate the household economy. "Men provide the seed, but women bear and raise the children. Men provide the flour, but women bake the bread and get the breakfast."[8] Through the evocation of "the most traditional values—religion, motherhood, home, and family"—women are relocated at the center, and men at the periphery, of daily life.

The American Woman's Home is a good example of the way in which "home as mother" can be an advance rather than a retreat, not a sequestering of the woman, or the "mother," but an assertion of her foundational political role.

And there was also, of course, the influence of Stowe's most famous book—a book whose title situates it in the humblest of houses. *Uncle Tom's Cabin* has been described as "the most important book of the [nineteenth] century," "the *summa theologica* of America's religion of domesticity," and also as "the story of salvation through motherly love."[9] Stowe parlayed her book, with its lowly "cabin" in the title, into the purchase of a mansion in the Northeast and an orange plantation in Florida, despite the fact that her copyright and publishing arrangements were not advantageous: the book was unimaginably successful. But its success was forgotten, or resisted, by literary history. Tompkins tellingly begins her account of the importance of *Uncle Tom's Cabin* for American literary history by remembering a reverential visit she made to the Mark Twain House when she was a student living in Hartford, Connecticut. There was another house nearby that she did not bother to visit, since she did not regard its former resident as a major American author. The house was Harriet Beecher Stowe's.

No Place Like Home

At the same time that commercial culture was encouraging the female consumer to "make a home" for her husband (or father), political and popular culture was celebrating the selflessness of the mother in the home. John Howard Payne's "Home, Sweet Home" was regularly cited throughout the later nineteenth century and into the twentieth as the song that "inspired encouragement under many a lowly roof." His ringing phrase "there is no place like home" seems to have struck a note of egalitarian promise; it was not wealth or power that counted most, but character and family.

Payne, an American actor, playwright, and poet celebrated on both sides of the Atlantic, wrote the lyrics to "Home, Sweet Home" for his highly successful play *Clari, The Maid of Milan* (1823). With the perpetual bad financial luck that dogged him throughout his career, Payne sold the play outright, so when his sentimental song became a national favorite he derived no profit from its popularity. Perhaps this was all too just, since the song itself famously exalted the home, "be it ever so humble," over the material blandishments of "pleasures and palaces." The editor of *Golden Thoughts on Mother, Home and Heaven* (1878), a typical anthology of Victorian prose and verse, expresses his pleasure at the fact that a monument to John Howard Payne stands in the chief public park of the borough of Brooklyn that was home to them both.

This winning combination of mother, home, and heaven, the emotional trifecta of late Victorian sentiment in America, served to focus and channel the erotic energies of "home" in a direction that still holds sway in the present-day language of family values. There was indeed "no place like home," in the sense that "home" was always a fantasy. The insistence on the "home" as an idealized portrait of spiritual rather than material attributes continued to dominate the ideology of American character development, generating a series of assertions that seem deeply split between sentiment and practicality. Thus even so practical a guide as *House and Home: A Manual and Text-Book of Practical House Planning*, one of a series of "home manuals" published by Lippincott in the 1920s on topics from canning and preserving to millinery and hygiene, begins its discussion of building, plumbing, heating, and grounds-keeping with a short account of the relationship between "house" and "home": "Home is not a house, nor a place, nor furnishings, but it is the hopes and memories which cling about the place of habitual abode. We make a home in a certain place, among material things, but not of materials."

The frontispiece of *House and Home* is indicative: a painting of a mother reading in a comfortable room adorned with oriental carpets, potted plants, and easel paintings, while her young son peers out the window at the street. The caption reads, predictably, "Home is Where the Heart Is." But the chicken-egg relationship between home-building and homemaking is, from the start, part of the story. "The home is a complex, built up of the emotions of the family, depending upon their characters and their experiences. But character and experience are shaped largely by environment, both physical and spiritual. The houses we live in are intimate parts of our physical environment . . . and, more important still, the house and its location to a large extent determine spiritual environment." Therefore this "home manual" proceeds, in a completely logical way, to a consideration of "sanitation, cost, social advantages, and aesthetic aspects" of "the house, its site, house plans, heating, plumbing, lighting, conveniences and labor-saving devices, beauty and materials."[10]

Yet the presence of innumerable conveniences and labor-saving devices could not make up for the "home" without a heart. One of the most powerful examples of this rhetorical tension between house and home can be found in Sinclair Lewis's *Babbitt*, the great novel of crass American middle-class culture, whose eponymous hero, George Babbitt, is in fact a real estate agent: "he was nimble in the calling of selling houses for more than people could afford to pay."[11] The Babbitts live in a residential district of Zenith known as Floral Heights, and their own Dutch Colonial house is typical, every detail declaring to the knowledgeable reader that this is just a house, a place of material display—and failed display at that—not a home:

The room displayed a modest and pleasant color-scheme, after one of the best standard designs of the decorator who "did the interiors" for most of the speculative-builders' houses in Zenith. The walls were gray, the woodwork white, the rug a serene blue; and very much like mahogany was the furniture—the bureau with its great clear mirror, Mrs. Babbitt's dressing-table with toilet-articles of almost solid silver, the plain twin beds, between them a small table holding a standard electric bedside lamp, a glass for water, and a standard book with colored illustrations—what particular book it was cannot be ascertained, since no one ever opened it. The mattresses were firm but not hard, triumphant modern mattresses which had cost a great deal of money; the hotwater radiator was of exactly the proper scientific surface for the cubic contents of the room. The windows were large and easily opened, with the best catches and cords, and Holland roller-shades guaranteed not to crack. It was a masterpiece among bedrooms, right out of Cheerful Modern Houses for Moderate

Incomes. Only it had nothing to do with the Babbitts, nor with anyone else. . . . It had the air of being a very good room in a very good hotel. One expected the chambermaid to come in and make it ready for people who would stay but one night, go without looking back, and never think of it again.

Every second house in Floral Heights had a bedroom precisely like this.

The Babbitts' house was five years old. It was all as competent and glossy as this bedroom. It had the best of taste, the best of inexpensive rugs, a simple and laudable architecture, and the latest conveniences. . . .

In fact, there was but one thing wrong with the Babbitt house: It was not a home.[12]

The particularity of observation here is devastating, from the pretentious materials ("very much like mahogany," "almost solid silver") to the unread book, the expensive modern mattresses, and the hotel-like ambience. "The best of taste," especially someone else's taste, is no substitute for character. That, despite its wealth of modern conveniences, the Babbitts' house is "not a home"—even before the unimaginative George takes the big leap into marital infidelity—is the ultimate, and ultimately damning, verdict on their marriage and their "values."

Paradoxically, the supposed nonmaterialism of the "home" has become one of its best commercial assets. Over time the word "home" became so value-laden (or "values"-laden) a term that some realtors stopped selling "houses" and started selling "homes." "The relation between 'house' and 'home,' " laments poet John Hollander, "has become complicated in contemporary usage by a number of ironic reversals of original meaning. The common—and, unlike many common expressions, vulgar—use of 'home' as a euphemism for 'house' is by and large the linguistic waste product of the American real-estate industry."[13] Thus, after a sightseeing tour of Los Angeles, a writer for the London *Guardian* reported with gentle irony, "In Beverly Hills and Bel

Air, we saw the homes (never called houses) of Jane Withers, Greer Garson, and Barbra Streisand."[14]

The Mother Is the Home

The longstanding symbolic association between houses and women ("to build a house is to create an area of peace, calm, and security, a replica of our own mother's womb")[15] is partly an extension of the cult of domesticity and partly a "literal" reading of women's sexuality as something enclosed and interior.

Much has been written about the Victorian ideology of the woman in the home.[16] What needs stressing here is not only that "a woman's place was in the home," but that she was in effect equated with the home space. Not only was she to be found "in" the home, she *was* the home.

In a book appropriately titled *The Madwoman in the Attic,* Susan Gubar and Sandra Gilbert take a critical view of the equation of persons—and particularly of women—with domestic spaces. They note "the tension between parlor and attic, the psychic split between the lady who submits to male dicta and the lunatic who rebels," that typifies the structure of Charlotte Brontë's *Jane Eyre,* a novel about a " 'haunted' ancestral mansion."[17] Rejecting Erik Erikson's notion of female "inner space," which he had advanced to account for little girls' interest in domestic enclosures, they resist the idea that houses are intrinsically either female or maternal, and point to a number of novels, poems, and stories—like Charlotte Perkins Gilman's 1891 "The Yellow Wallpaper"—in which the house becomes a prison, a negative kind of "asylum," a place of confinement rather than expression, for a woman of nerves and imagination.

Even when women are powerful and valued, they are often identified with houses not only by association but by a kind of insistent and anthropomorphic identity. In nineteenth- and twentieth-century novels the mother often *becomes* the home, to such an extent that when she dies the house itself seems to die as well. After the death of the vibrant and vital Mrs. Ramsay in Virginia Woolf's *To the Lighthouse* (1927), a lyrical and elegiac section called "Time Passes" intervenes between descriptions of human actions, and the novel comes to focus on the empty house:

> Nothing stirred in the drawing-room or in the dining-room or on the staircase. Only through the rusty hinges and swollen sea-moistened woodwork certain airs, detached from the body of the wind (the house was ramshackle after all) crept round corners and ventured indoors. Almost one might imagine them, as they entered the drawing-room questioning and wondering, toying with the flap of hanging wall-paper, asking, would it hang much longer, when would it fall? Then smoothly brushing the walls, they passed on musingly as if asking the red and yellow roses on the wall-paper whether they would fade, and questioning (gently, for there was time at their disposal) the torn letters in the waste-paper basket, the flowers, the books, all of which were now open to them and asking, Were they allies? Were they enemies? How long would they endure?[18]

This slightly unsettling, ghastly equivalence between the house and the *dead* mother calls to mind Sigmund Freud's analysis of the double psychological role of "home" in the life of an adult. Freud, very much a product of a Victorian bourgeois culture of domesticity, broadened the association between "home" and "mother" to encompass the crucial psychological functions of forgetting and repression. He noted that the definition of the word *heimlich* ("homey"), which begins by signifying "homelike and familiar," comes to take on the same meaning as its opposite, *unheimlich* ("uncanny"). "On the one hand," Freud wrote, "*heimlich* means what is familiar and agreeable, and, on the other, what is concealed and kept out of sight." He had noticed a tendency, in his male patients, to associate the idea of the uncanny with the fear of and desire for sexual relations with women.

> It often happens that neurotic men declare that they feel there is something uncanny about the female genital organs. This *unheimlich* place, however, is the entrance to the former *Heim* [home] of all human beings, to the place where each one of us lived once upon a time and in the beginning. There is a joking saying that "Love is home-sickness"; and whenever a man dreams of a place or a country and says to himself, while he is still dreaming: "This place is familiar to me, I've been here before," we may interpret the place as being his mother's genitals or her body. In this case too, then, the *unheimlich* is what was once *heimisch*, familiar; the prefix *"un"* ["un-"] is the token of repression.[19]

The prohibition against incest means that the child's first love object, the mother, must be renounced, and that what was once familiar must become unconscious.

Freud called "mother" the original object, the irreplaceable one, the thing that is always "lost," the very index of wishing, wanting, desire. What does it mean that the home should be "uncanny"? For one thing, it means that there is in more than one sense "no place like home"—that home is both phantasmic and unattainable. And for another thing, it means that "home"—unlike "house"—is always associated with the idea of a return.

What was once known and familiar has become, in the course of development, forgotten and repressed. The haunted house of gothic novels and films often functions as a figure for this structure (think of *Psycho* and *its* unforgettable mother), but even in novels less overtly gothic, the revival of unconscious memory can be represented by the uncanny familiarity of a house. The mystery novel genre is particularly fond of this figure, often combining a house, a missing mother, and a relatively broad-brushed but effective "Freudianism" to bring about its effects. Here is one example.

In an Agatha Christie mystery called *Sleeping Murder* a young woman raised in New Zealand comes to England apparently for the first time, buys a house, sets about making architectural changes—a new doorway, a set of porch stairs—that in each case turn out to restore original features she had no way of knowing had been there. Gradually she discovers that this was the house in which she had lived as a child, and in which a crime had been committed. Christie artfully stresses the sensation of déjà vu of her heroine from the start: "Immediately Gwenda felt a throb of appreciation—almost of recognition. This was *her* house!" And " 'This is *my* house,' thought Gwenda. 'It's *home*. I feel already as though I know every bit of it.' " And yet again, as she is being shown around the property by the seller: " 'Isn't there another bedroom at the end of this passage?' There was—and it was just the sort of room she had imagined it would be."[20]

As an allegory about human memory this is uncannily apt. But as a story about finding the dream house it is also powerfully suggestive, because the dream house is both a fantasy of the future and a fantasy of the past. The murdered woman in Gwenda's repressed memory is her stepmother, barely known and long forgotten. (Gwenda's own mother died "a year or two" after she was born; it's suggestive that she doesn't even know the facts.) When the murderer is revealed, the uncanny sensation disappears—and is replaced by a house with feelings, a mothering house. "She isn't there anymore—in the house—in the hall," Gwenda says to her husband. "I could feel that yesterday before we left. . . . There's just the house. And the house is fond of us. We can go back if we like. . . ."[21]

Intimate Spaces

Freud's tendency to allegorize the body and sexuality is often today misread in a literal way that makes it easy to dismiss. It's a rare individual, male or female, neurotic or "healthy," who would openly acknowledge a desire to take up residency in the mother's womb. Thus, for example, a late-twentieth-century medical doctor who specializes in interpreting children's drawings can discount as far too broad the notion of the house and its rooms as female symbols representing the womb (an idea he attributes to Freud), but then, in the same breath, go on to acknowledge that "the association of womb and haven is undeniable," and speculate that "unconscious feelings may be rising to the surface as the child consciously draws a house."[22]

And when a "psychologist of houses"[23] *refrains* from using provocative phrases like "back to the womb," and indeed, from overtly gendering the house as female, the results of the "house test" are suggestive. "Asking a child to draw his house is asking him to reveal the deepest dream shelter he has found for his happiness," one French critic wrote in connection with an exhibition of children's drawings. "If he is happy, he will succeed in drawing a snug, well-protected house which is well built on deeply-rooted foundations." In many of these house pictures "it is warm indoors, and there is a fire burning, such a big fire, indeed, that it can be seen coming out the chimney."[24] Is this a psychological portrait of "mother"? Of "the womb"? Only in the most stereotypical ways. But snugness, protection, deep roots, and warmth are part of the language of "home as mother" as it has developed in our culture.

We might note that the term "cocooning" doesn't carry any similar psychosexual baggage about going back to the womb, and has become an acceptable term for a certain kind of dwelling search. Gaston Bachelard could ruminate on "images of comforting retreat" in his classic *The Poetics of Space* (1958), observing that "in our houses we have nooks and corners in which we like to curl up comfortably. To curl up belongs to the phenomenology of the verb to inhabit, and only those who have learned to do so can inhabit with intensity."[25] "Nesting" has had a consistently good press as a social ideal, from the "nest egg" (money put away, often in expectation of buying a house) to the "nesting instinct" and the subsequent sense of loss identified as "empty nest" syndrome. One of the edgiest of new shelter magazines, pledged to exploring "the obsessive collectors, the eccentrics, the artists and the excessively house proud,"[26] chose for itself the name *Nest*.

"Always, in our daydreams, the house is a large cradle," says Bachelard. "When we dream of the house we were born in, in the utmost depths of revery, we participate in this original warmth, in this well-tempered matter of the material paradise." And he does not shy away from what he calls "the maternal features of the house," in which the human being is "bathed in nourishment, as though he were gratified with all the essential benefits."[27] Few present-day Americans—perhaps few Europeans today—are born at home, or remain in touch with the first house of their childhood. Yet Bachelard's account is compelling because it tells us something we would like to hear: not only that we remember the house, but also that the house remembers us:

> The house we were born in is physically inscribed in us. It is a group of organic habits. After twenty years, in spite of all the other anonymous stairways, we would recapture the reflexes of the "first stairway," we would not stumble on that rather high step. The house's entire being would open up, faithful to our own being. We would push the door that creaks with the same gesture, we would find our way in the dark to the distant attic. The feel of the tiniest latch has remained in our hands.
>
> The successive houses in which we have lived have no doubt made our gestures commonplace. But we are very surprised, when we return to the old house, after an odyssey of

many years, to find that the most delicate gestures, the earliest gestures suddenly come alive, are faultless.[28]

The "house we are born in" thus sounds not a little like house-as-mother, "faithful," "organic," "open," "physical"—the original home. The phenomenological approach, by integrating memory and reverie, naturalizes the dream in the light of day. It is not the uncanny with its terrifying undertones of gothic surprise, but the cozy activity of daydreaming that is now at stake. "The house we were born in is more than an embodiment of home, it is also an embodiment of dreams. Each one of its nooks and corners was a resting-place for day-dreaming. And often the resting-place particularized the daydream."[29]

Bachelard is the champion of the corner, the nook, the drawer, the closet, the enclosed space. "Does there exist a single dreamer of words who does not respond to the word wardrobe?" he asks, rhetorically. "Every poet of furniture—even if he be a poet in a garret, and therefore has no furniture—knows that the inner space of an old wardrobe is deep. A wardrobe's inner space is also *intimate space,* space that is not open to just anybody."[30] The allusion to Poe's "Philosophy of Furniture" is not inadvertent. Poe is a great intellectual figure in France, and his droll and intelligent essay on "the soul of an apartment" concludes with an account of a dream space: "Even now, there is present to my mind's eyes a small and not ostentatious chamber with whose decorations no fault can be found. The proprietor lies asleep upon a sofa. . . . I will make a sketch of the room ere he awakes."[31]

As for the "wardrobe," of course it is also a "closet," the intimacies of which—as Bachelard declares, "not open to just anybody"—have been the object of much critical unpacking by subsequent writers. The original architectural sense of "closet" in English was a private room, a place in which secret documents and possessions could be stored, and to which the householder—usually the man of the house—could retire.

Bachelard is slightly dismissive of Freud, whom he does not name: "Who doesn't like both locks and keys? There is an abundant psychoanalytical literature on this theme, so that it would be easy to find documentation on the subject. For our purpose, however, if we emphasized sexual symbols, we should conceal the depth of the dreams of intimacy. Indeed, one is probably never more aware of the monotony of the symbols used in psychoanalysis as in such an example [of the lock and key]."[32]

Whether intimate spaces are deeper or less monotonous than sexual symbols is a decision perhaps best left to the reader, though it's worth noting that Bachelard's resolutely ungendered narrative (he is preoccupied with the experience of "the child," a personage never labeled male or female, but clearly representing the author's own normatively masculine younger self) ironically uses a vocabulary of intimacy that has become the stock-in-trade of "women's magazines." And the more resistant to psychoanalysis he gets, stressing the difference between it and phenomenology, the more he replicates the clichés about women and "the mother" in Freud. Every kind of object to which he is drawn— chests, caskets, nests, corners, wardrobes—is an enclosed space "*that may be opened*" (his italics). As the epigraph to his chapter on "Corners," for example, he chooses this, from Maurice Blanchard: "*Fermez l'espace! Fermez la poche du Kangourou! Il y fait chaud*" (Close space! Close the kangaroo's pouch! It's warm in there).[33] But there is a real difference in their approaches. For Freud sexuality and gender difference are crucial; for Bachelard, they are irrelevant—or invisible. Freud analyzes the child; Bachelard becomes the child.

What I want to stress, however, is the arbitrariness of priority here—the tacit but strongly held assumption that the mother is the ground and the house the figure. The logic of this kind of reasoning, which is the logic behind much "house as mother" sentiment, is that the mother *is* the home because the mother is *in* the home and *makes* the home. "Home" by this set of steps becomes an artifact of the family. Even allowing for the progress made by feminism in unsettling the home/mother pairing in the direction of house-husbands and "Mr. Mom," so that "home" is no longer where "Mom" is but where the "primary caretaker" hangs out, this logic insists that house and home are the dependent variables, the secondary rank of experience and emotion. A similar kind of elision shows up in much of our ordinary language. A child "from a good home" is really a child from a good *family*, a loving and attentive family. When we read a child's drawing of a house allegorically (the roof is the hair or hat, the second-story windows are eyes, the door is a mouth, and so on), we are performing the same kind of appropriation, making the *real* object the human being we think we see behind the makeshift hologram of the house. "The child draws another inscrutable house," in the phrase of poet Elizabeth Bishop.[34]

In a formulation like "house as mother" we look *through* rather than *at* the house. But what happens if we see the house as ground and the mother as figure? Let me for argument's sake reverse the paradigm. Not "home is where the mother is," but "mother is where the home is." The house, we could say, is acting out the mother function.

House Mothers

Artist Louise Bourgeois's series *Femmes-maison* ("House-Women"), some painted and some drawn, juxtapose elements of the female body with house forms. In one work a nude woman is depicted frontally from the knees up with a columned Southern mansion for a head. In another, a nude is seen from the side, her head a white-shingled wooden house. The wooden house has one window and a narrow slit that could be a window or a door. Flames shoot from the roof; the house-woman converses with another figure, whose head and trunk are a flower. In another of these images the house is a city brownstone with a flight of steps for a mouth—or perhaps for a ribcage; it's hard to tell, as with a naïve children's drawing, whether we are looking at a trunk or a head. Arms and legs protrude from the sides and base of the building, which seems to leap up, whether in fear or in joy. Yet another image presents a nude woman whose ribcage is centered on a staircase and flanked by pairs of arches. But the arches are in the "basement," which has no floor and on one side hangs over a void. Inverted semicircles for breasts mirror, in reverse, the empty archways. The house, a Colonial cottage reminiscent of the artist's country home in Connecticut, occupies the whole upper torso, and seems again to be both trunk and head.

Are these autobiographical memories, as some critics have argued? The houses reflect Bourgeois's own homes in Choisy-le-Roi, New York City, and Easton, Connecticut, where she and her husband raised three sons. Or are they a "metaphor for her own psychic makeup," as one French critic maintains, "an inner model rather than a feminist metaphor"?[35] Is it necessary, or even possible, to separate these two categories in analyzing the work of an artist known also as a feminist? Although, as critics have acknowledged, "quoting the philosopher Gaston Bachelard when discussing Bourgeois has become a veritable commonplace," Bourgeois herself rejects this comparison, claiming that she found his "deductive" philosophy "disappointing."[36]

"I never dream," Bourgeois has said. "I think, though I'm not sure, that my connection with the unconscious comes not through the dream but through real life."[37] In her own childhood her father installed his mistress, a young English governess, in the household, an arrangement tacitly accepted by her mother for ten years. If—as Bourgeois observes—art is "the experiencing—or rather the re-experiencing of a trauma," this event seems one plausible key to the enigmatic *femmes-maison*. Bourgeois's images (must we ignore the significance of the family name?) are disquieting exactly to the degree that they question the relationship of figure and ground. Bourgeois disconcerts our visual as well as our conceptual expectations. Are these portraits of the house as woman? Of the woman as house? Who *is* the "house-woman"? What is a house? Can the house be or contain a "mother"?

If we juxtapose these *femmes-maisons* to a celebrated cartoon by James Thurber, in which the house is a huge, scowling, and judgmental woman (from the point of view of the tiny husband hesitating at the door) we can see even more clearly how social and gender attitudes, and presuppositions about "mother," the house, and the household, may enter into the phantasmic depiction of the house. Thurber's cartoon reflects the midcentury "Momism" excoriated in Philip Wylie's corrosive *Generation of Vipers* ("megaloid momworship has got completely out of hand. ... Mom is everywhere and everything and damned near everybody, and from her depends all the rest of the U.S.").[38]

"The Thurber woman is most triumphantly herself as the back part of a house lunging toward an apprehensive male," notes Wilfred Sheed in an appreciative but balanced portrait of a man often said to have "hated women." In real life, Sheed adds, "Thurber was surrounded by his share of menacing women, starting with his mother, who set the trend."[39]

Whether feminist or misogynist—or neither—these conflations of house and woman, house and mother, speak in the most direct visual and thematic terms to the question of stability: what is the relationship between the mother and the "stable home"?

Home Makers

"We believe most of today's problems would be solved if more people came from strong, stable, and secure homes," declared the full-page paid advertisement. The message was not from a political organization, however, but from a building system company boasting of its trademark Silent Floors. Tongue-in-cheek (or perhaps in this case, tongue-in-groove), the makers cleverly extolled the value of "a stable home in an uncertain world," describing the pleasures of "a floor without squeaks, creaks and sags."[40] (Ironically, the most desirable floors today may be those *with* squeaks and creaks, the wide pine floorboards of modest and highly prized eighteenth-century frame houses.) But the association of the middle-class house with family values has been a hallmark of that most public and persistent of cultural fantasies, the American Dream.

"The design, layout, and style of the house were invested with a moral purpose," writes one observer of American middle-class domesticity. "The properly designed single-family house would protect and strengthen the family, shoring up the foundations of society and instilling the proper virtues needed to preserve the republic."[41] Magazines, advice manuals, and plan books all abetted this social strategy. So did the U.S. government, by making mortgage interest payments tax-deductible. The picket fence, the square of lawn, the barbecue pit, the attached garage with its basketball hoop—these were the signs of independence, security, and that paradoxical version of collective American individualism that the late fifties and sixties came to call "conformity" and that many Americans today, not all of them senior citizens, idealize as a lost, and perfect, ideal. Like "the mother." As a space of and for fantasy, a space both inside and outside the psyche, a house can function as if it were capable of being the original lost object capable of giving us what we want—the space of wholeness and completeness, of perfectability, of fulfilled desire.

Home is more than a place, and more even than an ideology in these uses: it is the ground of possibility, a place of beginning and ending (or, as the poets have it, of womb and tomb). But more and more it is also a conscious fiction. Today's cheerful welcome mat declares "at-homeness" in a conventional manner, but modern and postmodern dwellers are frequently not at home in actual fact. The answering machine takes the place of the card tray for the calling card (even "calling card" today means something to do with the use of the telephone rather than the literal paying of a house call), and the screening of calls takes the place of the servant who once declared residents to be "not at home" whether they were or not. "Homemade," when printed that way, in quotation marks, means "not made at home, but tasting or looking or pretending to taste or look as if it was made at home."

The same for "home cooking," the standard boast of diners and roadhouses but not of home cooks, who tend instead to pride themselves in using "professional cookware" and "restaurant stoves." Machines for making bread and pasta and for washing and drying clothes perform the function of the fantasy mother without doing any mothering.

In a way the power of this association between the maternal and the material home has, perhaps, never been greater than it is now, when the "traditional home"—itself in the United States largely an artifact of fifties postwar culture, the heyday of the stay-at-home mom—is an object of tremendous nostalgia. Our culture has a great deal invested in not separating these two ideas, in conflating the mother and the house/home. When realtors suggest, as we've seen, that the smell of baking bread at an open house will subliminally attract buyers, they are summoning up the specter of the mother, who welcomes you "home" to a house you have never entered before. To buy the house is to come home to mother. No wonder the real estate market is complicated.

THREE

THE HOUSE AS BODY

The House Is Us

A young woman who was a fellow of a prestigious academic society used to enliven the weekly dinners for herself and her dinner companions by asking these distinguished scholars—largely men of "a certain age"—whether they had had sex in every room of their houses. It was amazing, she reported, how eagerly and how fully they were willing to answer this impertinent question.

What is the sexiest room in the house? Despite—or because of—the ubiquity of phrases like "bedroom eyes" and "philosophy in the bedroom," it is anywhere *but* the bedroom.

As in the wicked fifties ballad of suburban lust in which the lovers were caught in the kitchen "playing Westport between the washing machine and thermostat,"[1] the idea of illicit sex in illicit places has its own allure in the world of sex and real estate. (Consider the evocative power of the phrase "sex in the Oval Office" and you will see what I mean.)

The kitchen table was once a favorite sexual venue for writers of steamy romances. (Even Freud perceived that "the most intimate details of sexual life may be thought and dreamt of in seemingly innocent allusions to activities in the kitchen.") *Someone's in the kitchen with Dinah, strummin' on the old banjo.* Do fictional heroes and heroines now have sex on the granite countertops or cherry-paneled kitchen islands (avoiding the elegant but inconveniently placed bar sink and faucet)? A Los Angeles production of Noël Coward's 1932 play *Design for Living* (about a triangular relationship among an artist, a playwright, and an interior decorator) scandalized purists in the nineties with its "steamy staging," including "sex against walls, sex on top of tables," same-sex twosomes and threesomes.[2] In modern films of suburban life, at least, the impulse to make love somewhere else than in the bedroom is a sign that real passion is at work— or at play. Should we call this "decorator libido"?

The actor Steve Martin, apparently the apotheosis of middle-class "normality" on-screen, has featured in a number of these comedies. In *Housesitter* he finds himself sprawled headfirst in an empty fireplace with the rather conventional, plaid-clad woman he has longed for all his life; her hand clutches at the damper in a paroxysm of anticipatory pleasure ("Light my fire?"). Earlier in the same film, touring the house he built for her (and that she rejects along with his proposal), she eyes the whirlpool tub, which is located right in the bedroom—very convenient, she notes, with the first stirrings of something like lust. Martin, the architect, points out with bumbling eagerness that it's a tub designed for two. In another of Martin's morality tales from the suburbs, *Father of the Bride 2* (1995), seduction in the kitchen is seen as a sign that middle-aged desire is not an oxymoron. In fact, the parents, who have learned that their married daughter is pregnant, cook up (via some impromptu lovemaking on the kitchen floor) an unplanned new baby of their own.

Once the storied rite of passage for American brides was to be carried across the threshold by their husbands. In folklore and myth, thresholds, like any transitional spaces, are dangerous, so this is a protective act, avoiding bad luck. And it also contains, tellingly, an element of mingled possessiveness and transgression.[3] Threshold-crossing, like many another folk ritual, lost its original sense of function ("my woman, my house"), became glamorized in popular culture (all those film brides in filmy dresses being threshold-crossed by the likes of Cary Grant), and fell into genial disuse, except in comedic reversals (bride carries groom; groom is too wimpy to pick up bride). But it has been succeeded by a new "custom": nowadays couples "initiate" each room of the house or apartment, or each substantial new piece of furniture, by making love in them or on them (or, in the case of dining room tables, under them).

Dirt, says anthropologist Mary Douglas, is matter out of place. And dirty pleasures—like that other pleasurable activity, "dishing the dirt"—come in part from doing what we know to be forbidden or frowned upon. The sexiness of sex outside the bedroom, popularized again by films and daytime television, is enhanced by the sense of its being "out of place," just as "love in the afternoon" is a phrase that evokes high and sometimes illicit passion, as if the proper time for lovemaking were only at night, and in the dark.

The Body as House

The representation of the house as a human body is a very old idea, one often reinvented in children's drawings, where the bungalow or cottage frequently comes to resemble a face. The roof is a hat or hair, the windows of the upper story are eyes, the door is a mouth. Variations on this figure abound in everything from allegorical writing to toys and animated cartoons. But whether expressed in literature, painting, theology, or architecture, this analogy between the house and the body has usually emphasized one of three elements: proportion, function, or sex and gender roles.

- *Proportion:* Architectural proportions modeled on human proportions, with the implication of natural design.

The Roman architect and engineer Vitruvius had early on developed the analogy between the human body and architecture: "for without symmetry and proportion no temple can have a regular plan; that is, it must have an exact proportion worked out after the fashion of the members of a finely shaped human body."[4] The proportions of the body were measured and used as models for architectural proportions ("The face from the top of the forehead and the roots of the hair is a tenth part; also the palm of the hand from the wrist to the top of the middle finger is as much; the head from the chin to the crown, an eighth part").[5]

Similarly, a stanza of Andrew Marvell's seventeenth-century house poem, "Upon Appleton House," expresses the ideal of measurement gleaned from nature:

> Why should of all things man unruled
> Such unproportioned dwellings build?
> The beasts are by their dens expressed,
> And birds contrive an equal nest;
> The low-roofed tortoises do dwell
> In cases fit of tortoise-shell.
> No creature loves an empty space;
> Their bodies measure out their place.[6]

The body is the instrument of measurement in the Bible as well as in ancient classical culture. There we find natural measurements like the cubit (from the Latin word for "elbow"), equal to the length of the forearm from the tip of the middle finger to the elbow. God instructed Noah to build the ark 300 cubits long, 50 cubits wide, and 30 cubits high (Genesis 6:15).

The ark may seem an odd kind of model home, but it was designed according to a highly specific plan, with three stories and various categories of beasts (clean and unclean), fowls, and creeping things. Indeed, Christian authors in the Italian Renaissance went on to allegorize the connection between architecture and the body, making it tell a moral and spiritual as well as a physical story. Noah's ark was described in terms of a parallel between human anatomy and human virtue, with the "higher, good openings and the lower, bad ones"[7] exemplifying the basic tension within mankind (as well as between man and beast). This kind of interpretation clearly pointed in the direction of a *func-tionalist* reading, explaining the house as a working body as well as an emblem of natural design.

- *Function:* Bodily functions and how the house reflects them, metaphorically and literally.

The functionalist metaphor of house as body is hierarchical, dividing it into "lower" and "higher" functions overseen by the "head," which is both man (husband, patriarch) and mind. We might note that this is usually a single body—"*the* body"—and that it is unmarked by gender difference. Its differences are differences *within* (high, low, thought, feeling, eating, elimination, etc.).

The purpose of such an anatomy of the house (both literally and figuratively) is to point toward organic wholeness; the different parts work together, "naturally," to make the organism—and the house/household—function. In medieval and Renaissance literature the house is often a "body-castle," fortified against assault by sin and desire, at the same time that it possesses an effective internal economy. The House of Alma in Edmund Spenser's *Faerie Queene* is an extreme and ingenious example played out in great detail: the mouth is a barbican (literally a "gate-with-holes"), the stomach a big dining hall, and waste is disposed of "privily" through a small door at the back. Other Renaissance examples of the body as castle or citadel abound, from Seigneur du Bartas's *Divine Weeks* to Phineas Fletcher's *The Purple Island*, described by Leonard Barkan as "probably the most exhaustive poetic treatment of the human body ever composed."[8] Again there is an emphasis on high versus low functions and on reading the well-organized household as a model of the healthy and morally fit body.

This is a figure that goes back at least as far as Plato's *Timaeus*, where the part of the soul "which is endowed with courage and passion and loves contention" is located "nearer the head, be-

tween the midriff and the neck," so that "being obedient to the
rule of reason it might join with it in controlling and restraining
those desires when they are no longer willing of their own accord
to obey the word of command issuing from the citadel." By contrast, "the part of the soul which desires meats and drinks and
the other things of which it has need by reason of the bodily nature" is placed "between the midriff and the navel, contriving in
all this region a sort of manger for the food of the body." Like a
wild animal within the human frame, "who was chained up with
man and must be nourished if man was to exist," this "lower creation" is confined to a specific place in the body "in order that he
might be always feeding at the manger, and have his dwelling as
far as might be from the council chamber [i.e., the brain and
mind], and make as little noise and disturbance as possible."[9]

It's clear from this account that various regions of the house,
like the corresponding regions of the body, are imagined in a hierarchical relation. The manger—a feeding place for animals—is
as far away as possible from the council chamber, so that the
thoughtful deliberations of human beings will not be disturbed
by animal appetites. And yet all of these rooms and regions are
part of the human body.

- *Sex-gender:* Architecture as reflecting and producing sexual law and morality, and guarding (or enshrining) female
  virtue.

Here the differences are *between,* not within. The number is
two, not one. Man is the "head" of the house; woman is its
"heart." We may note that it is almost impossible to use the
metaphor of woman as a house, or to extend the figure, without
implying some law about her. Which does not keep the metaphor, whether expressed in painting or in poetry, from being,
often, very beautiful.

The body is a house, the house of the soul, claimed a medieval
treatise on the interior of the body. But since a woman's body was

"open," its boundaries convoluted, the inside-out version of a man's, she needed a second "house," a building, to contain her and protect her soul.[10] It is not so much that the building is being thought of as a body, says Mark Wigley. "Rather, the body is thought of as a building. The discourses of space and sexuality cannot be separated."[11]

The relation between the house and the gender and sexuality of its occupants was the implicit or explicit subject of some architectural treatises, like Leon Battista Alberti's influential fifteenth-century work, *On the Art of Building in Ten Books.* Women are to be sequestered deep within the house for their own protection: "any place reserved for women ought to be treated as though dedicated to religion and chastity; also I would have the young girls and maidens allocated comfortable apartments, to relieve their delicate minds from the tedium of confinement. The matron should be accommodated most effectively where she could monitor what everyone in the house was doing."[12] And again, in Alberti's earlier *Della Famiglia:* "the woman, as she remains locked up at home, should watch over things by staying at her post, by diligent care and watchfulness. The man should guard the woman, the house, and his family and country, but not by sitting still."[13] The man moves; the woman remains at home. In essence she *is* the home.

Alberti draws closely upon the ideas of the fourth-century B.C. Greek writer Xenophon, who insisted that the gods made women for indoor, and man for outdoor, pursuits: "Thus for a woman to bide tranquilly at home rather than roam around is no dishonor; but for a man to remain indoors, instead of devoting himself to outdoor pursuits is a thing discreditable."[14] As Wigley comments, "The virtuous woman becomes woman-plus-house, or, rather, woman-as-housed, such that her virtue cannot be separated from the physical space."[15]

Thus Alberti suggests that the spaces in the house are to be arranged in order to restrain and control sensual "appetite" and to conceal or regulate the physical nature of the body. Much of its architectural design—like that of the modern house—is concerned with decisions about what is to be shown and what is to be concealed.

Not only sexuality but also washing and elimination come under this rubric of ordering and regulating. As both customs and technology evolved, certain behaviors that had gone without questioning came under scrutiny. "The body now needs to be cleansed. Or rather, social order has to be cleansed of the body. Architecture is established as such a purification." Washing, dressing, withdrawing in order to perform activities that were not previously imagined as needing to be separated from the public eye—the house and its architectural design become "the agent of a new kind of modesty."[16] The word "closet" now evolves as a term both for a privy and for a study or library, private spaces for the "lowest" and the "highest" functions. It is another "renaissance," the birth of privacy. Bedroom, study, privy—these were the architectural locales of privacy, the places where the body worked and played.

The history of architecture over the last four hundred years has been a history of consistent negotiation between public and private spaces, indoor and outdoor, secret and open, male and female.[17] As we will see in more detail below, the rooms of our houses correspond to, or are at least ostensibly designed for, the containment and performance of specific bodily functions: washing, eating, sleeping, reading, having sex, eliminating bodily waste. But the boundaries of these locales and their "proper" activities have always shifted. The bedroom, for example, was a state chamber for Renaissance royalty and nobility, coded "public" rather than "private," a place where business was transacted and guests were welcomed.

Although from any one contemporary vantage point it may seem as if there is a clear and self-evident line of demarcation between what is in sight and what is out of sight, history gives the lie to such "presentist" views. To be able to attend a king's defecation was once an honor accorded to a dignitary given the title "Knight of the Stool" (the stool in question was a bodily product, not a piece of furniture). The Knight of the Bath was originally a Knight of the Bathtub, whose initiation took place in a tub, attended by esquires who poured water over him and knights who imparted the secrets of chivalry.[18]

But for less august personages, the privy, or medieval necessarium (necessary house), or, equally euphemistically, garderobe (wardrobe), was, as its names and the proliferation of coy euphemisms suggests, usually (if one were not a king) a private space. As one historian of the water closet notes, wryly, "Many of the 'hiding holes,' 'priest's holes,' 'oratories' and 'private chapels' beloved of National Trust guides were in fact garderobes." One supposed "altar slab" in a supposed "chapel" has a hole in it.[19]

But the late twentieth-century sense of "bathroom" as a place on which to expend serious money has been going on for at least a century. Marble tops, paneled woodwork, Ionic pilasters, cast-iron fixtures, floral enameling, brass fittings—all were in vogue in the late 1800s, when "bathrooms" were often converted bedrooms, not "closets" in any but the oldest sense of the term. The word toilet, too, in fact, charts the transit between public and private. Today it is commonly used in the United States as a synonym for lavatory—euphematically "the smallest room" in the house. But in the eighteenth century to be received in a woman's toilet, or dressing room, was a fashionable mark of favor.[20]

This question of the public and the private, the displayed and the hidden, the low and the high, has real implications for the story of the house as a body, and the body as a house. Our present-day concern with the material and materials of houses and with the roles and conventions of particular rooms within the house can be understood, at least in part, as a way of retelling this oldest human story.

One of the ways we have of making things modern—or post-modern—is to scramble up the "laws" of the house-as-body, turning the conventions of the house inside out, rearranging functional spaces in new—and often playful—ways. But if pleasure comes (at least in part) from flirting with transgression or excess, the very possibility of transgression comes (at least in part) from our acceptance of and dependence upon the old metaphor. Our sense of *im*propriety depends upon a notion of the proper and the appropriate, confirming, even as we seek to flout or deny, the conventions of functionality and containment.

Front to Back

What sociologist Erving Goffman called "front and back regions"—parts of the house (or the stage, or the workspace) that are, or are not, meant for public display—have always been susceptible to invasion or conversion. To be coded "front"—as in the old-style "front room" or "front parlor," also known as the "best room" or "best parlor"—was to be condemned to respectability and neglect. The family gathered not in the front but in the back. The front was for "company," or visitors. The "graveyard parlor" or "Sunday go-to-meeting parlor," formally arranged, stiffly and uncomfortably furnished, came in for criticism by the middle of the nineteenth century, when Calvert Vaux wrote that the company parlor "becomes a sort of quarantine in which to put each plague of a visitor that calls; and one almost expects to see the lady of the house walk in with a bottle of camphor in her hand, to prevent infection, she seems to have such a fear that any one should step within the bounds of her real every-day home life."[21]

Of course, there has always been *some* room or other in the typical middle-class house that was forbidden territory except on state occasions. Once it was the front parlor, to which "company" could be shown. Around the turn of the century certain rooms of the house became unfashionable, unnecessary, or both, for middle-class Americans. The parlor was one of the first to go: once the place for decorous courtship under the watchful eye of a parent or chaperone, it was now regarded by writers in *House Beautiful, Ladies' Home Journal,* and *Carpentry and Building* as "outdated, pretentious, and a waste of space."[22] The daughter of the house was far more likely to want to be elsewhere—out of the house—with her boyfriend.

By century's end a proponent of the "artistic cozy corner," with Turkish hangings, "Bagdad" curtains, and a divan defiantly placed diagonally, could celebrate the end of the era of the "best room," with its "haircloth-covered set of furniture" and its "funereal aspect," such that "one never entered without a chill."[23] Gradually such informal, highly decorated nooks and corners— a refuge from the formality of the parlor—gave way to a large, open room in the front of the house: the modern living room.

Based in part on the "living hall" of the Queen Anne house, at once reception area and family gathering space, this room traced its architectural roots as far back as the Elizabethan great hall, with its fireplace and multiple social functions (the great hall was later to be reborn as the "great room" of late-twentieth-century American home construction). The living room was the largest space in the new dwelling, "the heart of the house," "the room where the family gathers, and in which the visitor feels at once the warm, homelike hospitality."[24]

Above all, the new aesthetic declared, "the living room is meant to live in." It would offer the greatest possible contrast to the old parlor and drawing room. As such, it could be "a little shabby here and there, perhaps, but all the more satisfactory for that," Elsie De Wolfe declared in *The House in Good Taste,* and Emily Post concurred: the living room was the most personal of rooms. "The drawing-room demands a certain degree of formality alike in our occupations, our behavior, and our clothes, whereas the living-room is equally welcoming to us no matter what we happen to be doing, how relaxed our spines, how casual our dress, or how easy-going our character." Don't rush to reupholster worn living room furniture, she cautioned, "even a patch or two will do no harm." If the living room needs to look perfect, it's not really a living room. "Then let us call it a parlor or a drawing-room, since a genuine living-room it is not."[25]

This may have been true in the early part of the century, but I'd hate to have had to quote Mrs. Post to my mother's friends in the fifties and sixties. For these women the living room was often in fact the "best room," where "a patch or two" would have been unthinkable, and "redoing the living room" was a favorite social ambition.

The suburban living rooms of some of my schoolmates' families in the far-away fifties were decked in plastic slipcovers—a sign that this was what another era would have called the "best room." You either slid on these slipcovers (in cool weather) or stuck on them (in warm weather). I remember perching uncomfortably on the plastic in my friend Cheryl's house—it was quite thick—and wondering whether her mother had forgotten to take the wrappings off the furniture when it arrived from the store. Since the covers remained for months and indeed years, they seemed to be there on purpose, though I could never quite figure out what the purpose was. But we were children, and never attended any social events in the living room, so I never got to see whether Cheryl's parents' friends spilled drinks on the plastic slipcovers. Instead we were relegated to the knotty-pine-paneled family room in the basement (I think it may have been called a rec—for recreation—room).

In fact, by a principle of natural migration, the place of the old-fashioned parlor was supplied by the new living room. In many households, though not in all, the living room itself began to be a front region—not the place where the family "lived," but where they entertained. Another "back region"—the "family room"—was needed, and named.

Gwendolyn Wright points out that a concern with special spaces for special activities—playing the piano, sewing, reading—had been a major factor in the design of Victorian houses, where nooks, porches, windows, and window seats all had their roles, and a "music room," "nursery," and "library" could be found even in modest homes. "The names of these many rooms were a further statement about family life. Debates about sitting rooms, family rooms, parlors, living rooms, and living halls filled builders' guides as well as many novels."[26]

By the middle of the twentieth century, as Wright reports, two new rooms had appeared in the moderate-cost house: the utility room (for the washer and dryer) and a room first known as the don't-say-no space and then, after a piece appeared about a model house in a 1947 issue of *Parents' Magazine,* as the family room.[27] (Despite the promising original name, which I associate with the days of Nancy Reagan, it was clearly to a child, and not a lover or a mind-altering substance, that one was supposed to not-say-no.)

Presumably the living room was the place where you *could,* and perhaps even *should,* say no, which is why the modern living room has often been the deadest room in the house. For no less an authority than Miss Manners has declared the old-style living room dead. The living room, she remarked with customary wit, is "considered a nice place to have and to furnish, but not to live in."[28] Nor is the living room the only defunct household space. "The kitchen is used to entertain guests so they don't have to use the living room. This entertainment now consists of letting the guests watch what used to be the preparations for entertaining guests."

It seems almost as if the stepped-up pace of modern living increased the rapidity of the turnover, for succeeding decades gave us not only the family room but the rumpus room, the den, the television room (usually one of the smallest rooms in the house, and, except for the kitchen, the most frequently in use), and its more technologically sophisticated cousin, the media room.

The den ("a small room or lodging in which a man can seclude himself for work or leisure") had been around since the eighteenth century as a male or bachelor preserve but was losing some of its cachet as it became a commonplace in middle-class homes. Emily Post rued the fact that in order to express "manliness" this room "must be known as a 'den'" and "furnished with an overstuffed sofa that would support an elephant and with chairs obviously made for baby hippopotamuses."[29] By the middle of the twentieth century, the author of *Auntie Mame* could mock it, through the eyes of a ten-year-old boy, as a pretentious holdover from a more robust era. ("Mr. Babcock cleared his throat and said he believed we'd have Our Little Talk now and we'd go into the Den so the maid couldn't snoop. The Den sounded very interesting but it was just a little room full of books on banking and even hotter than the other rooms had been.")[30]

Meantime, at least in the United States, the "great room" became fashionable for new construction: often double height and with a fireplace, this was the "casual" living room that replaced the formal living room, which had replaced the front parlor. (In the United Kingdom, with its medieval and Renaissance architectural heritage of the "great hall," the phrase "great room" has not—or not yet—caught on.) The "eat-in kitchen" in many houses has replaced the dining room, often called the "formal dining room," as well as the informal "breakfast nook" and "dining alcove."

Back to Front

Inevitably—such is the nature of unruly desire—it became "exciting" to do "back" things in the front of the house, whether this meant snacking in the living room or necking in the parlor. A number of turn-of-the-century paintings show the erotic potential of the music room, whether the "master" was teaching his female pupil the piano or the violin. In the supposedly staid fifties, while the children's room or the rumpus room might have offered a private space for flirtation and experimentation, teenage lovers took amatory possession of the living room couch (or, if they were really willing to tempt fate, the parental bedroom).

But what has happened more recently is that rooms formerly coded "back"—like the kitchen and the bathroom—have become, in an odd way, "front." These are the spaces on which we spend huge amounts of money, whether in top-of-the-line appliances or in limestone and granite tile. "Is it a fireplace or an oven? That depends, do you feel like making love or baking?" inquire the manufacturers of the Tulikivi, a versatile soapstone fireplace (and bake oven). "It isn't every household fixture that can satisfy two of humanity's more pressing needs."[31]

The Victorian kitchen was a workplace and a gathering place for servants. No upper-class or even middle-class householder would have thought of eating there. In a move toward apparent democratization, like the rise of the living room as informal "heart of the house," the kitchen gradually took over as family eating space from the more formal dining room. The present-day nostalgia for the "country kitchen," as Mary Gilliatt points out, is a somewhat fanciful one, since in the English countryside until the 1920s "most well-to-do families possessed kitchens that they hardly ever thought of, let alone visited." What we mean when we say "country kitchen" is "the larders and kitchens of farmhouses and cottages where for centuries they were in fact general living rooms."[32] It is, in other words, a dream of classed-down "simplicity"—supported, these days, by the most expensive materials, often carefully crafted to look "distressed." Phrases like "eat-in kitchen"—in realty-speak, EIK—suggest spaciousness (as contrasted, say, with the tiny "galley" or "Pullman" kitchen, adapted from the close quarters of a ship or train) but they also conjure images of the family gathered around the table for meals, a heart-tugging picture from the memory bank of the past. But just as readily, the pendulum has swung back, making the "informal" kitchen the costliest, and often the most glamorous, room in the house, rivaled only by the formerly humble bathroom for pride of place, outsize proportions, and the latest in fixtures and cabinetry.

Not only are the kitchen and the bathroom the most extravagant rooms in many houses, they are often (as a consequence) the most displayed to visitors. And not only are they *marketed* as "sexy" (in the loose general sense of "desirable" and "expensive"), they have become places we think of as suitable for assignations:

with a spouse, a lover—or that most seductive of partners, the room itself.

An issue of *House & Garden* devoted to "Perfect Powder Rooms" and "Bathing Luxuries from Soaking Tubs to Fabulous Fixtures" opens with a two-page frontispiece ad from American Standard Plumbing that pictures a romantically candlelit tub, sink, and toilet. The headline reads, "A great place to read ROMANCE NOVELS or for that matter to RE-ENACT THEM." In smaller type the ad copy continues, "This is the sort of bathroom with which a person could form a long, loving relationship. For more information on these and other similarly seductive bathroom fixtures, call. . . ."[33]

Notice that it's the *bathroom* itself, not another person, that is imagined as offering the possibility of "a long, loving relationship." Once again material culture provides both seduction and romance. "I love bathing in the middle of the day, when everyone else is at work or at school," confesses author Jane Smiley, but "the best time to take a bath is before bed." Smiley says her "most intimate bathroom relationship" is with the tub ("my preferred tub is by Kohler, called 'the Greek' ").[34] Smiley's cherished baths are solo events—she has scathing things to say about "master bath syndrome" and the double sink—but the bathroom, emulating "the Greeks" or, even more likely, the Romans, is increasingly becoming a shared play space, at least in fantasy.

"You wouldn't believe what people are putting into their showers," says an Oklahoma distributor of luxury bathroom fixtures. One couple in Rancho Santa Fe, California, installed three television sets, two whirlpool tubs, two toilets, a bidet, and a steam shower "for eight of their closest friends." Marble, limestone, Baccarat crystal, polished nickel, and that old favorite, gold, now ornament the once-humble bathroom. An "adequate budget" for a handsome master bath is now about $50,000. "People want to be coddled," says a New Jersey certified bath designer. "There's no place in the world I'd rather be," testifies a woman whose comfortable suburban house contains five bedrooms. Her favorite room is the bathroom, which has a fireplace, glass doors leading to a wooden deck, and a built-in sound system.[35]

In the kitchen, too, new appliances are changing the way people fantasize their lives. With the advent of the "integrated refrigerator" that masquerades as a drawer or cabinet, you can stash your Granny Smiths among the lingerie. No need to tiptoe past the kids' rooms at night in search of a quart of Rocky Road. Instead you can keep your sinful tastes under control, and under wraps, by storing your treats in the bedroom. "The kitchen is moving out of the kitchen," reports the editor of *Remodeling* magazine. People these days "want to reward themselves, not necessarily with an object, but with a leisure experience."[36] And that leisure experience, while it might conceivably take place in the playroom, the media room, or the home gymnasium, often winds up in the master bedroom suite. "As the kitchen becomes more public, the theory goes, many affluent homeowners are retreating to the bedroom," away from children and houseguests.[37]

"What has enchanting, 600-count, Egyptian cotton sheets, a sitting room, and a library?" asked *Design Times* of its readers. It answered, "If you ask the nation's leading designers, it's your bedroom." In fact, and not surprisingly, the bedroom turns out to be "an opportunity to create a space that is not just about sleeping, but also a uniquely private living room," outfitted "to accommodate dreaming, reading, primping, snacking, channel-surfing, [and] faxing" as well as romancing between those high-thread-count Egyptian sheets.

In fact, the role of the bedroom has come full circle, from the all-purpose chambers of the past in which people once slept, ate, and lived, to a bedroom that—in a desperate search for "privacy"—regains its function as eating and living space.

The bedroom, after all, is a fairly new invention. Most of the families of medieval Europe shared a single room for living and sleeping, and the bedrooms of the rich and famous in the Renaissance were often state chambers where public visitors were

received. Powerful personages transacted business in their bedrooms: the *ruelle* was the space between the bed and the wall,
where secretaries could bring documents and visitors gossip. The
king's *levée* was a state, not a private, event. Beds both at home
and on the road—at inns, country houses, and palaces—often
accommodated more than one person, and the bedfellows were
sometimes strangers. England's famous Great Bed of Ware, ten
feet eleven inches square, slept any number at once.

In the houses of the nobility and the rich, suites of rooms,
called apartments, were assigned to individual persons, each of
whom might have his or her own great chamber, drawing room,
dressing room, and sometimes also a "closet" or private study.
Occupants could move for greater comfort and privacy into
smaller adjoining rooms—heating a large public chamber with
fireplaces was never easy in winter—but only gradually did the
bedchamber separate itself from the withdrawing (or drawing)
chamber.

The term "bedchamber" itself dates from the mid-sixteenth
century, marking the fact that the new space was used mainly for
sleeping and no longer as a bed-sitting room. By the eighteenth
century the drawing room had "ceased almost entirely to be attached to individual bedrooms," and by the end of the century,
in most of the larger houses in England, bedrooms, which had
formerly been located on the ground floor, had been moved upstairs. As Mark Girouard notes, "People began to feel that
upstairs bedrooms were part of the order of things." The Victo-
rians made sure that bedrooms for children were near those of
their parents, and many country houses had a self-contained
family wing, "with the nurseries up above the parents' boudoir,
study, bedroom and dressing room, and a little private stair to enable a fond mother to run up from her boudoir and see how the
children were."[38]

In the twentieth century more and more people had fewer and
fewer servants. (The return of the "nanny" is a self-conscious af-

fectation in terminology, though regarded as a child-care necessity for some financially comfortable two-career households.)

To a certain extent there has been a return, in high-end construction and interior design, to emphasizing the notion of separate "apartments," at least in the spatial separation of the parental quarters from the "children's wing." You can now find romance in your own home—neatly confirming, as you do so, the early architects' and philosophers' desire to keep women safely and monogamously within the house. As in a certain kind of drawing room comedy, it turns out that the transgressive affair you are having is with your husband or wife, in disguise. Modern real estate ads stress the opulence of the "master suite," often described in terms like "sumptuous," "lavish," "sensuous," "breathtaking," "fantasy," "baronial" (or "Texas-sized"), "royal," "Hollywood-inspired," "right out of the Arabian nights," "practically sinful," or (with no "practically" about it) downright "sinfully indulgent."[39] "Master suite features a snuggle-up fireplace" is suggested as a catchy come-on for buyers seeking a fantasy romance (with their spouse or partner) in a dream home. The twin conduits of desire—for a lover, for "possessions" or material goods—go hand in hand in this merchandizing of fantasy space, in which the buyers and the sellers are "in bed together," as the saying goes.

What Women Want in Their Bedrooms

What Women Want in Their Bedrooms sounds like the title of a best-selling self-help manual. (This was underscored for me when I mislaid the volume and had to report to some friends—who could barely control their amusement—that I had lost, or couldn't find, *What Women Want in Their Bedrooms*.) But the book in question is actually the product of a survey taken by *McCall's* magazine during the late 1930s and early 1940s on the "Home of Tomorrow," culminating in four separate competitions in 1943. As the magazine soberly noted, the contest "was partly fashioned by war conditions." Its purpose, almost unimaginable in the light of today's consumer-driven marketplace in luxury goods and services, was to *deny* or *avoid* the engendering of desire. The prizes for contest winners were war bonds and stamps.

The magazine's reluctance to "stimulate" the reader into untimely "buying wants" at an unpropitious time for the country was itself rather provocative, as were the titles of the individually published volumes in the series: *What Women Want in Their Dining Rooms of Tomorrow, What Women Want in Their Living Rooms of Tomorrow, What Women Want in Their Kitchens of Tomorrow,* and, inevitably, *What Women Want in Their Bedrooms of Tomorrow.* "Tomorrow" here meant not some far-off future (as in Disney's Tomorrowland) but as soon as the war was over.[40]

In short, this was a survey that, under the guise of delaying or displacing desire, in fact produced it, predicted it, and promised it to retailers. And in the course of doing so it answered, at least on the material plane, what no less a figure than Sigmund Freud had notoriously called "the great question"—a question for which he himself admitted he had no answer despite his "thirty years of research into the feminine soul": "What does a woman want?"[41]

Contestants were asked for each product item (down puffs, linoleum floor, built-in cupboards, antiques, early American reproductions, etc.) to check one of four boxes: "I must have and will buy as soon as possible"; "I like and may get—but not sure"; "I have now—don't need—won't buy"; or "I don't like and won't buy."

Inevitably the volume on bedrooms contained its share of double-entendres, like the section on "Chest Style Preference—Modern vs. Traditional." But the straightforward assertions were in a way more surprising than the unwitting witticisms. "Bedrooms," declare the editors of *What Women Want,* are "primarily a place for rest. On that one point the 'Modern' and 'Traditional' women agree. But the two style camps are by no means agreed on what rest means. For the 'Traditional' voters, 'rest' is 'sanctuary,' for the 'Moderns,' it is 'freedom.' "[42] And even here things were not exactly what they seemed. A Modern woman in search of freedom—at least in the pages of *McCall's*—found it not in sexual experimentation but in lighter housekeeping duties. "Bare floors with scatter rugs because they are easy to clean; light simple furniture because it is easy to dust." And many respondents, whether Modern or Traditional, regarded the bedroom as essentially women's space, where "she goes for 'a good cry' "—or, as one "understanding husband" put it, "okaying" a pastel color scheme, "with two sons where else can you indulge in a little feminine frippery?"

McCall's offered its readers a chance to vote for one of two photographed bedrooms, assuring them that both were "in good taste" and that the question was only which they preferred. The choice between Traditional and Modern in this case included a choice between twin four-poster beds separated by a night stand (Traditional) and what at first looks like a contemporary queen-sized bed with tables on either side (Modern). Indeed, the magazine's fictional spokeswoman for the Modern camp, "Sally," comments in her descriptive copy that "the oversize double bed is a dream." But on the contest entry form, neat lettering across the foot of a line drawing of the same double bed contradicts her: "two single beds" it says. Like the beds my parents slept in (which dated from the same era) this double bed is actually two beds pushed together under a single spread.

What women were expected to want in their bedrooms of tomorrow did not, apparently, include a double mattress. The twin bed, a cultural innovation that dates to the late eighteenth century, when a Sheraton design was adopted "to keep lovers cool during the hot summer months,"[43] reached its heyday in the United States in the decade of the fifties, the decade of *Pillow*

Talk, when the proportion of twin beds bought by Americans skyrocketed to 68 percent of the market.[44] But not everyone approved this trend. In fact, the word on twin beds was that—far from producing twins—twin beds produced divorce.

"This movement towards twin beds must stop," opined the director of the Family Relations Institute in 1947. "The change from a double bed to twin beds is often the prelude to a divorce."[45] "Twin Beds for Divorce," flatly declared the title of another article deploring the same socially deleterious fashion. Yet if in life twin beds could cause divorce, in Hollywood they were the very emblem of marriage. "Twin bed marriages," writes Parker Tyler, a historian of sex in films, "actually mark a whole Hollywood epoch of bedroom customs."[46] One of the ironclad rules of the Hays Code, self-imposed on U.S. movies since the early 1930s, was that, though a man and a woman could be shown alone together in a bedroom, even in their nightclothes, "there couldn't be a double bed waiting to accommodate their conjugal embraces; rather, there had to be *twin beds.*" So common was this association that the arrangement favored by my parents and selected as the "modern" option by *McCall's,* two single beds placed side by side with a common headboard, became known as the "Hollywood bed."

It's all too easy to conclude that Americans of the forties and fifties were prudish and unimaginative about sex, as prudish and unimaginative as the Hollywood code. In European hotels and foreign films of the same era the double bed reigned supreme. But in fact the "Hollywood" scenario now looks paradoxically erotic. Think of having to cross that boundary line, deliberately, visibly getting out of one bed and into another. It's almost like making love in a forbidden place, not the same old conjugal bed. If poet Robert Frost could muse that writing poetry without rhyme was like playing tennis with the net down, what might he have to say about the provocative barrier posed by that yard of empty space, occupied only by night table and lamp, that kept the two beds apart? Could it be that some Americans chose twin beds, not because they held sexuality at a distance, but because twin beds were *sexier*? Might we indeed live long enough to see a retro revival of the twin bed in the annals of cultural style?

A half-century after *McCall's* disclosed *What Women Want* in their bedrooms, living rooms, dining rooms, and kitchens, another "home" magazine was inspired to sponsor a similar survey to find out "what our readers really want in their dream house." Since this was the nineties, not the fifties, both men and women were invited to reply, but gender was still clearly an issue. The master bedroom, for example, was "an area of some differences of opinion, but not for the obvious reasons." It seems that what both men and women want most in their bedrooms of tomorrow is a *closet*. But more women than men wanted separate dressing rooms and a fireplace in their bedrooms, while more men than women sought to satisfy baser appetites: 30 percent of males, and only 19 percent of females, wanted an area set aside with a small refrigerator and a coffeemaker for breakfast and snacks.[47] This interest in eating spaces extended to what the magazine called "a full dining room," which came "at the top of the men's list of desired rooms." *Colonial Homes*, aiming to distinguish male taste from female taste—the survey was part of its special issue on men, a new target demographic for shelter magazines—speculated that "a man truly feels like a 'king in his castle' when he is sitting at the head of a family table." The old image of the body as a castle—and indeed, the man as the "head"—here returns as a scenario set *within* the house. But not, we might note in passing, within the "king bed."

What is certainly making a comeback, if the anecdotal evidence of younger friends is to be believed, is what is known in modern parenting circles as "the family bed"—the bed that contains Mom, Dad, and the kids. All at the same time. Not just for Mother's Day breakfast, but all through the night. "What about intimacy?" asked an article on modern parenting, posing the Big Question. "You have two choices. Be quiet, or be creative." Or, it turned out, abandon the bedroom to the kids. A couple with two children, a three-year-old daughter and a three-week-old son, sleep in their king-sized bed with the whole family. So they bought a convertible sofa-bed for the living room. When they wanted intimacy, they moved *out* of the bedroom. "It's kind of romantic because the fireplace is in the living room too," said the wife. "Now if we could just get rid of the dog and two cats!"[48]

The House as Self

Increasingly, for a generation of consumers whose appetites and ambitions are only matched by their (not so) secret feelings of insecurity and fears of unworthiness, the finding, furnishing, and exhibiting of the perfect house has become a *psychic* goal that can be realized in *material* terms. "Get rid of everything in your house or apartment that doesn't represent who you are," counseled quotable style guru Quentin Crisp. "You should regard your home as your dressing room."[49]

"Your house, to be perfect, must delight and express *not your decorator, but you,"* Emily Post had advised. "If the house expresses the architect or the decorator and *not* the owner, then its personality is a song out of tune."[50]

The notion that a house had a "personality" that could be expressed through home decorating began to gain favor at the end of the nineteenth century. On a highly successfully lecture tour of the United States in 1882–1883 the personable and charming Oscar Wilde, aged only 27 at the time, added a talk on "The House Beautiful" to his public lectures on "The English Renaissance" and "The Decorative Arts." Wilde, it is said, "metaphorically walked through the house, commenting on the mistakes he had observed."[51] Audiences flocked eagerly to hear him lay down the law about carpeting, tile, artificial flowers, blown glass and Dutch porcelain stoves. (It was this same Wilde who much later in his life, disgraced, mortally ill and with only a hint of his old bravado, famously quipped to a friend in Paris, "My wallpaper and I are fighting a duel to the death. One or the other of us has to go."[52] A month later Wilde was dead.)

As historian Karen Halttunen notes, around the turn of the century "*personality* displaced *character* as the dominant conceptualization of the self."[53]

"Personal decorating," the attempt to decorate houses as an expression of personality, became a dominant theme in the period from 1900 to 1930, inspired by books like Elsie De Wolfe's *The House in Good Taste* (1913) and Emily Post's *Personality of a House* (1930). De Wolfe, one of America's first interior decorators, an actress, an international hostess, and a woman with a big personality of her own, was given to bold pronouncements. Journalists loved to quote her words on first seeing the Parthenon: "It's beige—my color!" Convinced that "A house is a dead-giveaway, anyhow, so you should arrange it so that the person who sees your personality in it will be reassured, not disconcerted,"[54] she tried to imagine what it would be like to peek into the identical rooms on different floors of an apartment house and see what decoration had done to them. "How amazingly different they are! How amusing the suggestion of personality, or lack of it!"[55]

Character had meant something innate, value-laden, unchanging. *Personality* was, as De Wolfe saw, a matter of having fun. And personality went hand in hand, or hand in purse, with consumerism, for the era of handicrafts was, for the time being, over. Buying things, in short, became "the way to exhibit personal taste."[56]

Words like "anxiety," "status," and "fulfillment" were part of the decorator's new arsenal. Masculinity and femininity, "the kind of a room a man likes" (dark colors, heavy furnishing, bold patterns) and "the kind of room a woman likes" (floral and chintz, frilly curtains) could be expressed—through the art of the decorator—in the rooms of the family home.

Terms like "effeminate," "feminine," "charming," "masculine," and "manly" appear with great frequency as ways of describing, and accounting for the popularity of, various historic as well as modern styles.

The 1920s saw a new interest in color, which had to be articulated, it was thought, through the services of a trained designer.[57] Even bathroom plumbing could express the true you. By the end of the twenties manufacturers had learned how to color plumbing fixtures, and the previously all-white "sanitary" bathroom bloomed with shades of orchid and mint green. By 1937 you could choose a toilet in red or navy blue porcelain as well as in pastels.[58]

Emily Post wrote ardently of "color as a background for personal becomingness," dividing blonde women into four types (the noonday blonde, the moon blonde, the drab blonde, and the red-haired blonde) and warning the husband of the pallid "moon blonde" that his own masculine room should not have "heavy Tudor or Jacobean furniture if she is to be admitted— ever."[59] Brunettes and "mediums" were likewise subject to a detailed color analysis in which "psychology" was much in evidence.

"If you are very reserved—purposely, perhaps, or possibly inarticulate by nature—would gray or gray-blue-violet increase your innate aloofness?" If you are overenthusiastic and excitable, would the "perpetual stimulant of red" on your walls and furnishings "increase your own tendencies to the point where nervous breakdown threatens?"

In any case, age was a factor. Young women could get away with almost anything, but "when one grows older, choice of becomingness is essential. A woman whose skin is inclined to be at all red should avoid green like the plague." Women whose hair is fading in middle age should not fill their rooms with fashionable modern steel furniture, since steel makes their hair look "mousy-yellow."[60]

The idea that the house was a symbol of the self, an expression of "personality," thus led to a psychologizing, or pop-psychologizing, of decoration and furnishings that lasted through the middle of the century and may have reached its peak in the 1970s. Karen Halttunen cites the proliferation in that decade of books with titles like *What Your House Tells About You, What Do You Say to a Naked Room?*, and *Psycho-Decorating*. As she notes wryly, "These manuals explain, for example, that while glass-top tables reveal aggressiveness, burled wood indicates a strong sense of social justice, and patchwork quilt patterns betray a tendency toward self-criticism."[61] *Psycho-Decorating*, Halttunnen points out, also offered a portfolio of "Living Rooms of Different Personalities," including rooms that declared themselves and their residents (or their designers?) to be Achieving, Deferent, Exhibitionistic, Dominant, Heterosexual, or Friendly. And a cartoon in a 1978 *New Yorker* showed a man confiding to a woman seated next to him in a bar, "I've tried to express myself clearly, but for a truly definitive statement of *me* you'd have to see my living room."[62]

A new color craze contributed to the sense of self-realization. "Doing your colors" ("I'm a summer!" "You're an autumn") became fashionable, both in clothing and in home décor; books like *Color Me Beautiful* (1984) hit the best-seller list, reinventing Emily Post's color analyses for a new and fascinated audience. Analyses like Joan Kron's *Home-Psych: The Social Psychology of Home and Decoration* (1983) took intelligent cognizance of this trend. For the "me generation"—and, somewhat differently, for the Woodstock generation—self-expression had become a family value.

Material Pleasures

The pleasures of "doing," or "doing over," a house are often deprecated as self-indulgent, trivial, and consumerist, while the notion of "making a home" implies an ethical or moral commitment that transcends mere things, mere "stuff," from collectibles to plumbing fixtures. But for many people—and I am one of them—the two activities are intimately related, the one an imaginative spur to the other. The chandelier, the sconce, the perfect wallpaper for the baby's room, the eat-in kitchen with its "farm table" that allows us to imagine ourselves in a country setting even in the heart of the city—these are minor but crucial household icons, artifacts that are part fact and part art, all part of the story of who we are and what we love.

It's often the material things that provide the essence of memory: the smell of the kitchen, the unevenness of the paving stones (as Proust discovered), the edge of the too-small table as you crowd around it for a holiday dinner. Nostalgic memory is a sudden encounter with the thingness of the thing that has been forgotten, not the conscious desire for possessions, whether past, present, or future.

"There is a logic that has joined the priceless and the priced, the familiar and the unfamiliar, the world of goodness and the world of goods—in nineteenth-century terms, the dwelling place and the marketplace," suggests Jean-Christophe Agnew. The name he gives to that logic is "commodity aesthetic," a logic that celebrates those "moments when the very boundaries between the self and the commodity world collapse in the act of purchase."[63]

But perhaps the commodity aesthetic has had to keep resisting its own success, since it constantly threatens to make too available items that need to be unique in order to be valued. Attempting to distance itself from the "manufactured 'good taste' of mail-order supplies like Pottery Barn and style police such as Martha Stewart," *Elle Décor* plumped for something it called "postmaterialist glamour."[64]

It's partly for this reason that household furnishings, like just about everything else, are being marketed with an eye to their sex appeal.

"It has strong, sturdy legs just in case it makes you feel weak in the knees," proclaims a caption accompanying the image of a hefty and curvaceous chair in Thomasville Furniture's Encounter

Collection. The chair in question is named, with conscious double entendre, the Encounter Chair. And indeed the whole Encounter advertising campaign has the same gamesome flavor: "It's smart, attractive, and gives you all the space you need. Too bad you can't date it," says the running head above the picture of a cabinet with tambour doors (the Master Chest); and, in an inside foldout page, "Finally, a bed that doesn't just lie there," describing, needless to say, the Encounter Bed.[65]

"What strong arms you have," murmurs a furniture store ad to its Big Bench sofa.[66] "Eros invades every room of the house with seductive chairs and slithery sofas," announces an article on new furniture designs. "The seductive turn of a leg, the come-hither look of a slick vinyl chair. . . . Hemlines are up, legs are bared."[67]

Before we dismiss this as mere shelter-magazine sensationalism flaunted under the provocative headline "The Joy of Sexy," let's recall that the legs of Victorian pianos were draped and covered with fabric because it was thought indecent to let them show. Had they been called posts or props or stanchions, sensibilities would not have been offended. But "legs" they were, and legs required camouflage. There's no inevitability in labeling these appendages—the relationship of cause and effect (name and consequent prudery or prurience) is not so clear as it may seem in hindsight. It's almost as if the naughty pleasure of bare "legs" and "arms" was sought in order to be disavowed.

These blatantly seductive come-ons demonstrate more than the typical conventions of advertising, the "eroticizing of consumption."[68] The jokingly anthropomorphic chairs and sofas are inviting promises, and promising invitations. They supply exciting narratives, fantasies, and daydreams to go along with the materiality of chair or bed.

By providing not only love objects but love stories, love scenarios, the house and its furnishings are doing our living for us. The house itself—rather than any of its occupants—becomes what greets us when we come home.

FOUR

THE DREAM HOUSE

A glance at any magazine, realtor's guide, or bookstore shelf will make it clear that "dream house" is the most familiar of clichés. Shelter magazines like *House Beautiful* and *Design Times* offer layouts of "Dreamy Bedrooms," and a real estate book offers all you need to know about *Your Dream Vacation Home.* "Fulfill a Fantasy," invites an issue of *Country Living* ("One woman's dream cottage becomes reality, and so can yours with house plans available in this issue"). "Dream" in a phrase like "the American Dream," where the word means, or at least encompasses, the dream of home ownership, is so familiar that we don't really hear it. But what, if anything, do houses have to do with dreams?

Modern psychological accounts of the house frequently begin with Carl Jung's celebrated dream of himself as a house, a dream that Jung thought central to his development of the notion of the "collective unconscious." The dream occurred in 1909 at a moment in the relationship between Jung and Freud when their former collegiality had turned to resentment and rivalry. The disciple, Jung, now sought to distinguish himself from his mentor, and the dream of a house was crucial, he thought, in marking the difference between them.

This was a dream that became part of Jung's repertoire of stories. The more he told it, the longer it got, the more elaborate the description of the house and its rooms—and the more irritating and inept the figure of Freud. The version often quoted is from his memoirs, recorded and transcribed when he was an old man of eighty-one. But the most direct and succinct is probably the one Jung offered during an English-language seminar on analytical psychology in 1925.

As I have said, Freud was able to interpret the dreams I was then having only incompletely or not at all. They were dreams with collective contents, containing a great deal of symbolic material. One in particular was important to me, for it led me for the first time to the concept of the "collective unconscious." . . .

This was the dream. I was in a house I did not know. It was "my house." I found myself in the upper story, where there was a kind of salon furnished with fine old pieces in rococo style. On the walls hung a number of precious old paintings. I wondered that this should be my house, and thought, "Not bad." But then it occurred to me that I did not know what the lower floor looked like. Descending the stairs, I reached the ground floor. There everything was much older, and I realized that this part of the house must date from about the fifteenth or sixteenth century. The furnishings were medieval, the floors were of red brick. Everywhere it was rather dark. I went from one room to another, thinking, "Now I really must explore the whole house." I came upon a heavy door, and opened it. Beyond it, I discovered a stone stairway that led down into the cellar. Descending again, I found myself in a beautifully vaulted room which looked exceedingly ancient. Examining the walls, I discovered layers of brick among the ordinary stone blocks, and chips of brick in the mortar. As soon as I saw this I knew that the walls dated from Roman times. My interest by now was intense. I looked more closely at the floor. It was of stone slabs, and in one of these I discovered a ring. When I pulled it, the stone slab lifted, and again I saw a stairway of narrow stone steps leading down into the depths. These, too, I descended, and entered a low

cave cut into the rock. Thick dust lay on the floor, and in the
dust were scattered bones and broken pottery, like remains of
a primitive culture. I discovered two human skulls, obviously
very old and half disintegrated. Then I awoke.[1]

Annoyed to discover that Freud, who regarded all dreams as
wishes in the unconscious of the dreamer, was more interested in
the identity of the skulls than in the allegory of the house (for
him the question was, "Whom did Jung wish dead?"), Jung decided that it was up to him to "find the real meaning of the
dream." The meaning he offers is one that sees the house as an
allegory of the relationship between the conscious and the unconscious mind.

> It was plain to me that the house represented a kind of image
> of the psyche—that is to say, of my then state of conscious-
> ness, with hitherto unconscious addition. Consciousness was
> represented by the salon. It had an inhabited atmosphere, in
> spite of its antiquated style.
>   The ground floor stood for the first level of the uncon-
> scious. The deeper I went, the more alien and the darker the
> scene because. In the cave, I discovered remains of a primitive
> culture, that is, the world of the primitive man within my-
> self. . . .
>   The dream pointed out that there were further reaches to
> the state of consciousness I have just described: the long un-
> inhabited ground floor in medieval style, then the Roman
> cellar, and finally the prehistoric cave. These signified past
> times and passed stages of consciousness.[2]

What was the *subject* of Jung's famous dream? To him the
answer is clear: "It obviously pointed to the foundations of cultural history—a history of successive layers of consciousness.
My dream thus constituted a kind of structural diagram of the
human psyche. . . . it was my first inkling of a collective a priori

beneath the personal psyche."[3] Distinguishing himself from Freud, Jung regarded these dream images as coming not from a personal source (like his own individual associations, his reading, the unconsciously recalled words of an acquaintance) but instead from a common wellspring of "primitive" human experience, a "re-echo of the prehistoric and the ancient."[4]

We might want to point out that his dream design is for a rather European-looking house, and that the progression from "Roman" to "medieval" to "rococo," too, seems more regionally specific than it does universal. An American from the Midwest, or an Arab from the Middle East, might dream about a very different kind of house. But the dream of the house was for Jung the story of a history of consciousness. The house in his dream was an image of the mind—the collective mind or collective psyche. The house was an allegory, a story: a story with "stories," upper and lower.

When he came to build his own house in Bollingen on the upper lake of Zurich, Jung externalized these symbols. "From the beginning I felt the Tower as in some way a place of maturation—a maternal womb or a maternal figure in which I could become what I was, what I am and will be. It gave me a feeling as if I were being reborn in stone." He insists that "during the building work, of course, I never considered these matters. I built the house in sections, always following the concrete needs of the moment. It might also be said that I built it in a kind of dream."[5]

In effect Jung was building the house of his dreams—and of his famous dream. After his wife's death, he writes, "I suddenly realized that the small central section which crouched so low, so hidden, was myself! I could no longer hide myself behind the 'maternal' and the 'spiritual' towers. So, in that same year, I added an upper storey to this section, which represents myself, or my ego-personality. Earlier, I would not have been able to do this; I would have regarded it as presumptuous self-emphasis. Now it signified an extension of consciousness achieved in old age."

———

It's striking that later readers of Jung's "dream of the house" have tended to see it as a dream about *houses*, rather than about consciousness. By literalizing the dream—much as Jung did when he analyzed his own lakeside edifice complex—they have taken a figure of speech and translated it into a statement about archetypes and architecture. And it's not only psychologists who have seen meaning in houses, meaning that reflects, or refracts, the full panoply of human desires.

In a book called *House as a Mirror of Self* Berkeley architecture professor Clare Cooper Marcus explains that she was so impressed by Jung's dream of the house that it led her to a new phase of her career, training in Gestalt psychology and learning to use role-playing as a means of uncovering feelings about "the house interior and its contents as a mirror of our inner psychological self." Marcus spent twenty years exploring "the deeper meaning of home" by interviewing individuals in the San Francisco Bay area, inviting them to draw pictures of "home" with crayons and felt-tip pens and then to address the house they had drawn. "House—the way I feel about you is . . ." Then she would ask them to switch roles and speak back to themselves as if they were the house. The crayons and Magic Markers allowed a regression to childhood feelings and memories. For her, Jung's "multi-level house" is "the symbol of the self," and the ground floor, cellar, and vault are "a symbol of the collective unconscious, part of the self-house and yet, too, part of the universal bedrock of humanity."[6]

French analyst Olivier Marc's *Psychology of the House* cites Jung's dream to account for his own instinctively aversive response to an automatic sliding door at Orly airport. His reaction, he concludes, "went back to the most ancient part of my own inner house." The phrase "inner house," like the more familiar "inner child," is a Jungian coinage that suggests a true identity longing to be expressed: "I explored my inner house with its many rooms and wings of different styles." Marc is committed to the notion of a "collective psyche" in architecture, insisting, in a language that seems today almost a parody of Jungian style, that "to build a house is to create an area of peace, calm, and security, a replica of our own mother's womb," and that, for example, "the timeless spiritual message of the house with patio is that the fountain playing at the centre of the pool is the phallus in perpetual coitus, constantly impregnating the universal womb; it is Masculine and Feminine eternally united."[7] Marc's dream house was an enclosure, threatened somehow by the mechanical door that opened and shut apparently of its own accord.

Door, Fence, and Gate

"How many daydreams we should have to analyze under the simple heading of Doors!" exclaims Gaston Bachelard. "The door schematizes two strong possibilities, which sharply classify two types of daydream. At times it is closed, bolted, padlocked. At others it is open, that is to say, wide open."[8]

One of the most common house dreams is the dream in which we are locked out, barred from entry, unable to "go home." In a dream of this kind "home" could be body, mother, lover, homeland, or any other fantasy of completeness and plenitude. What is chiefly important, so important that it has become a standard trope of poetry, fiction, and saga, is the sense of the threshold— clearly a threshold of consciousness as well as of dream desire. And the emblem of that threshold, very often, is a fence or a gate. It is suggestive that Homer and Virgil described the portal to dream as "two gates of Sleep," the gate of horn and the gate of ivory; the translucent polished horn was the gate of true dreams, and the ivory gate the gate of false dreams, delusions, and deceptions.[9]

The image of the fenced or walled garden, the *hortus conclusus*, as the very sign of femininity, sexuality, and love is a favorite of early authors. Indeed from the time of Adam and Eve the image of lovemaking in the garden has been central to culture—and to fantasy. "A garden inclosed is my sister, my spouse," says the King James translation of the Song of Solomon, one of the great erotic poems in literature, and the invitation is clear: "Let my beloved come into his garden, and eat his pleasant fruits." Standard Christian interpretations of this unruly poem gloss the "inclosed garden" as "a symbol of the Immaculate Conception of the Virgin Mary," an association that, while less straightforwardly erotic, marks the enclosure just as clearly as a sign of virginity—as does the "closed gate," another sign of the Virgin in Christian art.[10]

The medieval French *Romance of the Rose,* a classical allegory of courtly love, is the story of a dreamer, a wall, and a rose. The youthful narrator describes his dream of being introduced into the walled Garden of Mirth, where he falls in love with a rosebud, but is prevented from touching it by the combined efforts of Danger, Shame, and Slander, and finally by the walls of a castle built by Jealousy.

Chaucer's virginal Emily, in *The Knight's Tale,* is walking in a walled garden when two young men catch sight of her from their tower prison and fall instantly in love. And in *The Merchant's Tale,* his darkly comic story of the marriage of old January and his young bride May, Chaucer describes the "garden walled all of stone" where in the summer season the lecherous old man would take his wife,

> And thinges whiche that were nat doon abed
> He in the gardin parfourned hem and spedde.

As the narrator observes, not even Priapus, the phallic god of fertility and lasciviousness, here slyly called only "the god of gardens," could describe so beautiful a spot. When May takes a young lover, she arranges to meet him in the garden and give him "the clicket [key] of that smale wiket [gate]." Whether or not we read the gate and key in anatomical terms (and we might recall that even today keys and locks are ordinarily described as having male and female parts), we can see that May invites her lover to make a double entry: first into her *husband's* walled garden, and then into her own.

"The orchard walls are high and hard to climb," says Juliet wonderingly to her Romeo when she finds him unaccountably in her garden, and he replies, "With love's light wings did I o'er-perch these walls,/For stony limits cannot hold love out."[11] And in Edmund Spenser's English epic *The Faerie Queene,* Guyon, the Knight of Temperance, arrives in an erotic landscape known as the Bower of Bliss. The bower is surrounded by a handsome fence, but further inspection reveals that it is so "weake and thin," and closed off by so "light" a gate, that this apparent barricade is really just a sham (or a tease), designed "Rather for pleasure, than for battery or fight."[12]

Medieval lore maintained that the only sure way to catch a unicorn was to lure him with a virgin. As a thirteenth-century bestiary explains, "Hunters can catch the unicorn only by placing a young virgin in his haunts. No sooner does he see the damsel than he runs toward her, and lies down at her feet, and so suffers himself to be captured."[13] The famous Unicorn Tapestries at the Cloisters Museum in New York depict the hunt and the fabled beast's capitulation, concluding with a scene of the unicorn in captivity amid a carpet of flowers, surrounded by a white picket fence. The male unicorn with his single horn was a sufficiently noble and phallic beast to satisfy any fictional regime. Here the logic of the dream casts the damsel in the role of both bait and huntress. The fence is at once her virginity and his (internal) prohibition.

The paucity of unicorns in captivity today should not, per-

haps, be blamed on a shortage of virgins, but rather on an apparent cultural shift in the use and meaning of walls and fences.
"Gated communities" now offer a different kind of dream, a fantasy of wealth, seclusion, exclusivity, and security. "Because the
desire for privacy is a top-class sign," wrote Paul Fussell in a
wickedly clever little book on social class distinctions in America, "high walls—anything higher than six or seven feet—confer
class."[14] Today's expensively re-created white picket fences evoke
bygone days of neighborliness and small town living. Stone
walls, once the farmer's way of disposing of the unwelcome
obstacles that met his plow, are now expensively constructed
from imported rock. But despite the commercialization of the
dream—and in part because of the heritage of visual and literary
culture that supports it—there remains no more "sexy" piece of
real estate today than the walled garden, bower, or enclosure, as
purveyors like the well-named catalogue distributor *Gardener's
Eden* have discovered.

Dream sequences in literature are often called "dream visions,"
after the common medieval practice of enclosing a fantasy
within the anchoring space of a dream. Modern authors have
also deployed this allegorical way of thinking, sometimes when
they are expressing ambivalence about a state of earthly affairs.
And here too house dreams tell interesting tales of doors closed
and doors open.

"I have sometimes thought that a woman's nature is like a
great house full of rooms," wrote Edith Wharton in an early
short story:

> There is the hall, through which everyone passes in going
> in and out; the drawing room, where one receives formal vis-
> its; the sitting room, where members of the family come and
> go as they list; but beyond that, far beyond, are other rooms,
> the handles of whose doors are never turned; no one knows
> the way to them, no one knows whither they lead, and in the

innermost room, the holy of holies, the soul sits alone and waits for a footstep that never comes.

Adds a biographer quietly, "This is the first indication in the fiction of the twenty-nine-year-old Edith that she finds married life lacking."[15]

Perhaps the most moving evocation of human life as a house can be found in John Keats's famous comparison, in a letter to his friend John Hamilton Reynolds:

> I compare human life to a large Mansion of Many Apartments, two of which I can only describe, the doors of the rest being as yet shut upon me.—The first we step into we call the infant or thoughtless Chamber, in which we remain as long as we do not think—We remain there a long while, and notwithstanding the doors of the second Chamber remain wide open, showing a bright appearance, we care not to hasten to it; but are at length imperceptibly impelled by the awakening of the thinking principle—within us—we no sooner get into the second Chamber, which I shall call the Chamber of Maiden-Thought, than we become intoxicated with the light and the atmosphere, we see nothing but pleasant wonders, and think of delaying there for ever in delight: However among the effects this breathing is father of is that tremendous one of sharpening one's vision into the heart and nature of Man—of convincing one's nerves that the World is full of Misery and Heartbreak, Pain, Sickness and oppression—whereby This Chamber of Maiden Thought becomes gradually darken'd and at the same time on all sides of it many doors are set open—but all dark—all leading to dark passages—We see not the balance of good and evil. We are in a Mist—*We* are now in that state—We feel the "burden of the

Mystery." To this point was Wordsworth come, as far as I can conceive when he wrote "Tintern Abbey" and it seems to me that his Genius is explorative of those dark Passages. Now if we live, and go on thinking, we too shall explore them.[16]

The sublimity of Keats's prose, and the power of his imagination, expand the biblical "in my Father's house are many mansions" to a dream house that is an allegory of the poet's soul.

Daydreams and Nightmares

It's significant that for Bachelard the central dream is the daydream, for a daydream, after all, is a conscious wish, a happy thought, a dream of gratified hope or ambition. Not your unconscious sneaking up on you. Thus he can write, "The house is one of the greatest powers of integration for the thoughts, memories, and dreams of mankind. The binding principle in this integration is the daydream." And again, "If I were asked to name the chief benefit of the house, I should say: the house shelters daydreaming, the house protects the dreamer, the house allows one to dream in peace."[17]

In fact, not only does the house *shelter* daydream, the house *is* a daydream—the quintessential daydream. Or, as the *Oxford English Dictionary* describes it, a "castle in the air." "The young daydreamer built castles in the air for himself," says Thackeray in *Pendennis,* and John Addington Symonds alludes to "daydreamers and castle-builders."[18] "They built Castles in the air, and thought to do great wonders," wrote Sir Thomas North. A "castle in the air," a "castle in the skies," a "castle in Spain." These are imaginary dwellings, synonyms for a grandiose imagination. We thus encounter a delicious tautology. To daydream is *to build a house in your imagination*—a house bigger and better than you can expect to have in life.

Yet if a house can be the stuff that (day)dreams are made on, it also clearly occupies the territory of nocturnal and involuntary and terrifying dreams, from *The Castle of Otranto* to *The Haunt-ing*. Novelists from Austen to Hardy, James, and Morrison have set their books in architectural spaces "haunted" by the imaginations of visitors or occupants. Indeed all of Bachelard's magical, womblike spaces—the corner, the drawer, the wardrobe or closet —are regularly exploited by the makers of horror films as places of surprise and terror.

But we do not need the works of Stephen King to understand the concept of a "dream house" gone wrong. The real estate "nightmare house" of fiction and popular culture devours the owners rather than fulfilling their fondest dreams. It is in a way the dark underside of the dream. If the house is a woman/mother here, it is the notorious *vagina dentata*, the devouring womb of dream and folklore. "The tree-shaded suburban mansion—a gracious white Colonial with big rooms and high ceilings—looked like the home of their dreams," said a typical review of the film *The Money Pit*, but "their lives turned into a comic nightmare." The most compelling testimony, though, came not from audiences but from the filmmakers themselves.

"Redoing my house gave me the idea," explained the screenwriter. "The house turns into this giant pit you just throw money into." And the production designer, who had been renovating a 250-year-old house for four years, told director Richard Benjamin, "I don't know what's in your script—but whatever it is, it's not worse than what I've been through." Creating the appearance of a house that was falling apart involved building three staircases (each at a different stage of disrepair), five bathtubs, and three sets of collapsing scaffolding, but the memories of unexpected demolition and cost overruns began to fade when the movie was finished. "It's like a real renovation," said one member of the production team. "You forget the worst of it and remember the good stuff."[19] Like a real renovation—and like the activity of "secondary revision" in a dream, which censors and rewrites the unacceptable thoughts, seeking, as Freud suggests, "to mould the material offered to it into something like a day-dream."[20]

American Dreams

Many classical analyses of the unconscious and its figurations through and of the house imply a kind of autobiography of house and person in which the *Bildungsroman* depends on a fixed, stable, and class-stratified "Buildings-*roman*" modeled on European upper(-middle)-class patterns of inhabiting. The "house you were born in." The "house of your ancestors."

But American patterns were and remain very different. The German poet Rainer Maria Rilke underscored his sense of this difference in a 1925 letter contrasting American "pseudo-things" with the "animated, experienced things" of a European culture he felt was at risk.

> Even for our grandparents a "house," a "well," a familiar tower, their very dress, their cloak, was infinitely more, infinitely more intimate; almost everything a vessel in which they found and stored humanity. Now there comes crowding over from America empty, indifferent things, pseudo-things. . . . A house, in the American understanding, an American apple or vine, has NOTHING in common with the house, the fruit, the grape into which the hope and meditation of our forefathers had entered. . . . The animated, experienced things that SHARE OUR LIVES are coming to an end and cannot be replaced.[21]

From its inception the United States has been a mobile, ambulant society, "settling" territories, colonizing, homesteading, moving inexorably west. Americans move on the average of every five years. Corporate relocation, as it is called, regularly moves American workers from city to city, or town to town, as part of the quest toward business success. Paradoxically, we might think, job "security" involves a willingness to *move house*. Typical American houses are built of wood, not of stone.

They go up and—sometimes—they come down. Sometimes the houses themselves actually move, improbably perched on the back of flatbed trucks labeled "wide load," trundled down the highway. The "American Dream," a phrase that has come to mean both economic success ("a piece of the pie") and home ownership ("a piece of the rock") often requires rapid and constant geographical mobility. Real estate and its attendant businesses ("housing starts") are anchors of the economy.

What does this do to the unconscious, or at least to the way the unconscious uses and is figured by house images? If "the house" is a major internalized image, it is a *second-order* image, derived from myth, art, folklore, psychology, and phenomenology—and from the concurrent development of what might be called the *consumer unconscious,* that is, the strategies of advertisement and merchandising that accompany or anticipate expansion in real estate and in the selling of high-end household goods and services. It is not that we dream less of houses than did the magisterial European writers of the early and mid-twentieth century. But we dream different dreams. For us their dreams are fantasy and nostalgia, "false memories"—though often also "memories" we would like to make come true in our own lives. This is where "dream," crucially, intersects with material-culture modern dreams. Late twentieth-century, early twenty-first-century dreams are dreams of the new house, even if the new house is someone else's old house. The omnipresence of the phrase "dream house" now becomes easier to understand. For it is *through the house,* and not *of the house,* that we dream our dreams.

Open Houses

The dream logic of "open and shut" can be found in social activities with a decidedly practical, if not overtly commercial, purpose. The *flânerie* of the nineteenth century, popularized by writers from Baudelaire to Walter Benjamin, has been replaced by the activity so suggestively called "house-hunting." Walking through someone else's house, whether it's a National Trust house or a Sunday real estate offering, provides a glimpse of other lives and a space for mental remodeling. From the house tour to the realty "open house," the private social "open house" (together with its cultural cousin, the literary salon), and the frankly commercial, though determinedly upscale, show house or "designer showcase," the flirtatious activity of window-shopping in people's houses has caught the public imagination. In them the dream house is transformed from an inborn memory to a cultural acquisition.

Here it's the house that does the seduction, offering us the eroticism of going freely into forbidden spaces.

At a performance/installation called "Dream House," the audience was given "permission to snoop" into the closets, cabinets, photo albums, and refrigerators of a "family," played by actors, who went through the motions of being in residence. The kitchen cupboard, for example, yields a can of "startled glances" and a package labeled "vague apprehension." The concept behind this interactive theater event, described as "almost virtual reality theater" by one of the artists who collaborated on the project, was "to make people realize how important a first house is, and how you carry the images all your life."[22]

Yet it's completely understandable that open houses (the very phrase, with its promise of secret places waiting to be discovered, makes my heart pound) should lure tourists. What is more pleasurable than peering into someone else's life? The real estate open house is a socially sanctioned license to daydream about what goes on behind other people's closed doors.

"Dear Fellow Lover of Beautiful Things," began a mass-market mailing that solicited subscriptions to a home magazine,

> I have a confession to make. . . . Right after we were married, my husband and I often spent whole Sunday afternoons touring Open Houses, many of them grand old homes we

couldn't possibly afford. We'd wander through elegant settings, admiring graceful archways, sunny garden rooms, delicate detail work and cozy reading nooks . . . imagining.[23]

Now that she—and her husband?—are able to afford some luxuries (like subscriptions to shelter magazines) the fictional correspondent presumably lets her fingers do the walking. Or perhaps she has graduated to the "house and garden tour," an upscale charity fund-raiser in which the owners of "grand old homes" open them for a fee, especially in historic districts like Charleston or Nantucket.

"House Maps of the Stars" for sale in the Bel Air section of Los Angeles. *Lifestyles of the Rich and Famous* on television. The British magazine *Country Life* with its irresistible estates. The childhood home of Louisa May Alcott, her pen resting on the desk as if its wielder will return at any moment to pick it up. Monticello, San Simeon, and Graceland, each with its larger-than-life owner, a brooding, absent presence. Invitations to peek where one could never peek when the occupant was in residence: glimpses of Elvis's interior decorator, folding hundreds of yards of fabric and tacking them to the ceiling of the billiards room.

Houses inhabited by the ghosts of the past often make the most enticing destinations. Who could resist a visit to "A La Ronde," in Exmouth, England, after a description like this from the National Trust Handbook:

A unique 16-sided house built on the instructions of two spinster cousins, Jane and Mary Parminter, on their return from a grand tour of Europe. Completed c.1760, the house contains many 18th-century contents and collections brought back by the Parminters. The fascinating interior decoration includes a feather frieze and shell-encrusted galley which, due to its fragility, can only be viewed on closed circuit television.[24]

The Stately Home or National Trust House has provided a kind of model for the designer and the entrepreneur. Presidential houses from Warm Springs to San Clemente and beyond have become virtual characters in the national drama—as, of course, has the White House itself. From Jacqueline Kennedy's televised tour to speculations about the guests in the Lincoln bedroom (or, indeed, in the Oval Office), the nation's attention has been trained on what goes on, and doesn't go on, within the public-private precincts of the First Family. Again, the topic here is really the "openness" as well as the house, the sense of legitimized violation, of cultural and culturally endorsed voyeurism.

Show Houses

Together with the house and garden tour, the phenomenon of the "decorator show house" has become a significant feature of the home lovers' landscape over the past decade. Often a large house that is about to be put on the market and is in need of up-dating and restyling, the show house is parceled out to designers room by room. Here is where the ladies-who-lunch come to meet and greet, while inspecting each other's epergnes. I've walked through dozens of show houses over the last few years, and have occasionally found really inventive and useful ideas. Perhaps the best was the remaking of a dead-end closet space— an area given to a particularly unlucky designer—into a keyhole frame that opened onto a wall-sized mirror and a half-round window, to produce the illusion of a full-round opening into the garden, replacing the original end-stopped wall.

On the other hand, the show house is often the site of the most extraordinary (and often misguided) fantasias: one blame-less and graciously proportioned nineteenth-century house was adorned with hallway "murals" that simulated torn wallpaper and peeling paint. Women and men who would never think of spending the morning at the mall line up obediently and take their turns walking through the maze of velvet ropes and kindly guides—as indeed they do on house and garden tours where the interiors are emphatically *not* for sale. (And you never know whether the owner is standing next to you when you cluck at a deplorable chandelier.) Many of the very same people who scoff at a television program like *Lifestyles of the Rich and Famous* are to be found here, taking notes. We have entered a world of virtual home-owning and virtual design, seeking to create in days and weeks—indeed on the Internet in seconds and minutes—traditions in the absence of history. Since many show houses serve a double function, as a designer's exhibition of skill and a benefit for charity—sponsored by the Junior League, the American Red Cross, the Cancer Research Institute, or some other socially valued nonprofit—you can even cultivate a sense of virtuous altruism to go along with your undisguised consumer prurience. The show house is the consumer version of the tourable stately home, a place where everything is for sale, including the decorator's services.

"You don't want rooms exactly like these," commented Grace Mirabella, the honorary chairwoman for one New York City designer show house. "It's whimsical. You might pull out some ideas, but mostly it just makes you smile."[25] The house in question, an eighteenth-century landmark mansion that had formerly been the carriage house on the estate of Abigail Adams Smith, included a Tavern Room outfitted for a faux-Thanksgiving feast complete with food "styled" by the same designers who did the food for the film *The Age of Innocence*. In the mansion's salon, visitors encountered a Japanese minimalist television room, a safari tent, computer monitors encased in antique frames, and Christopher Robin in bed. "With so much reality out there," remarked another show house official, "it's nice to see some creative fantasy."

But so over-the-top have some show houses become that a contest for the best "showcase design" held by *House Beautiful*

congratulated the winners for their *restraint:* "all our winning designers knew when to stop." In fact, *HB* noted with pleasure and
surprise, "some of the rooms were so low-key they felt not like
showcases, but rooms to live in."[26] An odd but ubiquitous mixture of old and new, frankly virtual and falsely "real," the show
house is both by nature and design a house of dreams.

The Culture of Desire

"Most every design—be it a simple product or an entire room—
that would otherwise astonish and make one dream has been
mined and merchandised ad nauseam in catalogues, magazines,
and television,"[27] lamented a writer in a special "glamour" issue
of the home magazine *Elle Décor.* The *fulfillment* of the dream
was not, after all, what was desired. Instead *ED* quoted *New York
Times* theater critic Ben Brantley: "Glamour is whatever you
can't have. It is best perceived at a distance, either literally or
emotionally. Knowledge kills glamour."[28]

This definition—that "glamour is whatever you can't have"—
is a perfectly distilled description of the culture of desire.
Bachelard tells the story of a poet whose descriptions of his
house in the country, with its garden, wood, wine cellar, and
other amenities, were entirely fictional, a fantasy of the house he
might have had, but never possessed. So eloquent was the poet's
account, however, that he received a letter from a man who, having read in the newspapers some of these precise descriptions of
the estate, was applying for the position of overseer.[29] This was
not a "dream come true," but rather an explosion of the dream.

Seen through a haze of plaster dust and plumbing parts, catalogues and swatches, the house of our dreams is never quite possessed, never perfect, never finished. "Keep the romance in your
marriage," urge the tabloids, "keep love alive." And so it is in the
relationship between us and our houses, those "other persons" in
our lives. This mutual and constant courtship, this ongoing rela-

tionship, imperfectly commodified and imperfectly consummated, is what produces both the anxiety and the enjoyment of owning a home. The keynote of much home design today is not character, not values, but desire. And desire, by its very nature, cannot be satisfied. It points always onward, toward the next redecoration, the next renovation, the next house.

FIVE

THE TROPHY HOUSE

First there were trophy wives. Then there were trophy houses and trophy apartments.

The "trophy" term took off in 1989, when *Fortune* magazine announced the ascendancy of "The CEO's Second Wife." The article featured cameo portraits of such notables as dress designer Carolyne Roehm, "Henry Kravis's second wife," and Susan Gutfreund, "the onetime airline stewardess who married John, 59, the CEO of Salomon, Inc.," who was so legendary for her extravagance that her Paris townhouse had a garage that looked like a ballroom. "Powerful men are beginning to demand trophy wives," reported *Fortune,* coining a term that gained instant currency. Self-made men, used to improving their circumstances, saw no reason to retain the "old, nice, matronly first wife" when she could be traded in for a sporty new model. The second wife "certifies her husband's status" and, whenever possible, "given the material she has to work with," proclaims his sexual vitality.[1]

That was then. But six years later, by the middle of the nineties, the trophy wife had undergone a makeover: "No longer just a walking testament to her husband's virility, today's trophy must be an intellectual companion as well," declared the same author in the same magazine. "Goodbye, bombshell. Hello, bluestocking. Make that sexy bluestocking." The poster women of 1989 had fallen on hard times; Henry Kravis was now on his third wife, "more her husband's size, physically and mentally." The only thing the new Mrs. Kravis didn't do, *Fortune* noted cattily, was (unlike her predecessor) design her own clothes. Susan Gutfreund was still married to John, but her husband, ousted by his firm, could no longer support her in the style to which she had become accustomed. She was now reported to be "chairing the benefits she used to turn down because she was too busy decorating her houses."

In fact, the trophy wife, old-style or new, bimbo or bluestocking (these were *Fortune's* terms), had given pride of place to what was inevitably dubbed by wits "the trophy house." But in a way the trophy house had preceded the trophy wife. "When I was writing the article [on trophy wives]," reported editor Julie Connelly, "I thought of the real-estate term *trophy building* for a premier place like the Plaza Hotel in New York, and I formed *trophy wife* based on that term."[2]

What is the relationship between the trophy wife and the trophy house? For Thorstein Veblen, writing in 1899, upper-class women were not only members of a leisure class but of a *vicarious* leisure class. They performed acts of "vicarious consumption," spending money their husbands earned. They displayed "vicarious leisure," their leisure a result of, and a testimony to, the success of their husbands' work. And their attention to the decorating and furnishing of houses, while it might more or less accidentally give pleasure, was largely a social sign of "the great economic law of wasted effort." Enter, almost a hundred years later, the "trophy wife."

We saw in Chapter 1 that the house could be a spouse—or a lover, or a beloved. In the dismissive society cliché of the trophy wife and trophy house the two status ornaments for a successful man are brought together. Each is a sign of his standing. But where in an earlier era the wife was *in* the house, these days she may not only be separable from it, she may even, when given a chance, possess herself of a trophy house of her own.

Olivia Goldsmith, whose novel and film *The First Wives Club*

were based on the "trophy wife" phenomenon, wrote of her passionate "affair" with a Georgian house on the Hudson River. Although she already owned a house in Florida and a cottage in
Vermont, and "had no intention of making any domestic up-
heavals," the house was so "beguiling" ("she reclines seductively
on four acres") that Goldsmith simply had to have it. The gendering of the house ("It is female, and, quite simply, a witch")
and the insistent metaphor of sexual conquest ("I needed a break
to reconsider my commitment. In the end, of course, the witch
got her way")[3] are testament to the seduction narrative. The
house was a Siren. Its call could not be resisted. "I believe this is
the last house I will ever 'do,' " Goldsmith concludes, "and it was
the only one I 'did' without a man as my partner." The Georgian
house, officially called Beaver Hall, was the First Wife's Last
Wife (and trophy house). At least for now.

The trophy husband, incidentally, is a more elusive character
than the trophy wife, but he does exist, at least in the fantasy
world of commodities. Commenting on the extravagance of a
furniture catalogue issued by the Sharper Image, one observer
notes, "Somewhere, a trophy husband is awaiting delivery of his
ornately carved $9,995 pool table."[4]

Trophies

The word "trophy" derives from the Greek word *trope,* a twisting
or turning—a word that also means a figure of speech (a "turn"
of phrase) like a metaphor, metonymy, or personification. And a
trophy house, like a trophy wife, is itself a figurative utterance,
something that, as we like to say these days, "makes a statement."

A trophy in ancient Greece or Rome was a monument erected
as a sign of victory in war, a lasting reminder of the fact that the
enemy had been turned or routed. Triumphal parades of victori-
ous returning generals were often processions of "trophies" won
in battle, including slaves, captive women, and statues. Over the

course of time it became the lavishness of the booty, rather than the victory itself, that drew the attention and awe of the people.

Veblen's *Theory of the Leisure Class* offered a Darwinian view of social status based upon this notion of the trophy as booty. "Gradually, as industrial activity . . . displaces predatory activity in the community's everyday life and in men's habits of thought, accumulated property replaces trophies of predatory exploit." "Property," wrote Veblen, is "of the nature of trophy," and becomes a "trophy of successes scored in the game of ownership." In fact property becomes the "most easily recognized evidence of a reputable degree of success," and therefore "the conventional basis of esteem."[5]

What is the achievement or quality of which the trophy house is a sign? Grandiosity? Self-doubt? Self-esteem? When Renaissance princes and popes wanted to leave an immortal legacy, they built palazzos and Palladian villas. In these ostensibly more democratic days, we can buy, sell, and rent them.

The trophy house was obviously the dream house blown up to unimaginable proportions, as much of the language describing it made clear. In the wake of the rising stock market, apartment residences designed "to fulfill the fantasies and affectations of the underserved super-rich" (with thirty-foot living rooms, twenty-two-foot bedrooms, libraries, servants' quarters, marble baths, and wine cellars) began to be built on New York's Park Avenue and Central Park South, "exploiting nostalgia for an age of sumptuous living that existed mostly in the escapist movies of the Great Depression."[6] "There's nothing left on a fantasy level anymore," said a Manhattan real estate broker when a twenty-room triplex on the top floors of the Pierre Hotel on Fifth Avenue and Sixty-first Street sold for just under $25 million, the highest price ever paid for a co-op. The penthouse with its "Sistine Chapel–type" ballroom had belonged to the Australian newspaper heiress Lady Fairfax. "Frankly, I've seen it and it's worth it, if you're into that kind of thing," said another broker.[7]

Of course there were losers as well as winners, what brokers called wannabe buildings, postwar white brick buildings on the Upper East Side that sought to rival the exclusivity of the grand prewar palazzos along Park and Fifth. (Notice that the building, and not its residents, is endowed with status envy.) But even the wannabes quickly became exclusive and excluding, thereby ensuring their own standing in a market where one buyer's rejection is another resident's sign of status.

Even rental properties could reach trophy status in a market where money is plentiful and executives can be top-drawer nomads. The *New York Times* tut-tutted about the comparative cheesiness of Donald Trump's rentable penthouse at 1 Central Park West, which lacked status-symbol appliances ("no Sub-Zero refrigerator, no Garland stove, no Miele dishwasher") and had "hollow Schlage door knobs and brass-plated hinges similar to those sold at Home Depot." Asking price: $100,000 a month. Comparable prices for rentals could be found in Hong Kong, Palm Beach, London, and Beverly Hills, to cite a few of the most sought-after locations. An apartment in a prewar building on Central Park West with nine rooms "and a handful of terraces" rented for $27,000 in a day. "These tycoons do not just wait around," observed the broker with satisfaction.[8] Where in former times millionaires flaunted their wealth, New York realtors claim these renters are "publicity-shy" and "want to make themselves invisible."[9] (By renting a duplex with a spiral staircase, four fireplaces, and five bathrooms?)

Though it has an American resonance, the "trophy" tag is in fact used around the world. Buyers "rich beyond imagination," in the words of the *Times* of London, throng the usually quiet London summer real estate market. "Grand trophy houses are what they crave, and as the rich seem to get richer, the houses they seek become ever grander."[10] Trophy purchasers can be found from the Middle East to the United Kingdom and Hong

Kong, paying millions—in Hong Kong before the Chinese takeover, as much as a billion dollars—for extravagant properties and spectacular views. Perhaps the most "international" of these trophy spaces are the shipboard condominium apartments, with private terraces, Jacuzzis, and daily maid service, now being marketed for prices from one to five-plus million dollars. "An incredibly sexy idea," said the U.S. president of the seller, World of Residensea. The 250 apartments will come equipped with Frette sheets and Christofle silver, and their kitchens will boast Sub-Zero refrigerators, Miele ovens, and Smallbone cabinets. At a dinner party she attended, "everyone was debating where they wanted to live for the rest of their lives," said a travel writer who signed up for a condo with her husband. "Suddenly I realized: I want to live out the rest of my life at sea."[11]

Inevitably, the rise in trophy properties has produced a new kind of trophy hunter, the "house-hunting impostor" or phantom buyer. Enterprising real estate scammers, oozing authority and connections, contact brokers and ask to see the most expensive properties. High-end house shoppers come provided with fake bank references and plausible stories. "It's entertainment and fun for people to go around and look at big, expensive apartments," reported one New York broker. Though real rich people tend not to drop names or numbers with such ostentation, nor to arrive for a house showing dressed to the nines, these impostors have succeeded in touring townhouses and condominiums in the city and horse farms outside it, with hovering realtors in tow. "You can't be too jaded," said another broker, "because there is a chance that it is for real."[12] Sometimes the "client" actually makes an offer, only to stop the check the minute he (or she) leaves the agency office.

The pleasure for such pseudo-buyers is presumably both in the house tour and in the "high" of the scam itself. A Soho architect I spoke with said a similar scam is practiced by clients in his business, who spend hours discussing plans, then disappear and are never heard from again. "Faking it," proclaimed the *New*

York Observer, neatly catching the sense of the broker's desire for a trophy sale and the "buyer's" seductive play-acting. But in this case—is it different from sex or the same?—it's the faker who may get the greatest pleasure from the act.

Utility and Futility

But when is a trophy not a trophy? When everyone gets one. We are always chasing a horizon that recedes. Veblen had seen clearly, and with his usual astringency, that "it is extremely gratifying to possess something more than others. But as fast as a person makes new acquisitions, and becomes accustomed to the resulting new standard of wealth, the new standard forthwith ceases to afford appreciably greater satisfaction than the earlier standard did." The result is "chronic dissatisfaction" and "a restless training to place a wider and ever-widening pecuniary interval" between oneself and one's neighbors.[13]

The trophy house, a symbol of victory in the Battle of Wall Street, rises in America every time the stock market enters a sustained period of expansion. It happened in the Gilded Age and in the 1920s before the crash. In the 1990s this phenomenon led to the proliferation of newly constructed "trophy houses" beyond Newport and Oyster Bay to suburbs and subdivisions all over the country. And with this democratization came a certain level of irony—if not from realtors and developers, then from the press.

"From San Diego to the eastern tip of Long Island," complained an editorial in the *Sacramento Bee,* "people living in posh ZIP codes are talking about the trophy house phenomenon." For anyone who had spent the last few years marooned on a desert island without newspaper or cable, the busy *Bee* included a basic definition:

> What is a trophy house? A trophy house is a big, big, really big new house. It typically offers every imaginable human luxury and costs one or several million . . . with six or more

bedrooms, exercise room, mahogany paneled library, formal dining room, and restaurant-style kitchen. Many people loathe trophy houses. Traditionalists see them as monstrous mishmashes of architectural types. Lacking any pretense to historic fidelity, the houses merely suggest older kinds of luxury housing.[14]

"Trophy houses are a dime a dozen these days," agreed Peter Passell in the *New York Times* Business section. "Practically anyone who was in on the ground floor at Cisco Systems or staked out a claim to a few dozen McDonald's franchises when Howard Johnson's still ruled the road can afford a faux-Palladian chateau in Holmby Hills or a rustic, 16,000-square-foot-cabin in Jackson Hole."[15] A builder asked to describe the period and style of his structures (were they Georgian? Victorian? Colonial?) told *House & Garden* magazine that they were "More like Ralph Lauren."

"They're not beautiful. They land like a bunch of spaceships out in a field. If there are any trees they mow them down," complained a realty-board spokeswoman in the suburbs west of Boston. "I don't understand who would want to live in them. They're just these stark monuments." A local official remarked in public that the super-sized houses were "testaments to the ego." In historic and formerly rural Concord, where these comments stirred controversy, there is some tendency to regard this as a clash between old money and new money. Older residents get together to shake their heads over the newcomers, whose homes often have elevators, tunnels, and indoor pools. But others are more sympathetic, and take a longer view. "People's homes have always been a reflection of their ego," said Concord's building commissioner.[16]

Indeed, one of the most striking elements of this tendency to architectural self-aggrandizement (or, as the old joke has it, the edifice complex) is the fact that it is hardly new. "What's happening now is very much what happened in the 20's and 30's," said one knowledgeable observer of the Greenwich, Connecticut, scene. "There's this profusion of mansion-building by New York City moneymakers and this almost hysterical prosperity. But it's a cycle. It will turn around again. Because by the 1950's and 60's, those mansions were crumbling."[17]

What accounts for the most recent boom in "luxury homes" (a phrase that, like "luxury cars," has become so much a commonplace that we never stop to think of it as odd)? The increasing wealth of the middle class, the mass production of luxury details like "Palladian" windows (now available in-stock from retail manufacturers like Pella or Andersen) and spiral staircases, and—I suspect—the memory of Levittown childhoods. Usages like "luxury liner" and "luxury edition" give some inkling of the modern sense of exclusiveness or privilege. It goes along with all those "you deserve it" and "I'm worth it" ads for status-enhancing consumer items like automobiles and hair-color. A "luxury home" is a gratifying self-indulgence, even though the term itself is a kind of status giveaway. If you need to say it, you're not there yet.

The purchasers of these houses are "the super-middle class," says a professor of economics and planning at New York University. "In income terms, they are upper income. But in class terms, they are middle class."[18] Their houses have nanny suites and home offices. And many of them are lifelong suburbanites following the dream. "We're kind of going on to the next step," said the purchaser of a 7,000-square-foot luxury house in a new subdivision. He and his wife were seeking a family-oriented community with split levels, cul-de-sacs, and backyard fences, like that of their suburban youth—only this time they wanted six bedrooms and seven baths.

A term like "luxury" can cover a multitude of sins—mostly sins of omission, like skimping on nails and retaining walls. "People just want drop-dead," said a Manhattan architect who previously worked as a project designer for Robert A. M. Stern. "They find it boring to spend money on foundations and stud walls. They'd rather spend it on what they can see." Stern, who is noted for the quality of his elegant upscale designs, concurred. "It appears that what sells houses depends on having a tub large enough for at least two people, and probably more; flashy stairs that make a racket as if a horse were climbing them, and other glitzy, totally unnecessary elements, as opposed to spatial or constructional quality."[19] "We're seeing more faux finishes for that Old World look," commented an architect in Palm Beach, Florida, another wealthy enclave. "People are not interested in the real dimensions of wood or what it can do, but just how it looks."[20] Some new houses, like some new cars, are available with "upgrades"—marble in the bathrooms, French doors (often with plastic mullions), granite or Corian countertops—that raise the basic price as much as $100,000.

As a representative of a design firm called Mansions and Millionaires (itself a sign of the expansive times) remarked, kitchens and bathrooms have become the most important rooms in the house: "The kitchens, not because you cook, but because it shows you appreciate good food. The bathrooms, they don't even call them bathrooms anymore. They have become more of a spa."[21]

In the trophy spirit for the mid-range buyer, U.S. Homes Corporation introduced its "Laureate" line of homes.[22] But how poetic are these Laureates? In many American suburbs mass-produced luxury houses, with "features once found only on true estates," are replacing the more modest tract houses of an earlier era. One man's (or woman's) Laureate house is, to those observers less kindly disposed to the phenomenon, another's McMansion. A Florida developer offers the "Versailles" model with four bedrooms, four baths, a den, a formal "dining area," a family room, and sliding doors leading to the lanai and pool.[23] (It's fascinating to imagine what Louis XIV would have done with a den and a lanai—and, for that matter, without a dining room.) "Starter palaces" is how one environmentally concerned couple dismissed these mass-market mansions and the wasteful habits of "boomers who take up more space and resources than they need." Another cited what has become a familiar saw: "We once lived in houses and worshiped in cathedrals. Now we want to live in cathedrals—what does this say about what we choose to worship?"[24]

The Suddenly Rich

Some of the most memorable trophy houses can be found not in life but in literature. Modern American readers who last read William Dean Howells's novel *The Rise of Silas Lapham* in high school might want to take another look. For Lapham, an upwardly mobile Boston businessman (one of those the novel calls "the suddenly rich," a man who has made his money in mineral paint), sets out to build himself what is clearly a trophy house.

"Howells is writing about Lapham," as Philip Fisher notes, "in order to describe a new phenomenon of wide social meaning, and, at the same time, to satisfy the curiosity of the public about such new self-made millionaires. Where do they come from? How do they live? What are their ethics?"[25] *The Rise of Silas Lapham* was published in 1885, just a few years before the appearance of *The Theory of the Leisure Class,* and Howells clearly shares Veblen's ambivalent fascination with conspicuous consumption and "pecuniary emulation."

"I've got the best architect in Boston," Lapham brags to a visitor, "and I'm building a house to suit myself. And if money can do it, I guess I'm going to be suited." Taking a deep breath, he expands upon his theme, while his daughter suffers an agony of embarrassment:

We spend more on our houses nowadays. I started out to build a forty thousand-dollar house. Well, sir! That fellow has got me in for more than sixty thousand already, and I doubt if I get out of it much under a hundred. You can't have a nice house for nothing. It's just like ordering a picture of a painter.

You pay him enough, and he can afford to paint you a first-class picture; and if you don't, he can't. That's all there is of it. . . . Yes sir, give an architect money enough, and he'll give you a nice house every time.[26]

But Lapham's own encounter with his architect is not so smooth as he here makes it out to be. In fact the initial conversation between architect and client is comic, revealing, and not so different from many such conversations today. The client begins with a clear sense of what he wants, and is persuaded, in a remarkably short time, to reverse every single preference. First Lapham explains "his ideas of black-walnut finish, high-studding, and cornices. The architect was able to conceal the shudder which they must have sent through him. He was skillful, as nearly all architects are, in playing upon that simple instrument Man."

"Oh, certainly, have the parlors high-studded," says architect to client. "But you've seen some of those pretty, old-fashioned country-houses, haven't you, where the entrance-story is very low-studded? . . . don't you think something of that kind would have a very nice effect?"

> "Then, were you thinking of having your parlors together, connected by folding doors?" asked the architect deferentially.
>
> "Yes, of course," said Lapham. "They're always so, aint they?"
>
> "Well, nearly," said the architect. "I was wondering how would it do to make one large square room at the front. . . ."
>
> "It'll be kind of odd, won't it?"
>
> "Well, I don't know," said the architect. "Not so odd, I hope, as the other thing will be a few years from now."

Likewise, when the architect suggests placing the dining room behind the hall, since that "gets you rid of one of those long,

straight, ugly staircases," his wealthy client is inwardly disconcerted: "Until that moment Lapham had thought a long, straight
staircase the chief ornament of a house." One of Silas's greatest
desires is for that fashionable black walnut paneling, which he
intends to install throughout the house (everywhere but in the
attic, which was to be "painted and grained like black walnut").
And this aesthetic vision too he puts forward, with a combination of aggression and wary deference that will be familiar to
many modern clients. (Recall that he has made his fortune in
mineral paint.)

> "I presume," he said, "you'll have the drawing-room finished
> in black walnut?"
> "Well yes," replied the architect, "if you like. But some less
> expensive wood can be made just as effective with paint. Of
> course you can paint black walnut too."
> "Paint it?" gasped the Colonel.
> "Yes," said the architect quietly. "White, or a little off
> white."
> Lapham dropped the plan he had picked up from the
> table. His wife made a little move toward him of consolation
> or support.
> "Of course," resumed the architect, "I know there has been
> a great craze for black walnut. But it's an ugly wood; and for
> a drawing-room there is really nothing like white paint."[27]

My own memories of *Silas Lapham*, dredged up from the dim
past when I was a tiresome teenage "idealist" eager to point out
the materialist follies of my parents' friends, recalled the protagonist as what one critic of the novel harshly calls "a newly rich
vulgarian."[28] Today, vulgarian or not, I am much more shame-
facedly sympathetic to Silas's ambitions and even, I have to say,
to his taste in furnishings. For what is perhaps most striking
about this exchange, beyond the faux-deferential manner so fa-

miliar in such power encounters today, is the way Silas's taste has come back into fashion. High ceilings, pocket doors, cornice moldings, woodwork "painted and grained like black walnut"— this is the stuff of glossy real estate brochures and shelter magazines.

What about "sex and real estate"? Let's not forget that Silas Lapham's house was his entry into the high society sweepstakes with the object of making good marriages for his daughters. His social failures lead, indirectly but inexorably, to the loss of the trophy house and (temporarily, at least) the trophy Brahmin husband. As for the elder Laphams, Silas and his wife, they retreat at the end of the novel to the old family farmstead in Vermont, where "the house was plain," with "no luxuries" and "no furnace in winter," furnished with all the "simpler" pieces from their former place in the city. Risen or fallen, from the point of view of contemporary style, the Laphams are, again, right on the money.

The Rich Are Different

There is no more poignant literary saga of the trophy house (and indeed, we might even say, of the trophy wife) than *The Great Gatsby,* a novel written during the same pre-crash euphoria as *Babbitt,* in which real and fake, surface and depth, genuine and spurious are notoriously difficult to disentangle. So often—and rightly—described as "the" or at least "a" great American novel, *Gatsby* in fact can really be read as a book about houses. One of the things that makes it a great *American* novel is its obsession with, and unerringly apt descriptions of, vernacular architecture as the sign and symbol of cultural desire.

Narrator Nick Carraway rents a house at West Egg, the "less fashionable" of two egg-shaped peninsulas jutting out into Long Island Sound. "My own house," he reports, is "squeezed between two huge places that rented for twelve or fifteen thousand a season."

> The one on my right was a colossal affair by any standard—it
> was a factual imitation of some Hôtel de Ville in Normandy,
> with a tower on one side, spanking new under a thin beard of
> raw ivy, and a marble swimming pool and more than forty
> acres of lawn and garden. It was Gatsby's mansion. Or rather,
> as I didn't know Mr. Gatsby, it was a mansion inhabited by a
> gentleman of that name.[29]

A "colossal affair," a "factual imitation," "spanking new," "raw
ivy"—in everything he says Nick underscores the sense of the
house as precisely a trophy for a parvenu, a nouveau riche. An
Hôtel de Ville is the provincial equivalent of City Hall.

> A brewer had built it early in the "period" craze, a decade be-
> fore, and there was a story that he'd agreed to pay five years'
> taxes on all the neighboring cottages if the owners would
> have their roofs thatched with straw.[30]

When the neighbors refused ("Americans, while occasionally
willing to be serfs, have always been obstinate about being peas-
antry"), the brewer went into an immediate decline and died.
"His children sold it with the black wreath still on the door." So
the house is a relic of someone else's failed social ambition: a trophy of a trophy.

How did the unknown Gatsby come to buy such an extravagant house? Nick has no idea. "Young men didn't—at least in my
provincial experience I believed they didn't—drift coolly out of
nowhere and buy a palace on Long Island Sound."[31] And indeed
Gatsby's ambivalent notoriety is such that rumor refuses to
imagine him as rooted anywhere, despite his largesse and com-
pulsive hospitality. "There was one persistent story that he didn't
live in a house at all, but in a boat that looked like a house and
was moved secretly up and down the Long Island shore."[32]

As a young man, poor and ambitious, an officer in the army,
Jay Gatsby (born Jay Gatz) had fallen in love with Daisy's fam-

ily's house, and—almost as if it were the same thing—with Daisy.

> He went to her house. . . . It amazed him—he had never been in such a beautiful house before. But what gave it an air of breathless intensity was that Daisy lived there—it was as casual a thing to her as his tent out at camp was to him. There was a ripe mystery about it, a hint of bedrooms upstairs more beautiful and cool than other bedrooms, of gay and radiant activities taking place through its corridors.

It's not by accident that he thinks of bedrooms, of course—for him the house is above all a place of sexuality and desire. "It excited him too that many men had already loved Daisy. . . . he felt their presence all about the house."[33]

Contrast Gatsby's wannabe "palace" with the home of Tom and Daisy Buchanan, located, it is almost needless to say, among "the white palaces of fashionable East Egg." The Buchanans, restless and rich, had just "spent a year in France, for no particular reason," but their house is no Hôtel de Ville. The only thing "French" about it is the stylish "French windows" that open onto the water:

> Their house was even more elaborate than I expected, a cheerful red and white Georgian Colonial mansion overlooking the bay. The lawn started at the beach and ran toward the front door for a quarter of a mile, jumping over sun-dials and brick walks and burning gardens—finally when it reached the house drifting up the side in bright vines as though from the momentum of its run. The front was broken by a line of French windows, glowing now with reflected gold, and wide open to the warm windy afternoon.[34]

At the house of Tom Buchanan the vines twine eagerly and naturally up the side of the house; this is no "thin beard of raw ivy" installed by a builder-gardener who wants the appearance of mellow age. Georgian Colonial, dating from the last decade of the eighteenth century, was a symmetrical and classical style of quiet and assured elegance.

The traditional "American Dream" really has two parts to it: the saga of the self-made man or woman and the fantasy of owning a house of one's own. *Gatsby*—like *Silas Lapham*—brilliantly combines the two. And the trophy house phenomenon brings them together in an inescapable logic of economic and cultural self-expression. What is often dismissed as an aberrant sign of the times—the thoughtless excess of "new money," a by-product of a bull market, the baby boomers' revolt against the Depression-era fiscal caution of their parents, a self-evident symptom of a loss of proportion and values—is as "American" as Silas Lapham, Jay Gatsby, or F. Scott Fitzgerald.

Celebrity Homes

For some purchasers, the house itself has receded from importance, its pride of place taken by the aura of the former owner or even the agent. We are now, it seems, even in the realm of trophy *brokers.* Transference begins with the realtor, a figure of trust, or glamour, or emulation—depending upon the market niche. "The agent is really the star of the transaction," says the president of Remax, a real estate company that puts agent's faces on yard signs for buyer bonding. These days some of the agents have agents, personal marketing companies that create television advertisements and brochures for realtors. Or, as one broker put it, "At the point of identification, the houses are the least important thing."[35]

Unless the house itself is a celebrity. For there is, of course, a thriving market in "celebrity homes"—houses that belong, or once belonged, to members of America's other royalty, the stars of film and entertainment.

Does celebrity sell houses? And is it the celebrity of the house or the celebrity of the (former) owner? If, as Daniel Boorstin once famously suggested, a celebrity is "a person who is known for his well-knownness,"[36] a celebrity house is a house known for already being known.

"There's an allure about a star living in a house. There's glamour there," says Elaine Young, described as "Beverly Hills's Realtor-to-the-stars." Candice Bergen bought Roger Moore's house. Eddie Murphy bought Cher's house. Johnny Depp bought Bela Lugosi's Hollywood Castle, a twenty-eight-room gray stone estate with turrets, iron trim, eight bedrooms, and seven baths—the former home of divorce attorney Marvin Mitchelson. Zsa Zsa Gabor bought a house in Bel Air that was once owned by Howard Hughes—and also ("not at the same time") by Elvis Presley. Madonna bought the former mansion of gangster Bugsy Siegel when she was involved with Warren Beatty, who starred in the film of Bugsy's life. Contributing her own ineffable touch, she took the "Mediterranean" estate and added yellow-and-rust-colored horizontal stripes "designed to evoke a Tuscan villa."[37] (Nonetheless, the house was resold for a reported $5 million, some $2 million more than she paid for it.)

A deadpan account in the London *Daily Telegraph* described the "highly original tastes" and "apparent desire to embrace a number of disparate architectural styles, including neo-classicism and rococo," of Sylvester Stallone's Florida waterfront estate, "once known as Casa Rocko," on sale for £17 million. Sotheby's International, which was handling the sale, explains that the mansion, with its two guest houses, boathouse, ballroom "fit for European nobility," and a "man-made ravine covered in cascading waterfalls and marble statuary," was "intended as a single man's environment," and was no longer suitable for the actor. "Now that Mr. Stallone has a daughter, he is looking for a family house."[38]

"Celebrities sell," announced a report in the *Wall Street Journal*. Madonna, who has spearheaded revivals in a number of "unchic" neighborhoods from Los Angeles to Miami, is described by one observer as "the celebrity with the most real estate clout."[39] Another declares that "Cher is by far the queen of celebrity real estate savvy."[40] On the other hand, one celebrity doesn't necessarily want to bask in the glow of another. Johnny Carson was distinctly unimpressed when informed by a realtor that a house she was showing him belonged to one of the Beatles.

Says a Malibu realtor, "Most of us can't afford to indulge our fantasies, but they can." In fact a surprising number of people *can* afford to indulge their fantasies, and the market for the houses of the stars is brisk. George Burns's house sold for $2 million after just one day on the market. Gig and Elizabeth Young were able to raise the price of their house by $50,000 just by including the bed that they had slept in. Liberace's house, with its piano-shaped swimming pool, was offered for over a hundred thousand dollars more than its neighbor, owned by *M.A.S.H.* star Mike Farrell. Sometimes the whiff of secondhand celebrity can be enough, even if the celebrity in question remains anonymous. "Recently owned by a famous actor," proclaims the blurb for a contemporary house with circular staircase, pool, and tennis courts in Alpine, New Jersey ("An additional amenity," adds the realtor, "is a unique surveillance-camera setup").[41]

What *is* the fantasy of owning a celebrity home? Does the buyer want to *be* the celebrity who used to live there, or to *have* the celebrity—whether as an indwelling presence, a trophy name, or a fantasy partner? What is it that the buyer seeks when he or she bids on a celebrity home? "Everyone wants to be a part of the entertainment industry, and buying a famous person's home makes people outside the business feel like they are somehow attached," says a Beverly Hills broker. "Some people come in and tell me that they only want celebrity homes." Mused an actress who bought the house of 1930s star Dolores Del Rio, whose husband had designed the Academy Award statuette, "Maybe it means that I am fated to win an Oscar."[42] "The Del Rio house," averred production designer David Gropman, "captured the essence of what it was to be a movie star in Hollywood, all the glamour and seduction of it."[43]

The psycho-logic here seems clear, if rudimentary. We could call the purchasers of celebrity homes "house-groupies," or fetishists. Or we could call them something nicer, like fans. The house becomes quite literally a dream or fantasy house for these buyers, who hobnob with the famous ex-residents, harmlessly at second hand, by walking the same floors and flushing the same toilets that were once used by their idols. Although "fan" comes from "fanatic" (from Latin *fanum*, temple) rather than "fantasy" (Greek *fantasia*, a making visible), both faculties are present here: enthusiasm and imagination. If "celebrity house" is a transferred epithet—if it's the former resident rather than the house itself that lends a haunting presence—then the buyers of celebrity homes forge a relationship with the aura of the previous owner.

But in some cases it is the house itself that is the celebrity. Houses in fiction, houses in movies, often take on a star power of their own. As one observer remarked about the house that is the title "character" in the Merchant-Ivory film of E. M. Forster's *Howards End,* "some actors would kill for such a sympathetic part."[44] The house in the *Psycho* films became younger or older depending upon whether the sequels were set earlier or later in time; like the actress who played a 100-year-old woman in *Titanic,* the house was "aged" with the use of special paint. Publicity materials for one of England's greatest "treasure houses," designed by eighteenth-century architect John Vanbrugh, boast that "Castle Howard has played many roles, some as a star, others as cameos or character parts," and circulate the castle's résumé.[45] About twenty to thirty modernist houses in the Hollywood Hills have starred regularly in films from *L.A. Confidential* to *Blade Runner,* not to mention commercials and fashion shoots. Since so many films are set in the interiors and exteriors of this finite group of contemporary houses—partly for the convenience of film crews—viewers often recognize them, as they do other celebrities, without knowing their names. The "Stahl house," the "Ennis-Brown house," "the Goldstein house," the "Del Rio house"—these are the architect-designed celebrities of our cinematic dreams.

Hotel Envy

In a genteel diatribe on "The Homelessness of Certain Married Women," Mrs. James F. Cox, writing in 1901 under the decorous initial "C.," inveighed against the fact that young married couples often chose to live, not in houses of their own, but in hotels. "Opportunity has come to me of late," she writes,

> to meet an unusual number of homeless young married people. They have good though moderate incomes, they are clever, in excellent health, active, energetic young men and women, and yet they have elected to live in boarding houses and hotels. Elevators carry them to upper stories of huge caravansaries, where they take possession of a bed-room, a parlor, and a dressing-room. Here they add to the rich but unmistakably "hotel furniture" the pretty trifles, easily transported, which were among their wedding-presents, and they declare themselves content. They partake of meals, always rich and indigestible, and often of doubtful origin, ordered from long bills of fare, cooked by foreigners, and sit at little tables observing and being observed with that long critical stare which is learned only in such surroundings.[46]

Mrs. Cox was adamant in her diagnosis: "There is no way in which either husband or wife can express themselves in the material things by which they are surrounded. These furnished rooms are to their personal characteristics like ready-made clothing to their bodies, and betray in one way and another that they are 'misfits.' "[47]

It may strike us as a rueful sign of the times (hers and ours) to see that "homeless" to Mrs. Cox meant being able to afford to live in a hotel. Certainly her home-grown xenophobia is on display in the account of the indigestible meals of doubtful origin cooked by foreigners of equally dubious provenance. But this account, published, we might note, in the same time period as *The Theory of the Leisure Class* and *The Interpretation of Dreams,* offers a vision of house and home as a "ground." Portable property, those easily transported wedding-present trifles, will not suffice to allow the husband and wife to "express themselves." Mrs. Cox's conclusion addresses both male and female partners, but clearly she blames the women most, as her title makes clear. A woman's job is to "make a home," not live in a hotel.

"The idea of the hotel is the perfect opposite of the home," declares anthropologist Mary Douglas, "not only because it uses market principles for its transactions, but because it allows its clients to buy privacy as a right of exclusion." Douglas regards the idea of the hotel as "the standard 'Other' " to the home. A hotel is a place "where every comfort has to be paid for, the mercenary, cold, luxurious counterpart against which the home is being measured." She cites the cry of the typical exasperated parent: "March in and out, without so much as by your leave; do they think this is a hotel?"[48]

But this, of course, is the great allure of the hotel, to parent and child alike. Anonymity *plus* exquisite personal attention. A "valet" to park your car and another to press your suit, your shoes shined overnight, a "concierge" in the lobby to recommend a place to eat: the complete Upstairs-Downstairs euro-fantasy now available to the middle class. And as for buying privacy, what commodity is more coveted? Room service at all hours (free "Continental" breakfast) and the Do Not Disturb sign ready to be hung on the door.

Hotels themselves have been quick to see that "homeyness," to a degree and for a price, would have its own appeal. "You know how you always gather late at night in the kitchen?" asked André Balazs of the Mercer Hotel in New York's Soho district. "Well, I wanted a restaurant that's like a big eat-in kitchen. It's always the place with the warmest feeling and the best conversation." He imagined a place where guests could be "padding down in their slippers and bathrobes" at all hours. The Mercer's lobby "feels like a super-chic living room," and the bathrooms have extra touches like nooks set into the tile walls and filled with votive candles to cast a soft glow on an evening bath. "It anticipates your needs," said Balazs. "You don't know when you might want to light them." Drawers built into the sink units contain useful sundries, "even a condom, on the same theory as those candles."[49]

A small hotel in Amsterdam is described as "like home; yet not exactly, unless at your house the sheets are always crisp, the bathroom is always gleaming, and the answer is always yes."[50] "That's what people want," said the director of public relations for the Pierre, "a home with all the pampering of a hotel."[51] "I know I can go back there after a long day and the bed will be made, the sheets will be clean," said one satisfied resident.

"I am at my most relaxed in palaces," says writer Fran Lebowitz.[52] Hers is a comment made for the times. This is the era of hotel envy. Rap star Hammer built his Vista del Sol mansion, with customized gym, indoor swimming pool, marble floors, mirrored bathrooms, and gold-and-black marble Jacuzzi in the bedroom to emulate the posh hosteleries he encountered on tour. The pop-up TV console in the bedroom, for example, was a hotel inspiration: "I got the idea at the Mirage in Vegas."[53]

Furniture designers and trend watchers have noted the crossover tendency to make houses look like hotels and hotels look like private homes. "While comfy chairs and squooshy sofas invade hotel lobbies, cafes and executive suites, 'contract' furniture—that sturdy stock made for offices, restaurants and other commercial and public spaces—is wending its way home."[54] Part of the pleasure is that of familiarity, and another part surprise, but a major element seems to be intimations, if not delusions, of grandeur. "People become enamored of furniture they see in the most unlikely places—mostly public spaces," says well-known restaurant and hotel architect and designer Adam Tihany. "When I ask a residential client to bring me pictures of things they like, I find that 50 percent of them are of hotel lobbies or famous buildings or offices with amazing pieces of furniture in them." Perhaps in anticipation of—or response to—a deluge of such requests, the Donatello, a small deluxe hotel in San Francisco, makes available to guests a detailed inventory of its "interior design, art & antique collection," including the four types of Italian marble used in the lobby and reception area.[55]

Fancy apartment buildings from Los Angeles to Dallas now come with services once found only in hotels—or in the homes of the servanted rich: wake-up calls, in-house dialing, a "property channel" that broadcasts news of the building and its residents, a quick-dial service for local restaurants that deliver. Multimillion-dollar "megahomes" in Florida are sold turnkey—fully furnished and ready to move into—to what a developer calls "impulse buyers," usually retired executives from the North seeking second or even third homes in the sun. And at least one successful speculator in the big-house market has refashioned the concept of "turnkey" into a hotel-of-your-own, equipping his new homes with monogrammed bathrobes, dining tables set with fine china, freezers filled with prime beef, and a fully stocked wine cellar. And in case you're too busy to bother collecting art and artifacts to personalize your new residence, the builder will do it for you, traveling the world to find one-of-a-kind teak sculptures and wall hangings—all included in the price of the showcase house.[56]

"Now that far-flung destinations are within easy reach, it's the home that has become the exotic refuge,"[57] trumpets a shelter magazine. It's certainly true that air travel, cruise ships, and safaris have "descended" to the point where they are affordable to middle-class travelers. (Veblen might have been amused—or not—to see that Darwin's Galápagos Islands have become a particularly attractive tourist destination.) And it's also true that some of the other "conveniences" of modern life, like the cell phone and the laptop computer, mean that even the most exotic of destinations doesn't free one from being in touch with civilization—or, more to the point, the office.

The combination of available money (or credit) and shortage of time has made the "dream house" into a hotel. Mail-order linen houses offer an 800 number, available twenty-four hours a day, that can supply you with "Hotel Luxuries" from English hotel blankets (crafted by "the same blanket maker that serves the Royal Palace") to French sheets, Turkish robes, and Italian terry towels. "Have you ever stayed in an exclusive spa or hotel and fallen in love with their luxurious towels and oversized robes?"[58] the brochure asks invitingly. "Now you can enjoy that same feeling of being on vacation in the privacy and comfort of your own home."

This is of course the point. It's not that people who would like to "sleep on sheets as extravagant as the ones used in the best luxury spas and hotels in the world"[59] don't occasionally stay in hotels, any more than people who have commercial or professional-style Viking or Garland ranges in their kitchens have stopped eating in restaurants. But the pleasures of home, at least at this end of the home-luxury scale, are really the pleasures of instant vacation, without the inconvenience of travel, packing and unpacking, tipping, and, above all, taking time off. What used to be called, in the familiar cliché, "all the comforts of home," are now the comforts of that fantasy "spa or hotel" where one can "fall in love" with sheets, towels, and (of course) "luxurious Sateen comforters." The "comforter" is a commodity, not a person.

The Real Thing

The "real" in real estate means both "immovable" and "genuine." Unlike furniture, jewels, and currency, real estate is not "portable property." But its "reality" has also come to be an imaginative quality. Compare it with phrases like "real money," "real world," "real life," the "real thing" (i.e., genuine love, not infatuation), "the real McCoy." The "real" in real estate means something you can touch. Something that is, somehow, authentic.

But what is the relationship between authenticity and material culture? Is authentic expression to be found in the disavowal of commodities and the embrace of "natural primitiveness,"[60] or in the cultivation of the tastes and desires of individuality as displayed by the intelligent consumer? "Ideals of authentic expression," writes cultural historian Jackson Lears, "began in yearnings for a more intense and palpable experience of the world than was available in commodity civilization, for a solid sense of truth beneath a tissue of misleading appearances." But through the advent of advertising and mass production, "the quest for personal authenticity," as Lears among others has observed, "became the project of assembling the right brand-name goods."[61] That emptiest of all commodities, Coca-Cola, after all, achieved global circulation by calling itself "the real thing."

Materialism might thus be the sign of authentic self-expression (the individual fulfills his dreams) or, contrariwise, of the manifestly "inauthentic self." The parody-paradigm case in American literature is that of George F. Babbitt, Sinclair Lewis's middle-class booster, for whom "what he believed to be his individuality" was established by advertising campaigns. "Standard advertised wares—toothpastes, socks, tires, cameras, instantaneous hot-water heaters—were his symbols and proofs of excellence; at first the signs, then the substitutes, for joy and passion and wisdom." And Babbitt, lest we forget, was a realtor. For a man who made his living selling houses, "none of these advertised tokens of financial and social success was more significant than a sleeping-porch with a sun-parlor below." A conformist before the term reached its journalistic high-water mark in the gray-flannel fifties, Babbitt even gets his "values" from outside rather than from within. As the narrator comments with devastating flatness, "It is not known whether he enjoyed his sleeping-porch because of the fresh air or because it was the standard thing to have a sleeping-porch."

It is easy to lampoon poor Babbitt, who is "enchanted" with his bathroom fixtures: "He looked at the solid tub, the beautiful nickel taps, the tiled walls of the room, and felt virtuous in the possession of this splendor."[62] And it is easy to critique the materialism of the surface, to decry "commodity fetishism" and "conspicuous consumption" as symptoms of status display. But take away the sense of invective here—too easily hurled by both moralists and journalists—and you will be left with a different kind of "reality": things, commodities, objects, consumable goods, are not only possessions but a kind of language. They are, like it or not, the way we communicate with each other, with ourselves, and with the world. If Babbitt's sense of "virtue" seems misplaced, it is not the fault of his water faucets.

The fact is, we conventionally *blame* goods, commodities, and shopping for everything from moral desuetude to the breakdown of the family. It makes us feel good, especially when the status symbols we complain about are the Joneses' rather than our own. And in a do-what-I-say-not-what-I-do culture, the bad faith here is half the problem. The condemnation of materialism is actually a misplaced permission to continue indulging in it. As long as we deplore it ("But it doesn't buy happiness!") we don't have to give it up. Instant diagnoses after the 1999 school shootings in Littleton, Colorado, focused on the fact that many families now owned more than one television set, allowing each member to watch the program of his or her choice, and rendering obsolete (or quaint, or nostalgically desirable) the scenario of the family gathering around the set in the living room to watch *Leave It to Beaver* or *All in the Family.* Indeed, family members were probably agreeing with this analysis in front of their multiple television screens all over the country. The adage, "We know very well but we do it anyway," is the beginning rather than the end of an analysis of our culture. Would an abstemious Babbitt in a cabin in the woods be a paragon of moral success? The things in our lives today are animate, animated, and animating. The absence of things alone does not confer virtue. And very few of those who claim that it might would be willing to live by their own precepts.

The house occupies a peculiarly powerful place in this logic of good and bad materialism. It is in some ways imagined as above the battle, since, as we have seen, house and home are culturally associated with all kinds of emotional things, from mothers to "selves," that we resist defining in material terms. Real estate was in law the opposite of personal estate, and "realty" to be distinguished from "personalty." A house outlasted its occupants, who lived there, died there, and in many cases passed on the house to their descendants. In European cultures where the house defined the "house" (the patriarchal lineage), people's genealogies were defined in terms of their relation to the family estate. The house was not a "commodity" in the sense that it was regularly traded or exchanged. Houses *contained* commodities and were a reason (or an excuse) for acquiring them.

Clearly houses did change ownership, sometimes drastically and precipitously, as a result of hereditary laws; in a number of Jane Austen novels daughters have to contemplate moving out of the family home to make way for the new male claimant. But the "real estate market" *as a market* is a fairly new phenomenon. In Britain an "estate agent" was formerly the steward or manager of a landed estate, but by the end of the nineteenth century the phrase had become a term for someone who buys and sells houses. In the United States the National Association of Realtors adopted "Realtor" as its professional title as recently as 1916. (George Babbitt, ever on the qui vive, was quick to get on the bandwagon: "We ought to insist that folks call us 'realtors' and not 'real-estate men.' Sounds more like a reg'lar profession."[63])

The real estate market substitutes for hereditary privilege the dream of purchase, ownership, and "moving up." The house becomes a commodity, and thus just as subject to all the anxieties of commodity culture from Puritan guilt to (what is its inverse and spectral double) "pecuniary emulation."

This is one reason, I want to suggest, why many people are so conflicted about their desire for bigger, more opulent, and better-appointed houses. Here are some others:

- Someone else's trophy house always seems extravagant. Because it is theirs.
- Someone else's trophy house always seems more perfect. Because it is theirs.
- The dream house, once realized, is no longer a dream.

In the twentieth-century culture of the celebrity, a new kind of "aristocracy" based on popular fame and even notoriety replaced an older, apparently "stable" image of hereditary privilege (itself developed, needless to say, in defiance of a close reading of history). And the twentieth-century culture of the house and home is in a way a chronicle of the house as star, whether in a home video or a Hollywood epic. The buying and selling of "celebrity homes" is a sign and an artifact of this new conceptual commodification of the house.

"Conspicuous consumption," "invidious comparison," "vicarious leisure," "waste," and "futility" were all analytic terms for Veblen, not moral ones, as he was at pains to explain and succeeding generations equally determined to forget. "Veblen is insistent—far more than Marx—on reducing aesthetics to economics," notes Adam Gopnik, who quotes a characteristic sentence: "The superior gratification derived from the use and contemplation of costly and supposedly beautiful products is . . . a gratification of our sense of costliness masquerading under the name of beauty."[64] But this cranky strain of cultural analysis is not the same as moral outrage, to which Veblen never either aspires or stoops. He doesn't think buying things is bad; he thinks it's a cultural symptom. It's perhaps equally symptomatic that, after a peripatetic career in a series of American cities and universities from Stanford to New York, he wound up living in a cabin in Northern California.

SIX

THE HOUSE AS HISTORY

What critic Walter Benjamin called the "aura" of a work of art can be compared to the "aura" of a house. An aura (the term is now familiar to us as a version of "star quality") is the "cult value of the work of art," the "unique phenomenon of a distance no matter how close it may be," and "the associations which . . . tend to cluster around the object of perception." And the aura is dependent, thought Benjamin, upon authenticity and history.

> The authenticity of a thing is the essence of all that is transmissible from its beginning, ranging from its substantive duration to its testimony to the history which it has experienced. Since the historical testimony rests on the authenticity, the former . . . is jeopardized by reproduction. . . . And what is really jeopardized when the historical testimony is affected is the authority of the object.[1]

Benjamin was wary of the fact that "the uniqueness of a work of art is inseparable from its being imbedded in the fabric of tradition." Was the inevitable result a kind of object worship? As "cult value" gave way to "exhibition value," and the work of art became, first and foremost, something to be displayed, its role in culture changed. With the advent of "mechanical reproduction" (Benjamin has in mind the invention, particularly, of photography and film), the notion of uniqueness and of the "original" began to make less sense.

So too with the house, once a uniquely historical object with its own pedigree and provenance. Such histories still attach to houses in the legal sense, since the paper trail of ownership (the "title search") functions as a kind of genealogy of the individual house, whatever its architectural interest. But the tract house, the prefabricated house, the "pattern book," and the (often costly and meticulous) historic reproduction have changed the way we relate both to houses and to history. In the United States, where there lingers some small vestige of a historical inferiority complex vis-à-vis the ancient cities and towns of Europe and elsewhere, the back-and-forth of new versus old is an old story. But it now seems possible, as never before, to buy a piece of history. As we've seen, landed "real" estate and portable property were initially two completely different property systems. Now that these have grown more and more alike—everything is becoming fully commodifiable (portable)—the very forces of mechanical reproduction that destroyed the aura of the castle are what enable people to achieve ever-closer approximations of it. In other words, once authenticity itself becomes a desirable commodity, it too can be advertised, imitated, manufactured, and sold.

Owning a Piece of History

One of the commodities most prized by American house purchasers is a little piece of history to call their own. In the film version of *Mr. Blandings Builds His Dream House* (1948), Cary Grant and Myrna Loy are beguiled by the house agent's claim that General Gates had watered his horses on "their" property before riding into battle. General Gates? Ah, yes, the Civil War, says Mr. Blandings vaguely. The *Revolutionary* War, corrects the agent, with conscious superiority. Before long Mr. Blandings has adopted the same story, and the same complacent, proprietary tone. What, I wonder, would he have done if confronted with an advertisement for an "Ante-Bellum Estate, Steeped in American History," which turned out to be "originally built in the 1920s," and "renovated by Stanford White for Ulysses S. Grant, Jr.," and was located not in the South but in upstate New York?[2]

Mocked, however gently or ungently, by authors from Henry James to F. Scott Fitzgerald for their fascination with the old stones and castles of Europe (some of which are now advertised for sale through Sotheby's, Christie's, and *Unique Homes*[3]), Americans have tried from time to time to re-create these English and Continental splendors on home turf. Thus, for example, the "Elizabethan-style manor" in Greenwich, Connecticut, a "replica of a 16th-century manor," replete with faux half-timbering, containing "12,000 square feet of exquisite Renaissance-style details." A "Castle-Like East Hill Mansion" in Englewood, New Jersey, describes itself as a "magnificent new French Normandy estate" (complete with "huge three-story stone rotunda," "massive staircases," "antique marble fireplace," Jacuzzi, and, in the eclectic American vein, "spectacular country kitchen"). "Build Your Palace Penthouse" invites a New York City realty firm that offers, as well, a "Castle in the Sky." Mansion buyers in suburban Nashville have their choice of "colonial," "Tudor," "Victorian," and "modern" models—all of them built yesterday.

"It'll be a kind of Italian villa," said the man who bought and tore down Jimmy Stewart's house, of the new dwelling he was planning to build on the site. "It'll look old, but be new."[4]

But though it's easy to tease the builders—and the buyers—for historical deficiency, the quotation marks around "historic" are, in a way, part of the authenticity effect. No one lives in a museum. When a ("real") old carriage house is turned into a delightful renovated residence for a modern couple, or an "early American" kitchen is equipped with new exposed "rustic" beams (crafted, naturally, of "old wood" reclaimed from "old buildings"), the imitation of the past is the sincerest form of flattery.

A cartoon in the *New Yorker* pictures a couple touring another's new house, which is adorned with candlesticks, old jugs, and antique fireplace tools. "In our first year of marriage we exposed our beams, too," the visiting wife says affably.[5]

Candlelight at dinner became "romantic" when it was nostalgic and optional. As Veblen noted in the 1890s, "The same could not have been said thirty years ago, when candles were, or recently had been, the cheapest available light for domestic use."[6] The displacement of an artifact from necessity to luxury is precisely what produces the historical effect. If we still used candles for light, they would not give us such a strong sense of the presence of history.

More than ten million viewers of *This Old House* watched the painstaking renovation of a 274-year-old antique Colonial house in Milton, Massachusetts, from the original wide-board pine paneling in the living room to the preserved beehive oven in the kitchen. But the builders added a "dream workshop" for the woodworker, a gym with a sauna, and a double garage with automatic doors. Clearly the folks at PBS felt confident enough in the historical verisimilitude of their Colonial original to augment it for present-day taste. Asked what was his favorite part of the house, the designer unhesitatingly answered, "the media room."[7]

And for every genuinely old "old house" there are lots of wannabes. "There is a finite number of old houses out there," said the editor in chief of *Country Home*. "Everybody wants one, but most people can't have them." In response to this desire there has developed a trend for the "new old" house, like those on display in a special show-house project in Greensboro, North Carolina. The houses are built to look and feel like antiques, using Palladian proportions from nineteenth-century pattern books and Greek Revival details. In this case the effect of "authenticity" requires the omission of exactly those modern and postmodern elements (sauna, media room) that were added to the real "old house" (though presumably the bathrooms are modern).

Instant Tradition

A hundred years ago America's wealthiest citizens went shopping in Europe for a "tradition" they felt they had to import, bringing home statues, walls, and whole houses and castles in boxes for reassembly. "Why Americans find it so fascinating to fantasize about owning a piece of English ancestry is for Ralph Lauren to know and for marketers to find out," notes a piece on the thriving trade in architectural antiques.[8] But is there really any mystery? Since at least the days of Henry James and Edith Wharton, Americans covetous of a more ancient European lineage have set about acquiring the past, brick by brick, fireplace by baronial fireplace (and sometimes nobleman by desiccated nobleman).

Henry James's biographer, Leon Edel, observes that "if one of his great themes was the chase of the American girl for her husband, another was the chase of the wealthy American for the artifacts of Europe."[9] Again sex and real estate presented themselves as twin fantasies of seduction and possession. In the Gilded Age of the American "collector," European art, furniture, and indeed architecture were the spoils of wealth and taste.

William Randolph Hearst built the vast castle of San Simeon near the coast of central California as a tribute to his mistress, the actress Marion Davies, and filled its cavernous spaces with marble. Every room was stocked with treasures brought from Europe: a marble doorway sculpted by Sansovino and bearing the crest of "the Warrior Pope," Julius II, a sixteenth-century French Renaissance fireplace constructed for the Château Le Jour and acquired from the collection of American architect Stanford White, a Gobelin tapestry from the "History of Alexander" set, a massive Gothic refectory furnished with five-hundred-year-old Catalonian choir stalls. After viewing San

Simeon, Irish playwright and socialist George Bernard Shaw is said to have remarked, "This is probably the way God would have done it if He had had the money."[10]

When film director Orson Welles and scriptwriter Herman Mankiewicz fictionalized the Hearst-Davies story in *Citizen Kane*, a 1931 *Fortune* magazine spread called "Hearst at Home" provided some of the inspiration for the stage set, though the Great Hall at "Xanadu," the film's version of San Simeon, was even more grandiose.[11] (Few people connected with the film had ever visited San Simeon much less been entertained there as guests.) A huge fireplace dominates the space, and is surrounded by a deliberately eclectic selection of artifacts: classical statuary, medieval gargoyles, a bellows from an English country estate, a candleholder that looks as if it belongs in a French church. "Our home is *here*, Susan," says Kane to his unhappy wife, gesturing at the huge, ceremonial space.

Isabella Stewart Gardner installed in her mansion on the Fenway in Boston, among myriad other wonders, medieval choir stalls, marble columns and capitals, Romanesque sculpture, and eight of the court balconies from Venice's Ca' d'Oro, the palazzo celebrated in John Ruskin's *The Stones of Venice*. She was assisted in her work as collector, connoisseur, and designer by Bernard Berenson, whose patron she became. Henry James used her as the model for the fanatical art collector Mrs. Gareth in *The Spoils of Poynton* (1897), and later, as Douglass Shand-Tucci notes, transformed her into the male figure of Adam Verber, "the public-spirited collector dedicated to bringing art to America"[12] in his late novel *The Golden Bowl* (1904). It was no accident that James's *Portrait of a Lady* (1881) offered as its protagonist an American woman of independent spirit and wealth who marries an impoverished dilettante with expensive and aesthetic tastes and goes to live with him in Rome. As Edel remarks, "Isabel Archer embodies a notion not unlike that of Isabella of Boston, with her motto *C'est mon plaisir*."[13]

At Gardner's harbor-front storage warehouse, packed high

with cases containing architectural fragments and old masters, the collector insisted on directing the unpacking herself. "Mrs. Gardner decided what case should be opened next; if it was at the bottom of a pile those on top must be lifted and placed at one side. . . . As each column, capital, and base was unpacked, she indicated the place in the storeroom where it should be put." When the job was finished, each base, column, and capital was in its place, "all arranged as she wanted them to stand at Fenway Court."[14] Gardner's achievement was a publicity coup as well as an aesthetic accomplishment, drawing notice as far from Boston as Kansas City and Florida. (With inadvertent architectural wit a Florida newspaper commented that "the Boston woman who is getting columns and columns of free advertisements out of her love for privacy is a genius in her way.")

Gardner's friends and admirers were given to praising Fenway Court as—precisely—a dream house. "Last night I dreamed that I was going into [Fenway Court] and you were waiting there & welcomed me, & I awoke with a sense of well-being, and of all the beauty that had been around me," wrote the Irish playwright Lady Gregory. The pioneer interior decorator Elsie De Wolfe wrote to her, "I shut my eyes close, to shut in all the beauty . . . of your beautiful things and shut out all the *banalité* and sordidness of our incredible present." And a young Boston acquaintance sent her a letter to say, "I dreamt of Fenway Court all night."[15]

But not every wealthy American collector of European artifacts was a Hearst or a Gardner—nor did most have a Bernard Berenson at their command. And some observers were more ambivalent about these wholesale "borrowings" from Europe. In fact Berenson's wife Mary once described Mrs. Gardner's Fenway Court as "a 'junk shop' of art 'ravished' from where it belonged, the 'horrid' result of 'snatching this and that away from its *real* home.' "[16] There were other pitfalls, too. Soon Emily Post would offer a helpful "word of warning" lest others "be led to follow in the footsteps of a New York woman, who, having bought a charming little putty-color-and-gilt room in one of the provinces of France, sent it home with orders to a certain cabinet-maker to fit it, and to fix it where necessary. The cabinet-maker fitted it very well, and 'fixed' it thoroughly. Finding the surface far from new, he planed it off as well as he could and sent for a painter to make a good job of it!

"As a matter of fact," Post pointed out genially to her readers, "we can—and do—produce these rooms in America. We can make them quite perfectly. But skill is lacking to duplicate the slight unevenness of surface produced by the softening of time—which is quite different from the mechanical repetition of irregularity."[17] The aura of history is precisely what can't be mechanically reproduced.

How are the pleasures of the instant past different today from what they were fifty to a hundred years ago? For one thing, the past has come to us: via the Internet, the ease of transatlantic travel, the relative democratization of the airlines and the airwaves. Lord Elgin became a British hero—and a villain to Greeks—when he high-handedly appropriated marble figures from the Parthenon frieze and brought them "home" to England. The poet Byron railed against what he regarded as Elgin's heedless plundering of another nation's treasury, as well as the immoral practice of "dilettanti" in despoiling "Phidian freaks,/ Misshapen monuments and maim'd antiques" in order to "make their grand saloons a general mart/For all the mutilated blocks of art."[18] Today every upscale homeowner can be his or her own Lord Elgin, ordering through designers or simply locating on the Internet bits and pieces of ancient European architecture.

Under headings like "Reclaimed Bricks" and "Antique Bathrooms," salvage companies offer up bits and pieces of the historic past. A seventeenth-century limestone kitchen floor from Bath, England, bought and shipped to New York; an oak-beamed granary dating from 1600, now dismantled and ready for shipping to your door. Does it matter if the history attached to it is not yours? Or is it just not yours *yet?* This phenomenon of *buying* the past seems a little like padding your résumé or adding a spurious aristocratic "von" to the family name. But it's also, more benignly, a way of getting, or keeping, in touch with the past. *Anyone's* past.

A dealer in County Westmeath, Ireland, advertises an Irish Georgian house "to be dismantled and relocated." The offering comes complete with the house's history ("the Rotherams, who were descended from a Yorkshire family, had been living in Ireland since the 14th century and were a well respected family"), a reproduction of the original owner's crest, learned observations about the special nature of the house's construction ("Crossdrum House is exceptional in that all four elevations are constructed of dressed stone, known as ashlar"), and an account of the terrain and landscaping, even though these are clearly *not* available for sale ("the practicalities of running a small working farm on the parkland meant, unfortunately, that most of the fine trees, including a magnificent copper beechwood avenue, were chopped down"). The dealer adds a telling note of pathos about the reasons for the present sale, calculated to remove whatever untoward sense of guilt a purchaser might have about buying and importing the dismembered building materials.[19] The purchaser, like Lord Elgin, will actually be *preserving* the past by taking it home.

Buying Time

But if the idea of packing up all those stones seems expensive and cumbersome, you can construct your own history effect with far less bother.

"What sells out there is anything that looks old," says the former proprietor of a design shop that carried old lanterns, tin sconces, and painted American furniture.[20] Locust Valley interior designer Tom Samet "gives newcomers' homes an instant old money look" with a judicious infusion of chintz fabric, old En-

glish and American furniture, and knickknacks from local con-
signment shops arranged to make them look like old family
pieces. And when an interior decorator for the magazine *In Style*
"propped" Christie Brinkley's new summer home in the Hamptons for a photo shoot, bringing in furniture from English
Country Antiques in Bridgehampton and adding various odds
and ends from flea markets, Brinkley bought the entire contents.
It felt like *her* house and *her* things—once she'd seen them all in
place.[21]

The effect of "instant tradition" can also be achieved on a
more modest budget. For a note of "urban country" flavor in a
model home in Chicago's Transportation Building, a designer
found a church pew at a flea market and "had the pew faux
painted," then placed it next to a glass-top table with plaster
columns for "a surprising contrast." She recommends mixing
vintage furnishings with contemporary ones. "Opt for genuine
items, such as kitchen gadgets from the 1930s, '40s and '50s, old
farm and garden tools, vintage knitting tools and handmade baskets."[22]

Faux-folk art is now a thriving cottage industry—quaint little
"dog-carts" made yesterday of old wood, perfect for petunias on
the front lawn, handcarved and painted wood replicas of turn-
of-the-century tailoring, or a 1910 watch dial "now adapted for
your wall. The distressed face is reproduced and découpaged
onto fiberboard." The classical past can also be purchased for a
fraction of its original price—like the Acropolis Fragment, a "bas
relief of Athena . . . crafted of reinforced plaster with an antique
wash," or the Grupo Putti, described as "a centuries-old Italian
artifact . . . reproduced in lightweight resin."[23]

And the illusion of antiquity is as close as your nearest Pottery
Barn, where decorative techniques like ragging, stippling, sten-
ciling, sponging, and colorwashing are taught in how-to kits.
Every new restaurant in town has a faux finish on its walls and at
least one piece of "distressed" furniture in the lobby.

Have you ever wondered why decorators and designers chose

so "psychological" a word to describe such a material characteristic? "A deep distress hath humanized my Soul," wrote the poet Wordsworth, feelingly. Would it have done the same for his love seat? (His contemporary Cowper did write a famous poem called "The Sofa.") The externalization of this apparently so inward sensation can be traced to the 1940s, when it appeared in a little work entitled *What Every Woman Should Know About Furniture.* "If you're a real antique lover you can even buy pieces with 'distressed' finish—that is, with simulated marks of age and wear."[24] Twenty years later the British *Daily Telegraph* made gentle sport of what it clearly regarded as a colonial inferiority complex: " 'We're using a lot of distressed furniture,' said the American designer solemnly. . . . the current vogue in America is for furniture that has been bashed or scarred to make it look like English antique."[25] "Age and wear," "bashed and scarred"—behind these images of neglect and domestic violence lies what might be described as *the pathos of furniture,* much more provocative in its way than what Edgar Allan Poe called the "philosophy of furniture." For however artificially induced the "distress," this is a metaphor that won't stay dead. A "heavily-distressed oak lowboy"; "antiqued, toughened and distressed leathers"; "a sofa covered in distressed pigskin, like the hides of retired footballs."[26]

The distressed sofa or sideboard or dining table is not "really" in distress; in fact, it is—like the famed damsel in distress of melodrama—actually enjoying its time in the spotlight. "Buff walls and nubby Berber carpeting make up the background for *lightly distressed* furniture, antiques, handmade baskets and plants," explains an interior designer, describing a model home with an "urban country" feel.[27] A San Francisco showroom has "copper lampshades that have been *bathed in acid* to turn them verdigris and powdery pink"; another displays "pretty little French provincial buffets and commodes . . . painted flat, milky pastels then *sanded, brushed and gouged to look as if they've been kicked around since the storming of the Bastille.*" A third collection offers "a primitive Philippine hutch . . . painted raspberry and *flesh pink* and *rubbed with a dark glaze to look worn.*"²⁸ The discreet note of S/M is not, I think, entirely an accident. These pieces of furniture are consensually sensual, suffering willingly on our account (and on our charge accounts). "Just when you think you'll go mad if you have to look at another beautifully bruised 18th-century walnut buffet," says a shopping guide to Provence, relief is at hand in the form of a store that features spare, angular modern furniture.²⁹

Here's a story a friend told me. A woman moving into a newly constructed house in an expensive Nantucket area of reproduction antique homes wanted her kitchen to look as much as possible like those in the 1800-era houses on historic India Street. She engaged the island's finest carpenters to design and build state-of-the-art cabinets of gleaming wood, a magnificent sight. Then she called in the "distressers." The cabinetmakers sat outside and literally covered their eyes as the experts went to work, flailing away at the newly installed doors and drawers with chains. But when the owner returned she was not satisfied. The cabinetry looked dented and bruised but not yet authentically distressed. She wanted another century of wear. Back came the distressers, lengths of chain in hand, and flailed away again. The finished kitchen, I'm told, is a marvel, extremely beautiful and "authentic" in style. It does indeed look exactly like the ones around the corner in genuinely historic houses. In this case "distressing" had the desired effect on the woodwork. I've heard no report about the psychological effect on the woodworkers.

There are also "antique" tools and gadgets, triggers for cherished new "memories"—even if you don't actually remember them. The latest chain of high-concept home-furnishing stores is Restoration Hardware, with its special emphasis on the detailing of the past. "Like Ralph Lauren, Restoration Hardware is attempting to elicit an emotional response by elevating and reinterpreting familiar but forgotten objects," noted the *New*

York Times. "Many objects for sale, though newly designed, are either historical-looking or rooted in earlier American iconography."[30] Words like "nostalgia" and "fantasy" are part of the erotic code of the everyday, from miners' lunch boxes to door knockers.

"We're not 'ye olde,' " said the founder, Stephen Gordon, "but I think a lot of us as we get older and have children want to make traditions and keep them, because it seems to add a lot of depth to our lives."[31] The desire to *make* traditions seems a peculiarly modern, or postmodern, boomer preoccupation. And what is equally of our time is the desire, in fact the determination, to found those traditions on or around material objects—"nostalgia-provoking, emotion-yanking objects" from the (supposed) past.

Each of the Restoration Hardware stores (there are almost a hundred nationwide) is laid out like a two-story American house, with furniture, gadgets, and tools in their proper places. Customers hunker down in leather armchairs and play house-of-the-past, or stand shoulder to shoulder gazing at the cleaning goods: Wax Remover for your tables, Sticky Wax to make your candles stand up straight, Beeswax Salad Bowl finish for your woodenware, and so on and on. Both male and female customers seem transfixed by these products. It's *better* than a living museum: you can buy things and take them home.

We might think of this obsession with instant tradition as a thing of the baby boomer generation. But lest we forget our *own* recent past, it's worth recalling the "historical" affectations of an earlier generation.

The Connecticut country house owned by the insufferably pretentious and tasteless Upsons, the over-the-top parody WASPs mercilessly exposed in Patrick Dennis's wickedly droll *Auntie Mame,* was "a low rambling field-stone affair with a hitching post in front, a string of sleigh bells hanging on the front door, and a pair of carriage lamps flanking it." "Isn't it *sweet,*" Auntie Mame cooed. "Almost like *Better Homes and Gardens.*" Decorated to a fare-thee-well in high-end department-store taste ("Downstairs is Sloane's and upstairs is Altman's," says Doris Upson proudly), the house, which has been named by its owners "Upson Downs," suffers from a condition of terminal cuteness that reminds me, a little too vividly, of the "finds" I have sometimes seized upon in my own auction and flea-market prowls:

> The downstairs, or Sloane Section of Upson Downs, was pretty much like the upstairs; very Quaint, very Country, very Colonial. There were carriage lamps, ratchet lamps, tole lamps, and lamps made out of butter churns, coffee mills, and apothecary jars. Bed warmers, old bellows, brass trivets, and gay samplers hung on the walls with Spy cartoons, hunting prints, yellowed maps, and daguerreotypes.[32]

As the ultra-urban, unerringly chic Auntie Mame takes the measure of this spectacle, she decides, for the moment at least, to get into the spirit of things: "You'll find me out in the sitting room reading *Oliver Wiswell* in one of those comfy Governor Winthrop chairs. It's just as though I *were* history in this little jewel of a house."

It's startling to recall that *Auntie Mame* was published in 1955. And more startling to see how much of the décor at Upson Downs can still be found on display in periodicals like *Traditional Home* and *Country Living.* As well as at country auctions.

Bidding on the Past

Auction going, and auction buying, has an enormous appeal, in part because what's on exhibit, and often on sale, is a piece of family history. Yours or someone else's. What we want is not only the thing itself but the story behind it—the pedigree, the provenance, the sense of continuity. These objects become fetishes, endowed with real power. I'm reminded of my favorite sentence from the work of psychiatrist Robert J. Stoller: "A fetish is a story masquerading as an object."[33]

The erotics of the auction are complete and satisfying. Here, if anywhere, is mimetic desire in play. (For a wonderfully wry example, consider the auction in *The First Wives Club*, in which a blond and clueless "second wife" candidate, all innocence and acquisitiveness, is deftly maneuvered into buying a Japanese plate for $140,000 of her middle-aged boyfriend's money. "Jackie Onassis had one just like it," her socialite guru—who is in league with the "first wives"—whispers in her ear when she hesitates. Up goes the paddle in a reflex action. "Sold.")

Why do those people want *that* chest of drawers, *that* armoire, *that* folk art pig, rather than the other one? Is it the dovetailing of the drawers, the bun feet on the armoire? Who could possibly want a large green bronze garden frog? Or an antique potty-chair (a surefire seller at country auctions)? That little side table, the one we said we had no use for, it's going really cheap. Up with the hand or the paper plate. We can always find a place for it. Gone! Your number please, the lady in the second row? You— you got it—it's yours.

One of the most delicious by-products of auction going—and one that doesn't cost any money—is a new vocabulary. Left bids. Rose medallion china. Firkins and dough tables. An old-er chair with new-er paint. This last is the auctioneer covering his vulnerabilities so that no one can protest being sold reproduction furniture (albeit at bargain prices) when they thought they were getting a "real" bargain, that is, a nineteenth-century immigrant's trunk for two hundred dollars. Summer tourist auction goers want a story—with themselves as Bargain-Man, the peerless antique detector—more than they want the item they're bidding on.

Auctioneers—perhaps especially auctioneers with captive populations, like summer tourists or island dwellers—make it their business to excel at storytelling. This "primitive chair" came from a house belonging to "one of the oldest families on the island"; that pencil sketch is from the hand of an artist "familiar to everyone on Nantucket"; the Pembroke table is walnut—"well, it looks to me like walnut"; the platter "appears to be old," or, again, "to have some age to it"; the Oriental rugs are selling for less than half what they would cost you *wholesale.*

If you can't get to Sotheby's or Christie's or to the local American Legion Hall or high school auditorium or wherever your regional auctions are held, you can settle down on your semi-antique couch and watch public television's *Antiques Roadshow.* An eclectic consumer crossover that combines the Home Shopping Channel, *Quiz Show, The Price Is Right,* and *Let's Make a Deal,* the *Roadshow* travels from city to city (Denver, New Orleans, Phoenix, Minneapolis) inviting folks to go exploring in their own attics, basements, and garages. Ordinary people like you and me bring their precious and semiprecious artifacts for an offstage audition and, if the artifact passes muster, they get a free, on-air appraisal from an attentive expert. The Mickey Mouse toy in its original box. The antique helmet. The unusual Tiffany lamp with its glass shade of plumed birds. "It was one of the most exciting moments of my life," testified the director of American furniture for Sotheby's, describing his first encounter with an eighteenth-century wooden card table brought to the show by a seventy-one-year-old woman. (She had bought it at a garage sale for $25.) "It took only seconds" for the experts "to seize upon it with pounding hearts." This was antique love at first sight. Metamorphosed, ugly-duckling or Cinderella-style, into "An Important Federal Satinwood-Inlaid and Figured Mahogany Demilune Games Table," the appraisers' find (formerly "a filthy, scorned item" and "the table no one wanted") fetched almost half a million dollars at auction.[34]

Money is one consideration here, and money is always sexy. The estimated price is the punch line of just about every encounter, displayed on the TV screen for those keeping score at home. But the *story* is what makes us watch the program—the story of its neglect, its persistence through years of undervaluation, and its triumphant restoration to glory. It's the story of the object as Cinderella, a "from ashes to palace" fairy tale or melodrama starring Aunt Ida's plush velvet button-back wing chair. Most of the people who bring in their treasured family heirlooms and garage-sale finds for appraisal seem (at least on camera) determined to keep the items, perhaps displayed in a more prominent place on the mantel or in the living room rather than the attic. These may be some of the same people who are now tracing their family genealogies, with the help of local librarians and computers. The connection with history and tradition is what they really want.

Historic Colors

History can, however, be a high-maintenance commodity.

When houses are located in "historic districts," any changes in their street appearance are subject to the judgment and regulation of a Historical Commission. This very serious panel, on which a number of concerned citizens sit, rules on matters like paint color (only a few "historic colors" are acceptable), fences, and virtually anything else that you may want to do to the "face" of your house. The boundaries of the historic district are sometimes a little arbitrary: around the corner from where I live in Cambridge several large houses are being renovated and expanded, installing media rooms and massive "Victorian" greenhouses, apparently without the need of a special historic blessing. But the houses along "Tory Row"—some of them in fact dating from the eighteenth century but quite a few much more recent upstarts—are under the eagle eye of the Cambridge Historical Commission. *American bald* eagle, of course.

"History," however, has a number of different meanings here. Our house, built in 1898, came onto the Historic Registry only in 1973 (the CHC itself was founded ten years earlier), by which time a good deal of damage had already been done. The wonderfully informative woman who came out for a site visit shook her head at the kitchen windows, a late sixties addition ("out of character"). Later, when she found in her files a photo of the house as it was in 1966, she called me triumphantly to come and see what the front porch had formerly looked like. Once it was double-width, handsomely columned, imposing—the proper entryway for the proper banker who built it. Now it was smaller, less formal, and with a peaked pediment that didn't—now that I saw the photo I was convinced—really "go" with the house. "They'd never permit you to do that now," she said sympathetically, referring to the "new" porch. The emotional pressure was instantaneous: it was our architectural and historical duty to restore the old porch. If we could ever afford to do so. (We're still waiting on this one.)

Reconstructive surgery to bring back the look of the past is part of the burden of being, and having, an old house. An application we made to put shutters on the kitchen windows and clapboards on an unsightly piece of asphalt-shingled roof between two third-floor dormers was turned down by the CHC because the shutters would call attention to the "inappropriate windows" and the clapboards would be "incongruous" with the "inappropriate dormers." But, as I wrote them, mustering all my epistolary deference, the windows and the dormers were already on the house, in all their glaring (to the CHC) inappropriateness, before we bought it. What we hoped to do was to bring the house into aesthetic conformity with its period—in other words, to make it look better. What I wanted to know, though I thought it better not to ask them directly in a letter, was whether the inappropriate dormers and the inappropriate kitchen windows were now protected by the Cambridge Historical Commission—since they had been on the house when it entered the historic rolls—as another piece of "history."

On another occasion, when the CHC interrogated the owner of a newly painted 156-year-old Greek Revival house, the hue and cry was about color: Why had the house, on historic Follen

Street, turned grayish purple instead of its former purplish gray? Armed with before-and-after slides and a can of purple stain, the commission's director pressed his point. At issue was whether the owners would be forced to repaint, at a cost of around $12,000, to conform to the neighborhood's historically accurate colors of stone-tinted gray or tan.

A representative of the Massachusetts Historical Commission noted that most historical districts don't regulate paint color because emotions run so high on the question. "The review of paint colors, in particular, tends to be an emotional, hot-button issue for a lot of property owners." Why should that be? Because, he said, "so many people consider it an expression of their individuality."[35] Other items over which the Historical Commission may have jurisdiction include fence height and type, curb cuts, and—the bane of all "historic" looks—window air conditioners. (In Nantucket, mercifully cooled by ocean breezes, air conditioners have been few until recently, and to preserve the illusion of period charm they were not permitted in the front windows of a dwelling. But tourism and trophy houses together have eroded the standard of "natural" comfort, and new construction, at least in nonhistoric areas, is now often centrally air-conditioned.)

The battle in such historic districts between "individuality" and "authenticity" resembles the battle waged in some Sunbelt condominium complexes and "new towns" over uniform dimensions, exterior paint colors, and the landscaping of common space. But what difference does "history" make here, in the complex of emotions you feel toward your house? In the Old Cambridge Historical District home owners must choose historically accurate paint colors and get a "certificate of appropriateness" for any significant changes. But when it looked into the use of color over the past three hundred years the Society for the Preservation of New England Antiquities discovered that "the dusty, washed-out tones we associate with colonial America were originally rich and vibrant."[36] So much for authenticity.

In the market niche occupied by "historic colors" the name

game is crucial. Sherwin-Williams Paints offers a "Preservation Palette" displaying colors from Colonial Yellow (1800) to chartreuse (1950). Benjamin Moore's "Historical Color Collection," featuring "significant colors from the 18th and 19th centuries," has delectable names (Georgian Brick, Abingdon Putty, Carrington Beige, Yorketowne Green) that evoke an idealized "Colonial" past. The manufacturers attest to the fact that "these rich, subtle tones have been matched to documented colors from historic homes and buildings throughout the United States," though they're careful to leave a loophole for your own modern reproduction or (to use the architect's term of veiled contempt) "builder's Colonial." For not only can "these handsome colors" restore "the charm of an authentic 18th or 19th century structure," they can also "give authenticity to a home inspired by this period of history." This wonderfully flexible vision of "authenticity"—imagined as a style or an effect rather than a pedigree—seems quintessentially American. It goes along with all those contemporary furniture stores selling "reproduction antiques" newly fabricated from old wood. But in a curiously contradictory move Benjamin Moore has changed the names (and precise hues?) of its Historical Color Collection, rendering the "historical," like the "authentic," a shifting category rather than a permanent attribute.

But the names do have an undeniable magic. One day I walked around Cambridge with a handful of HC (Historic Color) paint chips, holding them up against the clapboards of houses I particularly admired or coveted, to see what HC we should paint our own house, which seemed to us to have been painted by the previous owners a particularly unimaginative and non-Colonial yellow. This was a revealing exercise, proving that you can tell almost nothing from the color chips. Sidling up to the houses I liked best and surreptitiously slipping out our color samples, I felt like a voyeur overstepping the line. Had any of the owners emerged to find us stroking their clapboards there might have been a misunderstanding.

When we had our counseling session with the representative from the CHC (an entirely agreeable, indeed for me inspiring session, full of unexpected bits of historical lore, not at all like going to the dentist), we learned two things of particular interest: first, that the previous owners of our house had painted it in basic hues of yellow and bright white (against CHC urging) because the husband was colorblind and the wife thought those colors would be easier for him to "read"—something we would *never* have figured out on our own—and second, that the "original" colors of the house were in fact the colors we were trying to change it to now. According to CHC records, before its brief period of butter-colored glory the house had been "Colonial Yellow" and "Essex Green"—both standard, which is to say, deeply conventional, ready-made paint colors of the past. We were "restoring" colors that were very visible in the neighborhood (on, for example, the historic and magnificent Longfellow House) but which, in connection with our own house, were "new" to us.

In places like Nantucket that emphasize historical preservation the local hardware store displays a placard showing you the half-dozen or so colors you are permitted to paint your house, and the Historical Commission and zoning board sit for hours debating whether or not to permit builders of huge new houses to trim their shingled frames in white (more eye-catching and distracting on a big house).

People who build megahouses are often people who are used to getting their way in business, and it turns out that if you hire enough lawyers and experts you can often wind up persuading the Historical Commission. But when Mexican-American poet and novelist Sandra Cisneros repainted her beige house in San Antonio, Texas, in a Sherwin-Williams color called Corsican purple, the city's Historic Design and Review Commission ruled the new hue historically incorrect, and instructed Cisneros to change it. The author fought back. "What the house is saying is, 'I'm very Mexican, and I'm proud of it,' and that it's another way of being American," she said. Is purple ("*Corsican* purple") a Mexican color? Yes, said a member of the commission that oversees public art for the city. "The color purple is pre-Columbian."

Some neighbors liked it. Others, like a local banker, another member of the commission, whose nearby house is brown brick, called the purple paint "appalling." "It's not about ethnicity," he said, "it's about eccentricity." He charged that Cisneros, though she wrote so feelingly about the poor, was "acting like the privileged class that doesn't have to follow the rules." The commission suggested that the Purple House, as it became known throughout the city, become Plymouth green, or Colonial Revival tan—colors Cisneros rejected. Most of the nearby mansions in this Victorian-era district of San Antonio, built by wealthy German merchants, are white or beige, though some bungalows in the area sport brighter hues. The question here seemed to be one of conflicting notions of history: was it the *house*'s past or the *owner*'s that was to be faithfully restored?

The clash over colors, historic and modern, is not an exclusively American fetish—and may carry some unexpected social and cultural baggage. In Britain, city planning officials have prosecuted owners who return their houses to vernacular colors without getting permission. Theo Mayer's bake shop in Castle Cary was pink and maroon, then mushroom and black, and is presently lilac and violet. South Somerset officials threatened to prosecute him (and the man who painted the house) because new pavements had been laid and all the buildings on the street were supposed to coordinate with them by using "pastel-whitish" paint.

The personal preferences of regional officials often intervene, and are seldom historically correct. When a historic home in Sherborne, Dorset, was colorwashed lilac with gray detailing by its owner, a planning official denounced the original colors as "vibrant and garish" and arranged to prosecute. He himself liked "creams" but not "strong creams" or "rich colors." The Bath City Council criticized the rich, historically accurate door and window colors of Georgian terraced houses (like "invisible-green") as "jungle colors." In these cases, as in many others, the preferred tone was a brilliant white paint developed in the 1970s. The owners of a medieval and Victorian Gothic rectory, also in South Somerset, changed the brilliant white woodwork back to the historic green discovered by conservation consultants, but a planning officer tried to reverse the change, saying she didn't think the green was appropriate and "would prefer white." The Traditional Paint Forum remains embattled in its attempt to make planning boards aware of history. As an architectural conservation consultant commented, with (perhaps unconscious) double meaning, "There are some who really believe that Britain has always been white. And there are others who have continued to carry the torch of our rich colour heritage, traditional paints, and vernacular connections."[37]

Whose Castle?

A prize is offered to the first reader who correctly identifies the approximate date and source of the following quotation:

> People are spending more than ever on decorating their houses and the Englishman's home has become even more his castle. Nostalgia for the past is combined with the desire for increased comfort in the home as a bastion against the horrors of the world outside.

Give up? This is the voice of *Laura Ashley Decorates a London House,* published in 1985, when the horrors of the world outside Kensington Palace, near which the house in question is located, must have been striking indeed.

The fact is, I rather like Laura Ashley designs. They're not "me" (the dresses make me look like a tea cosy), but it's definitely a look. What strikes me, though, is how very serious we've gotten about reliving, and reloving, the past. It's not so long ago that Barbra Streisand could ask, sotto voce, "What kind of chair is a Morris chair?" and expect her audience to share her pose of faux-naïveté. But today "everybody" not only knows what a Morris chair is, but can recognize a Morris handblock wallpaper design—and order rolls of it sent direct from England.

The Ashley restoration book is historical and informative, full of references to nineteenth-century books of architecture and ornament, as well as photographs of things like (in the Morning Room) a "pelmet design taken from Thomas King's *Upholsterer's Guide* of 1848 in the Victoria and Albert Museum Library, . . . edged with Laura Ashley's dark green 'Nutmeg' "[38] and (in the Main Bathroom–Dressing Room) a "pair of oval, Victorian style wash basins . . . set in a marble top, and supported on a commode made from gothic pew doors from the demolished church of St. Luke's, Cheetham Hill, Manchester."[39] Not to mention (but how can we resist?) the "modern reproduction of a Victorian lavatory, with underglaze blue transfer-printed decoration . . . and fitted with a mahogany seat," versions of which have now become popular in many expensive plumbing lines. Ashley headquarters was not a museum, although "to complete the authentic appearance" (note the return of the concept of quasi-authenticity) Laura Ashley Ltd. did produce "a range of wallpapers, textiles, and a carpet, all copied faithfully from originals in museums" and extant period houses in England. Instead it was a show house of the past for the consumer of the present and the future, a touch of Upstairs without the Downstairs, since its "authentic appearance" was combined with convenience.

The "Laura Ashley look" has sometimes been conflated in the popular imagination with the cinematic style of Ismail Merchant and James Ivory, offering a certain "traditional" (if phantasmic) view of English civilization from *Howards End* and *The Remains of the Day* ("Some people think the décor *is* the film," commented director Ivory, wryly). In a published cartoon drawn by the film director Alan Parker, a pair of women exit from a Merchant-Ivory film, one saying to the other, "I can't stand these Laura Ashley movies." In Britain these days "Merchant-Ivory" is itself a kind of putdown, denoting a sanitized "historic" sensibility that falsifies, and prettifies, the grittier facts of the past. In the United States, however, the air-brushed view of history and the appeal of "authentic appearance" is arguably at an all-time high.

Cabin Fever

Nostalgia, literally "homesickness," is one of the most enduring forms of erotic relation to the past. Once regarded as a "real" illness—in the late eighteenth century doctors often diagnosed "the longing for home which the Physicians have gone so far as to esteem a disease under the name of Nostalgia"[40]—it became by the twentieth century a more metaphorical and sentimental condition embodying regretful, wistful longing for an earlier age. By its very nature, nostalgia was, and is, a kind of false consciousness, a *mis*remembering or embellishment, a nostalgia, as it were, for nostalgia itself, a longing for something that never was, something more "perfect," more satisfying, more whole and complete. The distinct contribution of our own time to this erotics of memory has come in the vogue for the "Colonial village," the "Main Street" and "the romance with the log cabin."[41]

One of America's favorite nostalgic sites is the log cabin, nurturer of presidents and values since the time of Lincoln and before. In fact it was Daniel Webster, in 1840, who in a campaign speech apologized to the American public for not having been born in one, confirming the popular notion that the log cabin was the proper site for the birth of a great American. "Gentlemen, it did not happen to me to be born in a log cabin, but my elder brothers and sisters were born in a log cabin, raised among the snow-drifts of New Hampshire. . . . Its remains still exist. I make to it an annual visit, I carry my children to it. . . ."[42] On the occasion of the 250th anniversary of the founding of Jamestown, in 1857, the governor of Virginia effused, "Here the Old World met the New. Here the White man first met the Red for settlement and colonization. Here the White man first wielded the axe to cut the first tree, for the first log cabin! Here the first log cabin, was built for the first village. . . ."[43] The log cabin became an immensely powerful political tool, since it mobilized the combined emotions of nostalgia, heroism, and "home" in a single image. Even today the "cabin in the woods" is associated with the American genius-as-loner, whether that loner is admired (Henry David Thoreau) or vilified (Theodore Kaczinski). Unabomber Kaczinski's Montana cabin (and, indeed, his Harvard dorm room) were read by the press as allegories of his disordered soul, knee-deep in paper, food remnants, and tools of the trade (mathematics, bomb-making). But the isolated cabin is also a traditional locus of inspiration and creativity, as writers' retreats like the MacDowell Colony have long suggested; the locus classicus in America, of course, is Thoreau's cabin at Walden Pond.

A series of articles called "Log-Cabin to the White House" traced the rise of Presidents Jackson ("Old Hickory"), W. H. Harrison ("Tippecanoe"), and, of course, Lincoln ("Honest Abe") from the rudimentary dwellings made of round logs that were considered the earliest form of indigenous Colonial architecture, a link to those English colonists who settled the east coast of North America from Newfoundland to Plymouth to Virginia and celebrated "the first Thanksgiving."

The problem with this comfortable mythology was that the English colonists did not, in fact, build log cabins at all, but frame houses of the same kind that they had left behind in England. The log cabin was a Scandinavian and also a German form, brought to this country by Swedes who settled in Delaware in 1638, but not much in use elsewhere until the end of the seventeenth century. Neither the English nor the Dutch built log dwellings. The Colonial log cabin, despite its crucial role in pa-

triotic mythology, was an invention, a myth of origins, established in the public mind not only by books of "history," but also
by popular illustrations that were "framed in schoolhouses
throughout the country, reproduced in textbooks, and mailed
home by tourists in the form of picture postcards."[44]

   American Log Homes. Build Your Own Low-Cost Log Home.
Building a Log Home from Scratch or Kit. How to Build and Furnish
a Log Cabin. A Dreamer's Log Cabin. Your Cabin in the Woods.
Shelter magazines like *Country Life* offer numerous kits, with accompanying videos, for planning and building "the log home of
your dreams." One New York City filmmaker built a log cabin
getaway (designed to look "like Abe Lincoln's cabin or even the
one shown on Log Cabin syrup")[45] on the roof of a city brownstone. Americans, or others, with cabin fever (a particular strain
of the disease of nostalgia) have no difficulty ministering to their
cravings at the local bookstore. Or, if they prefer, they can stay at
any number of log cabin lodges from Tennessee to Alaska, including some equipped with TV, VCR, cable, and telephone (eat
your heart out, Tippecanoe), easily located by "logging on" to an
Original Log Cabin Homes Website called "The American
Dream." I wonder, though, if I'm the only browser who finds
something out of kilter in the concept of a "three-story cathedral
ceiling log cabin."

Neotraditional Values

Nostalgia these days is more than a feeling—it's a lifestyle, as the
National Association of Home Builders has acknowledged,
pledging to "reflect that nostalgia in the area of design." "From
first time buyers to their more affluent counterparts, who may be
purchasing their third or fourth home, they are looking more
toward tradition for inspiration," said a designer from Irvine,
California. Buyers, he thought, were looking for communities in-
fused with "old world sensibilities."[46] (Like Irvine, home of high-
tech industry and a branch of the University of California?)

"The newest idea in planning is the nineteenth-century town," architect Andres Duany told a conference of Florida apartment developers in the early eighties. "That's what's really selling." And it's true. As Philip Langdon pointed out in the *Atlantic*, "Historic preservation, once considered a hobby of the elite, has become an industry. The interest in old houses has led many developers to incorporate in new houses some of the features that made the old houses appealing. If learning from the past has been valuable at the scale of the individual house, why not try it at the scale of a small town?"[47]

It's a version of the old question: does life imitate art, or art, life? But it's also powerful evidence of nostalgia as a cultural force. The design, construction, and settlement of what are called "neotraditional towns," instant tradition and instant nostalgia coupled with clean streets and family values, has been one of the most successful approaches to "acquiring a past" in the late twentieth century.

Prominent architects, sometimes working with dream factories like the Disney corporation, have designed a number of neotraditional towns, the most prominent among them, perhaps, two locales in Florida: Seaside, in Florida's Panhandle, designed by Andres Duany and Elizabeth Plater-Zyberk, and Celebration, near Orlando.

Some outsiders scoff at the idea of Mickey and Goofy as neighbors. Others may wonder whether what's being re-created is *Ozzie and Harriet, Picket Fences,* or the surreal and sinister landscape of *Blue Velvet,* with its own too-green yards and too-white fencing. But in these, as in other neotraditional towns (like Fairview Village, near Portland, Oregon; Harbor Town, near Memphis, Tennessee; Camden Park, near Chapel Hill, North Carolina; and Belmont Forest, in Loudon County, Virginia), the love affair with the past is ongoing. And it sells.

The success of Seaside, where prices are considerably higher than in neighboring towns, has led some to call it "an unrealistic enclave, a dream time, escapist." When it attained new celebrity as the (barely) fictional town of Seahaven in the Peter Weir film *The Truman Show,* Seaside in its cinematic debut was described by critics as "a hyper-idyllic planned community," "sparkingly antiseptic," and full of "architecturally tidy, strenuously pleasant dwellings."[48] Architecture critic Paul Goldberger came to the town's defense in a piece in the *New Yorker,* claiming that "the movie dolls the place up to a level of sweetness far beyond its normal state, then presents it as Truman's saccharine-coated jail.

"The brilliance of Seaside," Goldberger wrote, "is that it knows just how far to push cuteness, and then it stops. There is something about it that is hard to grasp—it is too real to be Disneyland, too entrancing to be any other small community. Its founders are proud of the fact that it lacks gates, and its tiny squares and plazas stand as symbols of public space at a time when that is becoming a scarce commodity. . . . [I]t is not an effort by a huge corporation to market sentimentality, as Celebration, the Disney-built town near Orlando, is."[49] So Seaside's neotraditional authenticity is defended by contrast to Celebration's sentimentality.

Celebration, developed by Disney and situated near the heart of the Magic Kingdom, has had to assert its own "reality" time and time again. The town's name was chosen by the developer from a list provided him by a focus group. "This is a real town with real people," says a Disney representative, "not a theme park." A spokesperson for McNally homes, which collaborated on some of the home designs, explained that "because the town of Celebration was founded on a nostalgic desire to revive ties between neighbors, a sizeable front porch was added to the plan. Homeowners can sit on the porch and chat with neighbors as they stroll by." (Whether this itself would be a fantasy or a "reality" remained to be seen since, as the lesson of Seaside had taught, back porches and side porches were in demand precisely because they offered greater privacy, a protection from the street.) A visitor found Celebration to be "a surprisingly normal place, albeit one that is self-consciously nostalgic, harkening back to an imagined America of small towns and traditional values." The residents, who number about a thousand and will ultimately, it is thought, reach a planned figure of 20,000 in ten to fifteen years, often say that they have "bought into that dream" of small town life. Critics fault it for a relative absence of racial diversity, for its power-washed streets (just like the Disney theme parks), and for what one local architect called "a totalitarian feel"—for him there was, paradoxically, "something fundamentally un-American about it."[50] Architecture critic Goldberger called it "an effort by a huge corporation to market sentimentality." For others, living "on Main Street and the Castle" *is* the American dream—and, as architect Robert A. M. Stern noted, it's too bad in a way that we equate clean streets with a lack of reality.

Nor is the neotraditional town an exclusively American phenomenon. The tradition-minded Prince Charles admired Seaside, and called upon Leon Krier, an architect who had built his own house there, to play a key role in developing the English "new town" of Poundbury, "an attempt to create a 21st-century community that looks like it grew up over time, with a long linger in the 18th and 19th centuries." Though some critics have derided Poundbury as "the freshly carpentered back lot for the latest big-budget clogs-and-shawls setting of *The Mayor of Casterbridge*," others, including architects, writers, and daytrippers, have discovered that what they call "Charleyville" has considerable appeal. "Overall, the effect is polite, elegant, and as English as a vicar's tea party," said the magazine *Homes and Antiques*.[51]

One can imagine an American clientele for this "look," though it might not be the same clientele as the one that is headed for Celebration. (Though, on the other hand, it very well might.) As with the new traditional towns in the United States, what seems to be aimed at, and perhaps even achieved, is the idea of living "in history" without the shawls, knee breeches, and other cultural quotations of living museums like Plimoth Plantation and Sturbridge Village. These new settlements represent nothing less than the desire to buy a way of life viewed with nostalgia and translated into architecture. The very market forces that have made it possible to construct these nostalgic towns are what have made them disappear as places to live—if they ever existed.

SEVEN

THE SUMMER HOUSE

Let's face it. When you're seventeen, you dream of a summer romance. When you're forty-seven (or thirty-seven, or fifty-seven), you dream of a summer home. Or at least a summer rental.

Second homes and vacation homes can be like love affairs and second marriages. They're a chance to reinvent yourself, to start again—without the emotional and legal strain of divorce or disentanglement. There's no enforced monogamy in today's American dream of home-owning. A second home, even for some fortunate or profligate few a third home, fulfills the "more the merrier" impulse to "play around" without, well—playing around. So you can get both the moral points *and* the transgressive frisson. And take the other members of your household with you.

Earlier, grander secondary residences, like the châteaux of the Loire Valley, the architectural glory of Renaissance France, were built to accommodate the great man's several households: his wife, his mistresses, his court. Built along the Seine near Paris, the *petites maisons* of wealthy, powerful men were elegant, extravagant private retreats designed for erotic pleasure. France's Henry II installed his mistress Diane de Poitiers in the magnificent Château de Chenonceaux, which he presented to her in token of his love. (After Henry's death his queen, Catherine de Médicis, forced her to give it back in exchange for lesser real estate.) In America neo-Renaissance princes of commerce and industry often did the same: the sprawling castle of San Simeon on the California coast was built by William Randolph Hearst for his mistress Marion Davies.

But today's second homes *are* the lovers or mistresses, the fantasy partners that represent glamour and dalliance, the play space of domesticity away from home. "I keep a house in Nantucket," reports columnist Russell Baker—and lest we think this is just an accident of phrasing ("I keep a car at the station," "I keep a spare set of keys under the mat"), he himself supplies a sexual subtext: "A house will never be seduced by a professor suffering midlife crisis."[1] There are lots of things Russell Baker understands better than I do, but the relationship between professors suffering midlife crises and vacation real estate may not be one of them. Although they can't afford the nouveau palaces he deplores ("normal house-size houses . . . are being reborn as mansions to advertise the power of warriors who have conquered Wall Street"), the professor-Romeos of this generation are as likely to flirt with saltboxes as with sophomores. It's not even displacement. It's real desire. The summer place is like a "kept man" or a "kept woman," that slightly anachronistic arrangement once thought conducive to a discreet and sophisticated sexual life among persons of a certain set.

Of course, summer romances can lead to marital bliss—repeatedly. "It's like their first marriage was to the Hamptons," mused a realtor in Washington Depot, a picturesque village in Litchfield County, Connecticut, about the influx of new summer residents. "Their second marriage, now that they've matured a bit, is to Litchfield County. Summer rentals have exploded."[2] In the eyes of this Connecticut realtor, it was the Hamptons that were being jilted, outgrown and replaced by a more suitably "mature" love. Washington Depot, located in the lush northwestern part of Connecticut's hills, has no beach to attract sunbunnies ("No, no, no beach," the realtor said, dismissively)—it was not a teenager's fantasy.

In the summer of 1998 it wasn't only tiny Washington Depot

that was attracting Wall Streeters eager "to explore a new place," it was Westport, Norwalk, Nantucket, Provence. Hamptons rents had peaked, celebrities were moving on, there was some sense of a need for change. Fidelity can be an aspect of vacationing—"we always go to the Jersey shore"—but so can variety.

"Right now, Locust Valley is at the top of the list for young people looking for a country house," says a man who has sold luxury properties in the New York area for two decades. "When people ask for Locust Valley, you know they know." One of the things they "know" is that Locust Valley, on the north shore of Long Island, has long been regarded as the setting of *The Great Gatsby*. "Welcome to Nick Carraway's cottage," said Charles Scribner III, a great-grandson of F. Scott Fitzgerald's publisher, to a guest who dropped in at his Locust Valley house. He acknowledged to a reporter that "the draw of the place is the fantasy of moving into the pages of [Fitzgerald's] classic novel." Since Gatsby himself was living a fantasy life of self-invention, it seems entirely appropriate that his story should generate fantasies in Fitzgerald's readers. But where Jay Gatsby saw posh real estate as a way of wooing Daisy Buchanan, latter-day city folk, though they still engage in "flirtation with the Hamptons,"[3] increasingly see Locust Valley itself (Gatsby's "East Egg") as the object of their desire.

House Swapping

"One of the most common reasons that people give for not buying a vacation home is that they will then have to spend all their vacation time in it," explained the author of a down-to-earth guide called *Your Dream Vacation Home*. But "this simply is not true," she noted. If you don't want to use the house, you can either rent or exchange it.[4] Unlike your "real" house or apartment, unlike your spouse or partner, your vacation house is *designed* to be exchangeable, at the same time that it embodies your fantasies of escape.

"Time-shares" have become a major staple of the real estate business—after all, they're made for swapping. A friend of mine was looking for an inexpensive vacation, and found a time-share company on the Cape looking to sell units. As is common for such ventures, they advertised a special deal: come down and look at our property, and we'll give you a free gift—in this case some rather nice-looking Samsonite luggage. The only problem was, the company would only give its sales pitch to married couples. And my friend had been recently divorced.

Determined (as a feminist, a would-be vacationer, a consumer, and a person of ingenuity) not to let this be an obstacle, she joined forces with a man she knew who was also divorced, and they descended upon Cape Cod wearing rings and chatting knowledgeably about "their" children. Despite some awkward moments—she recalls that he kept misremembering the children's names and ages—they spent their afternoon in the sun and returned, triumphantly, bearing luggage—some of which they divided among their former spouses.

The house swap itself has become a common feature of vacation planning. "Experience New England in the Fall. Swap our elegantly furnished, beautifully restored 5,500 square-foot Victorian home in prime Cambridge location for your comparable Manhattan apartment," invites one advertisement, while another urges, "Swap: our 2-bedroom modern Paris Latin Quarter for northeast shore in summer." Seldom, I've noticed, do these ads offer more than they seek. The opportunity to spend August in Paris rather than at the shore is less tempting than the same exchange proposed for December. But then, as they say, there's no accounting for taste.

It's almost irresistible to compare these benign social and economic transactions with the brief notoriety of "wife swapping" in the 1970s, a practice often engaged in, as part of suburban entertainment, through what were called "key parties." Ang Lee's mordant film *The Ice Storm* (set in 1973) depicts a chilling example: men drop their car keys in a bowl and women pick them out, going home—and presumably to bed—with the owner of the keys, and the house that goes with them. A house swap supplies something of the sense of surprise and luck, without the moral hangover.

Some summer places are for families; others are for summer love. As the pragmatic wife says to her husband in *The Return of the Secaucus Seven* (1980), "The way I feel, if we're taking the time to rent the place every summer, people ought to just strike up a relationship with whoever we put them in with." People who wouldn't think of sharing their winter quarters with virtual strangers sign on to rent "group houses" in Amagansett or Fire Island. It's an arrangement that usually works out pretty well, even if the housemates never see each other. Perhaps *especially* if they never see each other.

A Family Affair

For many people, though, summer means family, however they define that term. A hundred years ago, in *Summer Homes and Camps* (1899), Frank Lent wrote:

> The idea of home is entering more and more into arrangements for the summer. It is often the case that the members of the family see more of each other during the leisure of the summer than during all the rest of the year. Many families make it a point to gather under one roof at least every summer, and there are many cases where the summer residence is the only home, the family living there six or eight months continuously and spending the remainder of the year in travelling or living in hotels.

A century later this seems, for some folks at least, equally true. Summer is the time when people tend to vacation with others like themselves, whether ethnically, professionally, or socially. Gays and lesbians often "summer" in Fire Island or Provincetown; academics as well as shrinks gather in Wellfleet and Truro. "The psychiatrists are on Cape Cod, the black professionals are in Azurest on Long Island and the Syrian Jews are in Deal on the New Jersey shore," noted the *New York Times* at the beginning of one summer season.[5]

For an increasing number of people, the summer home can in fact become the family home. It is the only place where the extended family congregates in one place. An Italian family summering in New Jersey's Bradley Beach took pleasure in the mixture of the generations: "It's really nice for the kids," said a grandmother with pride. "When do you get the opportunity to wake up with your cousins and grandparents?" Bradley Beach, on the famed Jersey shore, has been the summer home for both Italian and Chinese families from New York's Lower East Side since the 1940s and 1950s.[6]

As with all family affairs, however, when it comes to questions of inheritance (or divorce) there's sometimes pain and conflict in the offing. The problem of how to split up family cottages, or, for that matter, how to maintain them in the style to which they have become accustomed, is being explored by sociologists like Judy Huggins Balfe, who wonders whether it's still the case that "family identity is more important than selling off the summer house" to split the profits.

Often a wealthy new buyer knocks down the old cottage and builds—you guessed it—a trophy house. "The people with a great deal of money," says Balfe, "don't face these quandaries. How can these trophy houses ever stay in their original families, anyway?" As a result, she's started a consulting service for families trying to split summer homes among many heirs—in effect, family therapy for the vacation house. A team of lawyer, accountant, and five family therapists makes site visits (can we call them "house calls"?) to try to keep things manageable. "A man on Martha's Vineyard was one of five brothers who inherited a house," she said. "One man's wife wanted to summer in Maine, so that made it easier for the four of them. I asked him if being four brothers made it easier as well. He said it didn't, but his wife chimed in and said it had everything to do with it."[7]

A young man I know is a third-generation member of a family that owns a summer house in a traditionally desirable East Coast locale. He attests to the complications of divvying up family vacation time, and also apportioning things like decorating choices. An aunt chose the wallpaper (a large floral print, with wicker armchairs to match), but he and his female partner got to choose the kitchen equipment and cabinets (Shaker-style simplicity). He's still working on getting the family to chip in on such unglamorous expenditures as having the windows cleaned. And there are proprietary issues, too. After he and his partner had been in residence for about six weeks another young couple arrived to begin their two-week stay. The two couples overlapped by a few days, and there was a quiet but intense battle about which were the hosts and which the visitors. From groceries in the refrigerator to competing dinner reservations, they vied for the role of householder.

For others, though, buying or renting a summer home is not going back to the family enclave but going forward to a new "tradition." "I feel like I really belong here," said one New York City woman whose family had been renting in Peconic Bay for the past four summers. "This is my real home, and my summer neighbors are my 'family.' " She felt so comfortable that it was as if she had "always" been there, and she was convinced that she "always" would be.

It's partly a change in the role of the summer house, or, perhaps, in the interests of summer house residents. Earlier generations often, though not always, "dressed down" when they "summered," preferring a more rough-hewn lifestyle: outdoor showers, casual clothes, secondhand furniture and dishes. But today's buyers often want "summer houses that make a statement about who they are"—or who they'd like to be. As one longtime resident of Cape Cod remarked, "If you paid $1 million or more for your property, you don't want a modest little summer shack on it."[8]

Increasingly the summer house is seen as what sociologist Roberta Satow describes as the center of "a whole ensemble of possessions that define a person's lifestyle and values." Of the more than 1,500 professional families Satow surveyed in 1991 in New York, Boston, Chicago, and Houston, half had summer homes. Eighty-two percent of them had not gone to family-owned summer homes when they were children.

Summer homes used to be stocked with castoffs from the first home—worn clothes, old furniture, chipped dishes. Many still are. But the trend, at least in some quarters, has been to really "do up" the second home, whether in "old style" or "new." Island and country house decoration has become itself a major subset of the design business—it's "let's pretend" come to life, enabled by bonuses and royalties. Lou Sagar, the man who founded Zona, the epicenter of the eighties' Southwestern decorating craze (with branches in Soho, Aspen, East Hampton, Florence, and Tokyo), noted, "many of our customers in the eighties were buying for their second homes. That's where they were *living*."[9]

The multiroom megahouse with theater and bowling alleys being built, and hotly contested, in the Hamptons, was, let us not forget, a second home for a man who—like most of his summer neighbors—spent the winter in the city. Because the wealthiest buyers are often business people rather than those with inherited wealth (who usually have also, like the Kennedys and the Bushes, inherited family summer homes), the "trophy" scenario is sometimes at its most fervent and fevered in the competition to build, buy, or renovate waterfront, country, or mountain property.

A realtor in the Hamptons reported that "70's and 80's contemporaries are out of fashion," along with "undistinguished houses on one-acre lots in the woods." While you can't get much in the upper echelons ("in the higher price ranges—over $2 million—there's hardly anything left"), you can still, apparently, get a little two-bedroom house in a wooded area. "They're actually quite pleasant," she said, "but not desirable for most of our buyers and certainly not to people looking for an address."[10]

Bear in mind that these highly desirable "addresses" are for *second* residences. By the middle of 1998, 52 houses sold in Nantucket in excess of $1 million, up from 29 in 1996 and 15 in 1995. August 1998 home sales were up 51 percent over 1997. As a regional senior vice president for Sotheby's International Realty saw it, investors who had done well in the stock market said to themselves, "enough delayed gratification, I owe it to myself." That's the reason, he thought, for the quadrupling of million-plus homes sold in just two years. Like the notion of needing a "good address" in the country, the idea that waiting a year before buying a mansion is "delayed gratification" may tell us something about the erotic pleasures and dangers of the second-home market, at least for CEOs and investment bankers.

The Play House

But in some ways it's the *concept* of the second home, the home away from home, the place of escape, that really counts. Some residents of New York City are apparently finding their home away from home in rented mini-storage. "Manhattanites often think of mini-storage just as they would a weekend home," reported the *New York Times*, "as a sanctuary, a place to tryst (two managers say they have walked in on couples coupling), to banish old towels, to putter around (hobbyists have installed workbenches). Or simply a place to catch a cool breeze. One woman reads in the air-conditioned splendor of her mini-storage room because her husband hates air-conditioning at home." And, the article quipped, "like the best summer cottage, Room 01-11-19 on 645 West 44th Street has a view of the Intrepid Air, Sea and Space Museum and the Hudson River. Price: $91 a month."[11]

The compact quarters may actually have enhanced the feeling of a holiday escapade. Although summer houses now regularly achieve trophy status and megahouse size (Russell Baker complained that formerly modest houses were being "gutted, rebuilt and expanded at the pleasure of people who use million-dollar bills to ignite their fireplace kindling"), their model, in concept if not design, is the *dollhouse*. The phrase "doll's house" often features, in an enticing way, in realtors' advertising copy ("just steps from Ocean Beach. A 2 bedroom doll house—antique flooring and interesting details"), and while this is an obvious ploy to describe a potential liability as an asset, it has a certain effectiveness. A "small carriage house" in the Hamptons rented for $15,000 for the season to a "professional woman from the city," and was described in terms that stressed its elfin charm:

> It's like a doll's house; a privet hedge, a rose arbor and an ivy-covered tree serve to frame the entrance; the roof has a saucy peak, a chimney and just below the peak, a small-paned arched window. It has a little bedroom and bath downstairs and a little loft upstairs.

The point of the account is that summer rentals are pricey, but the portrait, from the rhetorical flourish of "saucy peak" to the repetition of "little" ("little bedroom and bath," "little loft") suggests that the author, the realtor, or both share—or at least understand—the "professional woman's" fantasy of a fairytale dwelling. "She likes it so much it's her third year."[12] Anyone who has recently attended an auction and priced antique doll furniture or "salesman's samples" (miniature chests, desks, and chairs used by traveling salesmen as portable examples of what the customer can order for delivery, full-size) knows that small doesn't mean cheap. But the dollhouse provides an overview of the whole, a fantasy of control and mastery, and a site for play. The vacation house is a playhouse in which you get to be the child.

Maybe it's not a paradox, but a simple truth, that these old things, worn things, known things, are what really constitute a home. Like a child's (or pet's) favorite toy, the worn doll that has had to be restitched and patched together, it is the history in the things, and not just the things themselves, that make us feel "at home."

In what I like to think of as a droll version of this same dollhouse spirit, Britain's Landmark Trust buildings, available for holiday rental, include not only towers, gatehouses, stables, lodges, castles, villas, a priest's house, and a radio room (accommodations for one in a small building behind a walled garden), but also a pigsty with Ionic columns. The sty is fetchingly described in the Landmark Trust Handbook:

> Two pigs were the excuse for this exercise in primitive classicism, supposedly inspired by buildings seen by Squire Barry of Fyling Hall on his travels around the Mediterranean in the 1880s. . . . It is some decades since [the owners] went in for pig-breeding. . . . By the minimum of addition, and the insertion of glass here and there, we hope we have made it acceptable to a higher breed of inhabitant.

It's hard to say without visiting whether such a vacation spot is really a silk purse or a sow's ear.

Another version of this play space for adults is the tree house. As a Denver home builder noted in the sixties,

> The second home buyer is a little like a kid who builds his own tree house. The kid wants a private place away from the rest of the family and feels he has to earn it himself—so with great effort he builds his tree house. The second home buyer seems to want the same thing. He feels a little guilty about spending that much money on a luxury item. So, he buys a partially incomplete structure and bangs his thumb and sweats a little to justify the expenditure.[13]

In summer houses and second homes today, with the increasing proportion of two-earner households, there's often neither time nor inclination to do it yourself. But just try to get a contractor or painter to work on your summer place. They're all booked up till *next* spring.

And by the way, when was the last time you saw a tree house? I noticed the other day that one of my Cambridge neighbors was building one. The carpenter was adding dentilated trim and a mansardlike roof to this miniature structure, which when finished would have a door—with a lock—and a window. If this was for the pleasure of the residents' *child* or *children*, all I have to say is that Cambridge kids are even more precocious than they're generally thought to be.

It's probably not altogether an accident that these descriptions of dollhouse and tree house are gendered (though we have to allow some time lapse from the sixties). Women certainly imagine themselves in tree houses, and I know several men who own or rent tiny (dollhouse-sized) cottages in stylish vacation areas, but what this language is demonstrating is not gender bias (or personal history) but a *fantasy of childhood*. As one writer in *The Listener* observed—with a touch of acerbity—about children's books, "When grown-ups become passionately interested in them, some kind of nostalgia is involved."[14]

Perhaps for this reason, places in the country or at the shore are often described as "little," no matter what their actual size. This rhetoric of the miniature ("we have a little house in Myrtle Beach") used, often disingenuously, to describe a massive place in the country or at the shore, can be traced back at least as far as the monumental Newport "cottages" of the Vanderbilts.

The Cottage

"Summer house" was formerly a term that meant a rustic building in a garden. Now it means a shingle-style house in the

Hamptons or a contemporary glass-walled structure in the Vineyard's West Chop. A "cottage," originally a dwelling of small size and humble character occupied only by the poor who had no other choice, became in the late eighteenth and nineteenth centuries first a small country residence that "frees from all pretension and parade and restraint"; then a deliberately picturesque *cottage ornée*, often with verandas and French windows or doors; and finally, especially in the United States, a summer residence "often on a large and sumptuous scale" at a "water-place or a health or pleasure resort."[15]

Combined with the nostalgia for pastoral and rural settings, cottages on both sides of the Atlantic could be anything but simple. "The strong element of artificiality in the whole back-to-nature movement," writes Mark Girouard, "came into the open in one of its most engaging but also ridiculous products, the *cottage ornée*—the simple life, lived in simple luxury in a simple cottage with—quite often—fifteen simple bedrooms, all hung with French wallpapers."[16] The ironic idealization of the "simple life" by the rich is neatly exhibited in Jane Austen's *Sense and Sensibility*, when the self-indulgent Robert Ferrars, first encountered in a jeweler's shop ordering himself a toothpick case adorned with gold, ivory, and pearls, waxes enthusiastic on the romance of "a cottage."

I am excessively fond of a cottage; there is always so much comfort, so much elegance about them. And I protest, if I had any money to spare, I should buy a little land and build one myself, within a short distance of London, where I might drive myself down at any time, and collect a few friends about me, and be happy. I advise every body who is going to build, to build a cottage. My friend Lord Courtland came to me the other day on purpose to ask my advice, and laid before me three different plans of Bonomi's [Joseph Bonomi, a well-known architect]. I was to decide on the best of them. "My dear Courtland," said I, immediately throwing them all into the fire, "do not adopt either of them, but by all means build a cottage." And that, I fancy, will be the end of it.[17]

The situation was much the same on the other side of the Atlantic. With the growth of some of the major cities in the Northeast—New York, Boston, Baltimore, and Philadelphia—in the years after the Civil War, summer resorts developed on the eastern seaboard of the United States and on Chicago's lakefront. In areas like Newport, Rhode Island, as early as the 1840s "the expression of conspicuous consumption and surplus capital" led to the building of villas and "cottages" in the vicinity of the larger hotels.

The Breakers, the Vanderbilt cottage at Newport, was, like its neighbors, a vast and formal showplace, built for entertaining, staffed by legions of servants, and characteristic of the grandeur (some would say flagrant excess) of the Gilded Age. (Marie Antoinette, with her shepherd's crook and her brioche, might have felt right at home in many of these "cottages.") By the 1880s there had been considerable expansion. As Charles D. Warner observed in 1885, "the eastern coast, with its ragged outlines of bays, headlands, indentations . . . from Watch Hill to Mount Desert, presents an almost continual chain of hotels and summer cottages. In fact, the same may be said of the whole Atlantic coast from Mount Desert to Cape May."[18]

The term "cottage" became such a commonplace that in *Kipps: The Story of a Simple Soul* (1905) H. G. Wells could have his shopkeeper hero Arthur Kipps, newly possessed of a fortune, ruminate on whether he could properly call his new house "'Ome Cottage": "It's got eleven bedrooms, y'see," he says. "I don't see 'ow you call it a cottage with more bedrooms than four. Prop'ly speaking, it's a Large Villa. Prop'ly it's almost a Big 'Ouse. Leastaways a 'Ouse."

Back to Nature

In contrast to the elegance of some of these cottages, another kind of vacation house was often considered a place for "roughing it," or "getting back to nature." (Bear in mind that the cabin at Walden Pond was Thoreau's "second home," a few miles away from his residence—and the family pencil factory—in Concord.) Around the turn of the century wilderness novels, naturalist journals, and newly founded shelter magazines promoted the idea of the simple life, while the Arts and Crafts movement, popular in England from the 1880s, also caught on in the United States, urging a rejection of "bourgeois civilization and materialism" in favor of an ideal of simplicity. Citing such apostles of simplicity as Walt Whitman, Edward Carpenter, and the Russian social philosopher Kropotkin, Gustav Stickley's journal *The Craftsman* published designs for building "Forest," "Hillside," "Craftsman," and other bungalows. "Of late years," the journal declared in 1906, "it has become more and more the approved thing to own the country home or camp and to go there year after year."

Stickley's object was to appeal to rising young professionals who were building vacation homes in the "new wilderness areas."[19] The Craftsman bungalow in the United States, with its low roof and cobblestone fireplace, was a "close to nature" repudiation of capitalism and the excesses of urban life—though of course many of those who could afford to build them were, precisely, capitalists, or sons of capitalists. The degree to which their desire was linked to a kind of cultural fantasy of primitivism is clear from the opposition between the "artificial" and the "natural" in passages like this one, from a piece called "Vacation Homes in the Woods," addressed to an obviously affluent readership:

To those of us who live and work amid the artificiality of city life there is something irresistibly attractive in the idea of

being close to the heart of nature, wearing old clothes and living for a time the free and easy life which we like to imagine
was lived before the call of the city became insistent.[20]

That this is a fantasy of privilege, more easily engaged in by
those who have other clothes to wear and other lives to lead in
the city, has been rather sardonically noted by more skeptical observers of the "back to nature" trend virtually from the beginning. In 1911 Henry Saylor had described the bungalow, one of
most popular vacation-area dwellings, as "a fad for many wealthy
men who want some sort of retreat in the woods where they can
entertain as freely as in the city," and he cheerfully quoted someone else's definition of a bungalow as "a house that looks as if it
has been built for less money than it actually cost."[21]

Newly constructed log cabins likewise evoked simplicity while
providing creature comforts. An article in the *Women's Home
Companion* of 1916, quoted by Anthony King, announced, "The
old-fashioned log cabin is the new-fashioned summer camp,
with all the comforts of modern life and all the picturesqueness
of pioneer days." The wilderness "camp" was often adorned, as
King notes, with the "essential male" symbols with which "the
urbane, educated city-dweller" transformed himself into 'primitive man,' a Daniel Boone or a Davy Crockett"—fishing nets,
snowshoes, guns, hardwood chairs, shooting hats, "symbols of
what the Great Outdoors man, President Theodore Roosevelt,
called 'the strenuous life.' "[22]

Meantime in England the "Bohemian" cottage or bungalow,
located in the picturesque countryside or situated along the river,
enjoyed a similar vogue as the place for artists and others who
disdained—or could afford to disdain—the conventional life.

Pay Per View

Interest in the panoramas of nature has if anything increased
in the twentieth century, as the countryside has grown more

crowded. But sometimes you pay a premium for natural splendor, whether you intended to or not. Although "the best things in life are free" would seem to cover, precisely, the enjoyment of natural beauty, we live in an age when nothing can be taken for granted.

Some New York friends of mine scraped together the money to buy a modest contemporary house in the Berkshire Mountains of western Massachusetts to use on weekends. It was nestled in the woods, so it didn't have much of a view—until a tornado, a rare occurrence in the Northeast, tore a path through the forest and opened up a striking vista. Imagine their surprise when they were hit with a bill for the "view tax."

The same thing happened to a man whose expensive new home in Burlington, Connecticut, gave him a stunning outlook over some twenty miles of hills and valleys. To his astonishment the town of Burlington sent him a tax bill that included a surcharge of over a thousand dollars labeled "view."[23]

This creative innovation on the part of some local governments across the country, from California to Connecticut, adds an extra charge to your tax bill for the pleasure of looking. The California city of Port Hueneme made headlines, and legal history, when it imposed a tax on residents whose property afforded them a view of the Pacific Ocean. The assessment was in part intended to raise funds for the upkeep of a beachfront park that abutted the homes, but the phrase "view tax" struck a chord with the national media. "Why stop with a 'view tax'?" asked the *Tampa Tribune*, archly suggesting a "smell tax" for houses in the vicinity of a bakery and a "sound tax" for those in earshot of carillon bells.[24]

A Seattle real estate consultant told a story about meeting a broker from Southern California at a convention who asked him what type of view he had. "Gorgeous," he replied. But this was apparently the wrong response. The Californian looked at him incredulously, and explained that in beach cities properties are often priced by the type of water in the view. "A 'white-water view' (waves crashing, white-water foam) is much more expensive than a 'blue-water' view (one with no coastline). If you can barely make out water in the distance, it's called a 'horizon' view." The Seattle man thought his view should probably be characterized as "blue water and horizon," since, as he said, "we rarely have waves on Puget Sound." "Oh really?" said the Californian. "Why's that?"[25]

Despite the grumbles of property owners, most would acknowledge that a view does enhance the value and pleasure of the summer or vacation home. But not in all cases. When actress Katherine Cornell built her summer place, Chip Chop, on Martha's Vineyard, she made sure that there were no windows in the kitchen, just a large skylight. She was concerned that her guests, who included the Lunts, Noël Coward, Rex Harrison, and Laurence Olivier, be able to skinny-dip without being overlooked—or looked over—by the servants.[26]

The Name Game

Cornell's Chip Chop had a typical vacation house name, in a way—clever and apparently self-disparaging. The phrase means speaking "in a 'chopping,' or harshly consonantal way"—"our outlandish chip-chop gibberish," one early writer said of English, as contrasted with the more mellifluous Greek, Latin, or Italian. So for an actress "chip-chop" could mean harsh or awkward speech. But it also plays on the names of the two promontories of land on Martha's Vineyard known as East Chop and West Chop. The name was thus a double in-joke, for Vineyarders and actors, as well as a comic description of what was actually an elegant house.

In general Americans are far more likely to give names to their second or vacation homes than to their "real" ones. It's as if the vacation house is a pet, a toy, a plaything, or a fantasy—all of which, of course, are partly true. Though you might occasionally see nameplates on city or surburban houses, they're more likely to announce "The Smiths" than "The Hollies." It's in the country that all inhibitions seem to disappear, and all fantasies flourish.

"A house here is a luxury almost like a yacht," suggests a commentator on the neotraditional town of Seaside in the Florida Panhandle, "and many houses bear signs with their names, along with the names and hometowns of their owners, exactly as on the sterns of pleasure craft."[27] It was, he thought, precisely houses with names like Fantasia, Peach Delight, Villa Whimsey, and Precious, together with the rose trellises and gazebos of the neo-"Victorian" section known as Rosewalk, that "led some architects and critics to deride the town as cute and backward-looking, a brand-spanking-new replica of an idealized past."[28] Like boat names, house names are revealing bits of whimsy, vanity, and fantasy: Windswept, Moi et mienne, Nirvana, Lynn's Whim, No Vue, You Are My Sunshine, Toy Box, Gracie's Mansion (in this last instance, "Gracie" turned out to be a dog).

One irreverent renter of a house called Breaking Waves scandalized the neighbors by covering up part of the house sign and replacing it. The name he chose—to coordinate with Summer Wind across the way—was Breaking Wind. And—as the much-disparaged "Dunroamin'" suggests—the country house is also the last refuge of that universally despised species, the bad pun (Tooth Acres, Bedside Manor). Recall that the Connecticut place owned by the egregious Upsons in Patrick Dennis's *Auntie Mame* was named Upson Downs. "Isn't that *darling!*" Mame, the urban sophisticate, exclaims disingenuously. "I think it's just *terribly amusing* ... I wonder which one of them ever thought of anything so clever."

But as house prices go up, "twee" names have fallen out of fashion, at least for now. First-time second-home buyers these days often want their houses to sound antique and "authentic" rather than cute, and old rather than new. Just as the naïve Mr. and Mrs. Blandings were charmed by the idea of buying "the old Hackett place," so old family names—even, or especially, the names of families other than your own—confer another sense of "instant tradition." A friend who bought an old house in the countryside was thrilled to find that it bore a plaque proclaiming it the "James Litchfield house, 1847." One high-end vacation market now offers Gibb's Livery Stable (as it was known in the 1800s)—"today, with modern amenities, it accommodates island visitors as a charming guest house, but you may prefer to use it as a private residence"—and the Ebenezer Rand House as well as properties called Sea Horse, Joie de Vivre, Dry Docked, Seaward, and Spring Cottage.[29]

Advertisements occasionally try to lure buyers with the seduction of names, like this description of two newly constructed waterfront houses: "Close to the beach, 'Fame' and 'Harmony' share 2¼ acres of choice property in the dunes. 'Fame' has 3 bedrooms, 2 baths, modern kitchen, great living spaces, a fireplace and fabulous water views. Ready to move in. 'Harmony's' 3 bedrooms, 2 baths, 2 fireplaces and open great room await your custom interior finishing."[30] Is it an accident that Fame is complete and Harmony still awaits your custom finishing? I don't think so. Here in little is the allegorical story of the quest for the summer home.

When it comes to naming your house in Britain, "cottage" and "bungalow" still dominate the field. A survey by the nation's largest mortgage provider, the Halifax, disclosed that The Cottage is the nation's most popular house name, followed by The Bungalow (the national favorite five years earlier) and Rose Cottage, a perennial winner. "Cottages" (Willow-, April-, Pear Tree-, Ivy, Yew Tree-, Orchard-, and Holly-) easily outnumbered "houses," "villas," "manors," "rectories," and "farms." "Overall, the top 50 names are traditional and timeless," said the Halifax, though the *Times* (London) thought "boring" might be a better description.

Significantly absent in the listings are the dwellings of "devoted couples who live in neologisms created from syllables of their names" (like Casa Bevron, shared by Beverly and Ron, or indeed the grander and more celebrated Pickfair, the Hollywood home of Douglas Fairbanks and Mary Pickford), though My Way, Chaos, Bedlam, and Wits' End Cottage are all cited as unusual examples. Old favorites like Dunroamin' were likewise conspicuously missing. According to the Halifax, the conservative trend in nomenclature is an economic fact of life, since bigger houses, bungalows, and "period properties" are expensive, and likely to be purchased by older buyers. "The more mature the owners, the more conservative they are likely to be."[31]

Agatha Christie neatly skewered the practice of bestowing grand names on small structures in a tongue-in-cheek account of a raffish young film executive's country hideaway:

> Basil Blake's cottage, which consisted of all modern conveniences enclosed in a hideous shell of half timbering and sham Tudor, was known to the postal authorities and to William Booker, Builder, as "Chatsworth"; to Basil and his friends as "The Period Piece"; and to the village of St. Mary Mead at large as "Mr. Booker's new house."[32]

This is the inverse of the Newport ploy: instead of a mansion that calls itself a cottage, it's a cottage the builder calls a stately home. Balmoral and Blenheim are other favorite "stately" names for homely homes, and in the United States, inevitably, the White House. Yet it's worth pointing out that no one knew better than Christie the snob value of a good address; the central scenes of *The Body in the Library* (1942) take place in Colonel Bantry's Gossington Hall. She herself is described by a biographer as "ending her days as Dame Agatha, chatelaine of the beautiful Georgian estate of Greenway in Devon."[33]

The Romance of Real Estate

We may think that the drive to replace older homes with more grandiose structures is a recent phenomenon. But it goes back at

least two hundred years. That unerring observer of human en-
thusiasms and human follies, Jane Austen, spared a few moments toward the end of her career to glance with an indulgent
eye at a fashionable seaside resort-in-the-making, the town of
Sanditon:

" 'Everybody has heard of Sanditon,' " says the eager Mr.
Parker, who has invested heavily in this new pleasure spot,
" 'the favourite—for a young and rising bathing-place, certainly,
the favourite spot of all that are to be found along the coast of
Sussex;—the most favoured by nature, and promising to be the
most chosen by man.' "

" 'Yes—I have heard of Sanditon,' " replies his new acquaintance Mr. Heywood. " 'Every five years, one hears of some new
place or other starting up by the sea, and growing the fashion.—
How they can half of them be filled, is the wonder! *Where* people
can be found with money or time to go to them!' "[34]

It's easy to close your eyes and think you are hearing the voices
of current-day real estate speculators, however more elegantly we
may think Messrs. Parker and Heywood speak. But Mr. Parker is
indeed both an enthusiast and a speculator. In fact we soon learn
that he has traded in his charming old homestead for a newly
built, and pretentiously named, house on a hill (and in the wind).

" 'Whose very snug-looking place is this?' " asks one of his
fellow voyagers, "as they passed close by a moderate-sized house,
well fenced and planted, and rich in the garden, orchard, and
meadows which are the best embellishments of such a dwelling."

"Ah!"—said Mr. Parker.—"This is my old house—the house
of my forefathers—the house where I and all of my brothers
and sisters were born and bred—and where my own three eldest children were born—where Mrs. Parker and I lived till
within the last two years—till our new house was finished.—
I am glad you are pleased with it.—It is an honest old place—
and Hillier keeps it in very good order. I have given it up you
know to the man who occupies the chief of my land. *He* gets

a better house by it—and I, a rather better situation!—one other hill brings us to Sanditon—modern Sanditon—a beautiful spot. . . . You will not think I have made a bad exchange, when we reach Trafalgar House—which by the bye, I almost wish I had not named Tragalfar—for Waterloo is more the thing now. However, Waterloo is in reserve—and if we have encouragement enough this year for a little crescent to be ventured on—(as I trust we shall) then, we shall be able to call it Waterloo Crescent."

Mrs. Parker, who is riding with her husband in the coach, observes rather wistfully that the old place " 'was always a very comfortable house' . . . looking at it through the back window with something like the fondness of regret.—'And such a nice garden—such an excellent garden.' " But her husband regards such things as fruit and vegetable gardens, and indeed shade trees, as old-fashioned, no cause for regret. They can always buy their vegetables at Sanditon House. And " 'We have the canvas awning, which gives us the most complete comfort within doors.' "[35]

In this passage Jane Austen neatly summarizes the two desires driving the romance of the summer house: the desire to move ever onward, to find the bigger and better dream house just over the next hill, and the desire to return to the snug little family dwelling that one has left behind. But perhaps the drive to move on and the drive to move back are not so different as they at first appear. Not only is there an irony in the fact that the "snug-looking place" with its unspoiled orchards and gardens is many people's dream of the perfect "second home" today, but even such different-seeming objects as the house with modern and expensive toys ("the canvas awning") and the house with cozy and familiar features (the kitchen garden) may in fact both be visions of perfect satisfaction differently realized.

The lost origin and the future dream are both vanishing points where we imagine ourselves at peace, surrounded by comfort and harmony. But since such vanishing points are by definition just out of reach, the restless urge to find or build the perfect house will never be realized. The summer house, because it defines itself as a space for pleasure, comes to stand for that quest for the ideal "place." It is the ultimate "romance," the story we tell ourselves about who we are and who we wish to be. But this is really true for *all* the houses we allow ourselves to love. The house and all that it symbolizes is the repository of histories, memories, fantasies, self-images, aspirations, and dreams. That is why our romance with houses is—in every sense—such a consuming passion.

WHY WE LOVE HOUSES

Consider the following account, from *House & Garden*, of a love affair in Jean-François de Bastide's eighteenth-century French novella *The Little House.*

> The woman is chaste, demanding, and desirable. The man has something she wants, though she doesn't know it yet; in fact, she's furious that he would even think of seducing her. He's attractive, of course, a man of talent and taste. But that's not what tempts her. What she really wants is his . . . house![1]

Described as a combination of architectural treatise and erotic libertine novel, crammed with "luscious descriptions of forecourts and foreplay," *The Little House* (*La Petite Maison*) is the story of a beautiful woman and a man who sets out to seduce her. Mélite bets the wealthy Trémicour that she can take a tour of his *petite maison* without succumbing to his blandishments or to the allure of the house. The novella's language, as it details the couple's exploration of room after room, makes clear the power of transference: "so voluptuous was this salon that it inspired the tenderest feelings, feelings that one believes one could have only for its owner."[2] Thus Mélite, while proclaiming her virtue, is led further and further into temptation. (Her taste is distinctly "modern" and recognizable to today's upscale home buyer: she is overcome by the ineffable beauty of a marble bathroom.)

Trying to flee a place that had become far too threatening, she entered, alone, into a new room, even more delicious than any she had yet seen. Trémicour could have taken advantage of her ecstasy to close the door without her noticing and force her to listen to his words of love, but he would rather that his victory progress at the pace of pleasure.

The room that Mélite had entered was a bathroom, in which nothing was spared; marble, porcelain, and mousseline were in lavish display.[3]

In the adjacent dressing room, with its painted paneling and silver *toilette*, she feels weak with pleasure and is forced to sit down.

"I can not take this any longer," she said. "This house is too beautiful. There is nothing comparable on earth . . ."

Mélite's tone of voice betrayed a secret distress. Trémicour felt that she was nearly his.[4]

Finally, in a green boudoir lavishly furnished with "ottomans," "duchesses," and *sultanes* (cushioned seats, day beds, and chaise longues) she collapses into a *bergère* (literally, a "shepherdess," an easy chair with a loose cushion or upholstered seat), shudders, sighs, and prepares to lose her wager.

Seduction by architecture was not unusual in the erotic literature of the late eighteenth century, when the *petite maison* became a convenient and exotic locale for liaisons among the fashionable. We could say that very little has changed.

The use of the word "love" is neither surprising nor rare when homeowners speak of their dwellings, past and present. Courtship, flirtation, seduction, second thoughts and commitment all enter into the relationship between a person and a house, before and after they "go to contract." "The annual spring mating dance between home buyer and seller is well underway," observed a newspaper article on the "sizzling" real estate market, employing a familiar figure of speech.

Many stories have been offered to "explain" this relationship, stories based on anthropology, psychology, sociology, philosophy, phenomenology and economics. Even biological determinism (the "nesting instinct") has been urged as the reason why people love their houses. But none of these "answers" really touches the heart of our passion for houses and homes—our own and others. And no biological explanation can tell us why, for example, "empty nesters" sometimes want bigger houses, not smaller ones.

It's not really an explanation that we need.

Throughout these pages, it has been my contention that the house can be a primary object of affection and desire—not a displacement or a substitute or a metaphor. Phrases like "my dream house" and "the house of my dreams," which have become so familiar both in ordinary conversation and in the wish-language of real estate ads and shelter magazines, tell a profound kind of truth—the truth that human desire cannot be contained within explanation or need. The house is the repository of our unmet needs, our unfulfilled dreams, or our nostalgic longings. It cannot really satisfy any of them, but perhaps that is why we have so much satisfaction in making the attempt. In the process, we get to experience the very specific pleasures and pains that only a house can provide.

Perhaps increasingly, for busy people, space has come to substitute for time, and the house becomes the unlived life. In an era when the "welcome mat" and the "answering machine" all-too-often stand in for personal greeting and the human voice, the house—with its "living" room, "dining" room, "family" room and "media" room, is the place where we stage the life we wish we had time to live.

Once upon a time, "the earth moved" was the perfect sexual compliment. Now, it's likely to be the announcement—delivered with equal, sensual satisfaction—that the contractor has shown up and is on the job.

Notes

INTRODUCTION   *Sex and Real Estate*

1 Russell Baker, "Poor Old Mister Money," *New York Times,* January 16, 1998, p. A27.

2 Tina Cassidy, "Make Your Best Offer," *Boston Globe,* March 23, 1997, p. D6.

3 Frank Faulkner, quoted in Angus Wilkie, "Hudson Hawk," *Elle Décor,* May 1998, p. 173.

4 Dominique Browning, "Welcome: Turn on the Lights," *House & Garden,* September 1996, p. 29.

5 Richard Ford, *Independence Day* (New York: Vintage, 1996), p. 41.

6 Quoted in Janny Scott, "Bright, Shining, or Dark: American Way of Lying," *New York Times,* August 16, 1998, sec. 4, p. 3.

7 Tracie Rozhon, "Lover's Leap Mentality Hits Co-ops," *New York Times,* April 30, 1998, pp. C1, C13.

8 Randi Grossman, quoted in Tracie Rozhon, "A Hot Market Leads to Cold-Blooded Dealing," *New York Times,* May 25, 1997, sec. 9, p. 1.

9 Tracie Rozhon, "What's the Trendy Word at Co-ops These Days? 'Rejected,'" *New York Times,* September 24, 1996, pp. B1, B4.

10 John Tierney, "Two-Bedroom Quandary," *New York Times Magazine,* June 14, 1998, p. 34.

11 Lorrie Moore, "Real Estate," *New Yorker,* August 17, 1998, p. 67.

12 Amy Saltzman, "The Truth About Open Houses," *U.S. News & World Report,* April 5, 1993, p. 76.

13 Mary S. Ludwig, *Your Dream Vacation Home* (Blue Ridge Summit, PA: Liberty Hall, 1991), p. 159.

14 Ami Tanel, Avatar Development Corporation, quoted in Edward J. Blakely and Mary Gail Snyder, *Fortress America: Gated Communities in the United States* (Washington: Brookings Institute Press, and Cambridge, MA: Lincoln Institute of Land Policy, 1997), p. 18.

15 Mitchell Owens, "Mark Hampton, Decorator and Style Expert, Dies at 58," *New York Times*, July 24, 1998, p. A23.

16 Robin Pogrebin, "House & Garden Reappears on a Crowded Stage," *New York Times*, July 30, 1996, p. D5.

17 Audit Bureau of Circulation and Mediamark Research, as cited in Pogrebin, "House & Garden Reappears," p. D1.

18 Julie V. Iovine, "Helter-Shelter: New Look for Dream Books," *New York Times*, August 22, 1998, p. C8.

19 "The Hon Rosina Cobbhold," *Hello!*, June 27, 1998, p. 68.

20 Alan Emmet, "One Look Back and Two Steps Forward," *House & Garden*, March 1998, p. 96.

21 Stephen A. Kliment, "Island Themes Revisited," *Architectural Digest*, July 1998, p. 92.

22 Julie V. Iovine, "Currents," *New York Times*, November 13, 1997, p. C3.

23 Pogrebin, "House & Garden Reappears," p. D5.

24 Ibid., p. D1.

25 Dennis Hevesi, "The Art of Marketing Rooms at the Top," *New York Times*, January 18, 1998, sec. 11, p. 1.

26 David Silverman, "Builders Just a Bunch of Romantics," *Chicago Tribune*, February 3, 1990, Home Guide sec. p. 2.

27 Ford, *Independence Day*, p. 75.

28 Moore, "Real Estate," p. 67.

29 Ruth Simon, "Hit the Prospect at Every Emotional Level," *Forbes*, January 9, 1989, p. 310.

30 Julie V. Iovine, "Making the Imperfect Picture Perfect," *New York Times*, July 17, 1997, pp. C1, C7.

31 Verne G. Kopytoff, " 'Staging' a House for Prospective Buyers," *New York Times*, August 9, 1998, p. 34.

32 Simon, "Hit the Prospect at Every Emotional Level," p. 310.

33 Mary Cook, quoted in David Silverman, "Builders Just a Bunch of Romantics," p. 2.

34 Simon, "Hit the Prospect at Every Emotional Level," p. 310.

35 Hevesi, "Art of Marketing Rooms at the Top," p. 1.

ONE *The House as Beloved*

1 "Sag Harbor Sanctuary" (no author credited), *Country Living*, July 1998, p. III.

2 Realtors Linda Cutter, Gill Woods, and Nancy J. Connon, quoted in Ellen James Martin, "Emotion Can Blind House Hunters Who Fall in Love at First Sight," *Detroit News*, October 25, 1997, p. D26.

3 Tracie Rozhon, "Co-op Boards Twist the Screws," *New York Times*, October 23, 1997, p. C1.

4 These phrases are the headlines given to Martin, "Emotion Can Blind House Hunters," when it appeared in the *Los Angeles Times* (October 26, 1997) and the *Detroit News*.

5 Nena Groskind, "There's Much to Inspect Before Hiring an Inspector," *Boston Globe*, March 29, 1998, p. H.4.

6 Karen Curran, "Cape Escapes," *Boston Globe*, June 8, 1997, p. F.4.

7 Martin, "Emotion Can Blind House Hunters."

8 Richard Ford, *Independence Day* (New York: Vintage, 1996), pp. 51, 62, 70, 75, 86, 60.

9 Groucho Marx, *The Groucho Letters* (New York: Simon and Schuster, 1967).

10 Eric Hodgins, *Mr. Blandings Builds His Dream House* (New York: Simon & Schuster, 1946), p. 14.

11 Ibid., p. 36.

12 Jane Austen, *Pride and Prejudice* (1813; London: Penguin, 1972, 1985), p. 382.

13 Ibid., p. 267.

14 Ibid., p. 268.

15 Susan Watkins, *Jane Austen in Style* (London: Thames and Hudson, 1990, 1996), p. 84.

16 A. J. McIlroy, "Darcy's House Attracts a Romantic Following," *Daily Telegraph*, July 22, 1996, p. 20. These figures are for 1994–1995. In the following year (1995–1996) Lyme Park's visitors again increased by 42 percent, and those of Sudbury Hall, where the interior scenes at "Pemberley" were shot, by 59 percent. "TV Saga Fuels Surge in Tourism," *The Independent* (London), August 11, 1997, p. 2.

17 Nancy Mitford, *The Sun King: Louis XIV at Versailles* (New York: Crescent Books, 1966), p. 17.

18 Nigel Nicolson, *Portrait of a Marriage* (New York: Atheneum, 1973), p. 90.

19 V. Sackville-West, "To Knole. 1 October 1913," in *Poems of West and East* (London: John Lane, 1917).

20 Nicolson, *Portrait of a Marriage*, pp. 202, 208.

21 Honor Moore, "A House Too Can Be a Lifelong Companion," *Radcliffe Quarterly* 83, no. 4 (Spring 1998), p. 13.

22 Elsie De Wolfe, *The House in Good Taste* (New York: Century, 1914), p. 27.

23 Evelyn Waugh, *Brideshead Revisited* (Boston: Little, Brown, 1945), pp. 34‒35.

24 Ibid., p. 351.

25 Ibid., p. 217.

26 Ibid., pp. 226–227.

27 Daphne du Maurier, *Rebecca* (1938; New York: Avon, 1971), p. 23.

28 Ibid., pp. 53, 63, 65, 69.

29 Jennifer M. Nichols, "Reflecting Mira," *Boston Globe*, June 15, 1998, p. F1.

30 Adam Phillips, *Monogamy* (New York: Vintage, 1999), p. 42.

31 Bureau of the Census, Census Questionnaire Content, 1990 CQC-9 (April, 1993).

32 Florence Williams, "A House, 10 Wives: Polygamy in Suburbia," *New York Times*, December 11, 1997, pp. C1, C7.

33 James Laing of Strutt & Parker, quoted in Mary Wilson, "Who Gets the House?" *Times* (London), May 17, 1995.

34 Ellen James Martin, "Preparing a Property for Market," *Boston Globe*, April 26, 1998, p. F1.

35 Christopher Thomas, quoted in Alexandra Peers, "The House: A Hornets' Nest of Divorce," *Wall Street Journal;* reprinted in *San Diego Union-Tribune*, October 8, 1995, p. H-2.

36 Peers, "The House: A Hornets' Nest of Divorce."

37 Karen Ridgeway, "Hamlin, Johnson Settle Divorce," *USA Today*, March 16, 1960, p. 2D.

38 Kathleen Murray, "Odd Couples and Their Odder Divorce Settlements," *Cosmopolitan*, May 1996, p. 222.

39 Clare Garner, "Housing Boom Mirrors Marriage Break-Ups," *Independent* (London), May 31, 1998, p. 3.

40 Louise T. Truax and Melvyn B. Frumkes, quoted in Margot Slade,

"Spending It: Gainful Way to Splitsville," *New York Times*, March 8, 1998, section 3, p. 10.

41 Gary N. Skoloff, quoted in Tracie Rozhon, "The Perils of Owning a Home in Splitsville," *New York Times*, January 21, 1996, sec. 9, p. 1.

TWO   *The House as Mother*

1 Jane Davison and Lesley Davison, *To Make a House a Home* (New York: Random House, 1994), p. 24. Sigmund Freud, *Dora, An Analysis of a Case of Hysteria* (New York: Collier, 1963), p. 84. See also Sigmund Freud, *The Interpretation of Dreams* in *The Standard Edition of the Complete Psychological Works of Sigmund Freud*, ed. James Strachey (London: Hogarth Press and Institute of Psycho-Analysis, 1955), 5:357.

2 Ann Douglas, *The Feminization of American Culture* (New York: Avon, 1977), p. 55.

3 Frank Presbrey, *The History and Development of Advertising* (New York: Doubleday, 1929), p. 318.

4 Douglas, *Feminization of American Culture*, p. 79.

5 Ibid., p. 77.

6 Ibid., p. 86.

7 Jane Tompkins, *Sensational Designs: The Cultural Work of American Fiction, 1790–1860* (New York: Oxford University Press, 1985), p. 144.

8 Ibid., p. 145.

9 Ibid., pp. 124–125.

10 Greta Gray, *House and Home: A Manual and Text-Book of Practical House Planning*. (Philadelphia: Lippincott, 1923), pp. 1–4.

11 Sinclair Lewis, *Babbitt* (1922; New York: New American Library, 1991), p. 6.

12 Ibid., pp. 16–17.

13 John Hollander, "It All Depends," in *Home: A Place in the World*, ed. Arien Mack (New York: New York University Press, 1993), p. 37.

14 *Guardian*, October 20, 1973, p. 11; *OED*, "home," *sb.* 2a.

15 Olivier Marc, *Psychology of the House*, trans. Jessie Wood (London: Thames and Hudson, 1977), p. 14.

16 See, for example, Nancy Cott, *The Bonds of Womanhood: "Woman's Sphere" in New England, 1780–1835* (New Haven: Yale University Press, 1977).

17 Sandra M. Gilbert and Susan Gubar, *The Madwoman in the Attic: The Woman Writer and the Nineteenth-Century Literary Imagination* (New Haven: Yale University Press, 1984), pp. 87–88.

18 Virginia Woolf, *To the Lighthouse* (1927; New York: Harcourt Brace Jovanovich, 1955), pp. 190–191.

19 Sigmund Freud, "The 'Uncanny' " (1919), in *The Standard Edition of the Complete Psychological Works of Sigmund Freud*, trans. James Strachey (London: The Hogarth Press and the Institute of Psycho-Analysis, 1955), 17: 245.

20 Agatha Christie, *Sleeping Murder* (1976; New York: HarperCollins, 1992), pp. 3, 4, 5.

21 Ibid., p. 214.

22 Joseph H. DiLeo, *Interpreting Children's Drawings* (New York: Bruner/Mazel, 1983), p. 57.

23 The phrase is Bachelard's. He is describing the fine discriminations employed by psychologists like Françoise Minkowska, who studied houses drawn by children. Gaston Bachelard, *The Poetics of Space*, trans. Maria Jolas (Boston: Beacon, 1994), p. 73.

24 Anne Balif, *De Van Gogh et Seurat aus dessins d'enfants*, illustrated catalogue of an exhibition held at the Musée Pédagogique, Paris, in 1949. Cited in Bachelard, *Poetics of Space*, p. 72.

25 Bachelard, *Poetics of Space*, p. xxxviii.

26 Joseph Holtzman, editor of *Nest*, quoted in Julie V. Iovine, "Currents," *New York Times*, November 13, 1997, p. C3.

27 Bachelard, *Poetics of Space*, p. 7.

28 Ibid., pp. 14–15.

29 Ibid., p. 15.

30 Ibid., p. 78.

31 Edgar Allan Poe, "The Philosophy of Furniture," in *The Unabridged Edgar Allan Poe*, ed. Tam Mossman (Philadelphia: Running Press, 1983), p. 645.

32 Bachelard, *Poetics of Space*, p. 84.

33 Ibid., p. 136. The footnote refers the reader to *Le Temps de la poésie*, G.L.M., July 1948, p. 32.

34 Elizabeth Bishop, *Sestina* (1965).

35 Marie-Laure Bernadac, *Louise Bourgeois* (Paris: Flammarion), p. 24.

36 Ibid., p. 11n.

37 Quoted in Christiane Meyer-Thoss, *Louise Bourgeois: Designing for Free Fall* (Zurich: Ammann Verlag, 1992), p. 122.

38 Philip Wylie, *Generation of Vipers* (1942; New York: Holt, Rinehart and Winston, 1955), p. 198.

39 Wilfred Sheed, Introduction to James Thurber, *Men, Women and Dogs* (New York: Dodd, Mead, 1975), pp. 11–12.

40 Advertisement for Frame Works Building Systems made by Trus Joist MacMillan, 200 East Mallard Drive, Boise, Idaho 83706, in *Home*, June 1996, p. 132 (insert).

41 Clifford Edward Clark, Jr., *The American Family Home, 1800–1960* (Chapel Hill: University of North Carolina Press, 1986), p. 238.

THREE   *The House as Body*

1 "Westport," from *Take Five, a Julius Monk Review*, original cast recording with Pearl Bailey and Will Holt (c. 1952–1954).

2 Charles Spencer, "The Arts: Living in Sin with the Master," *Daily Telegraph*, February 23, 1995, p. 14.

3 Peter Stallybrass, "Patriarchal Territories: The Body Enclosed," in *Rewriting the Renaissance*, ed. Margaret Ferguson, Maureen Quilligan, and Nancy J. Vickers (Chicago: University of Chicago Press, 1986), p. 126.

4 Vitruvius, *De Architectura*, trans. Frank Granger (Cambridge, MA: Harvard University Press, 1955), 1:159. For more on the human body as image of the world, see Leonard Barkan, *Nature's Work of Art* (New Haven: Yale University Press, 1975).

5 Vitruvius, *De Architectura*, 1:159.

6 Andrew Marvell, "Upon Appleton House," lines 9–16, in *The Selected Poetry*, ed. Frank Kermode (New York: New American Library, 1967).

7 Barkan, *Nature's Work of Art*, p. 142n, describing an argument of Francesco Giorgi.

8 Ibid., p. 158.

9 Plato, *Timaeus*, in *The Collected Dialogues of Plato*, trans. Benjamin Jowett, ed. Edith Hamilton and Huntington Cairns (Princeton: Princeton University Press, 1961), 70a–e, pp. 1193–1194.

10 Henri De Mondeville (fourteenth century). See Carolyn Walker Bynum, "The Female Body and Religious Practices in the Later Middle

Age," in *Fragments for a History of the Human Body,* Part I, ed. Michel Feher (New York: Zone, 1989), p. 187; and Mark Wigley, "Untitled: The Housing of Gender," in *Sexuality & Space,* ed. Beatriz Colomina (Princeton: Princeton Architectural Press, 1992), p. 358.

11 Wigley, "Untitled: The Housing of Gender," p. 357.

12 Leon Battista Alberti, *On the Art of Building in Ten Books,* trans. Joseph Rykwert, Neil Leach, and Robert Tavernor (Cambridge, MA: MIT Press, 1988), 5:149.

13 Leon Battista Alberti, *Della Famiglia,* trans. Renée Neu Watkins as *The Family in Renaissance Florence* (Columbia: University of South Carolina Press, 1969), 3:207.

14 Xenophon, *Oeconomicus,* trans. H. G. Dakyns as "The Economist," in *The Works of Xenophon* (London: Macmillan, 1897), 3:231.

15 Wigley, "Untitled: The Housing of Gender," p. 337.

16 Ibid., p. 345.

17 Henri Lefebvre, in *The Production of Space,* trans. Donald Nicholson-Smith (1974; Oxford: Blackwell's, 1998), reflects on social spaces that are religious and political sites, places he associates in precapitalist societies with "the principle of fertility (the Mother)" (p. 34). For modern societies he urges a recognition of the "potential for playfulness" (p. 211) in what he calls "sensory-sensual" spaces, which are often animated by oppositions and contrasts like high and low, near and far, central and peripheral, including in his list of dynamic oppositions "paternity and maternity, male places and female places." And when he comes to speak of the relationship between town and countryside he again invokes this familiar pair: "by appropriating rural space the town takes on a reality which is sometimes 'maternal' (it stores, stocks or profitably exchanges a portion of the surplus product . . .) and sometimes 'masculine' (it protects while exploiting—or exploits while protecting; it holds the power; it oversees, [and] regulates . . .)" (p. 234). This use of gendered categories seems rather to reinforce stereotypes than to analyze them, yet Lefebvre, like Bachelard, is crankily resistant to psychoanalytic interpretations. Any interpretation of social space that is explained in terms of the incest taboo (which "separates the child from his mother because incest is forbidden") and the split subject (which "separates the child from its body because language in constituting consciousness breaks down the unmediated unity of the body") worries him because it seems to assume that language is prior to

space, and applies only to an "imaginary society." Yet he himself is eager to assert that in " 'real' societies" the omnipresence of *phallic verticality* (his italics) "cries out for explanation" (p. 36). And he sees that "walls, enclosures, and facades serve to define both a *scene* (where something takes place) and an *obscene* area to which everything that cannot or may not happen on the scene is relegated" (p. 36). The love-hate relationship with psychoanalysis that Bachelard cannot resist acting out is also evident in Lefebvre, whose response is that of the young fetishist who can't believe his mother lacks a penis ("I know . . . but still"): "It is true that explaining everything in psychoanalytic terms, in terms of the unconscious, can only lead to an intolerable reductionism and dogmatism . . . yet . . . there is such a thing as the 'unconscious' " (p. 36).

18 Lawrence Wright, *Clean and Decent: The Fascinating History of the Bathroom & the Water Closet* (New York: Viking, 1960), p. 57.

19 Ibid., p. 48.

20 *OED*, "toilet," 5b: "You shall introduce him to Mrs. Clerimont's Toilet" (Steele, *Tender Husband* 1.1.).

21 Calvert Vaux, *Villas and Cottages: A Series of Designs Prepared for Execution in the United States* (New York: Harper and Brothers, 1864), pp. 95–97; Karen Halttunen, "From Parlor to Living Room: Domestic Space, Interior Decoration, and the Culture of Personality," in *Consuming Visions: Accumulation and Display of Goods in America 1880–1920*, ed. Simon J. Bronner (New York: Norton, 1989), p. 162.

22 Gwendolyn Wright, *Building the Dream: A Social History of Housing in America* (Cambridge, MA: MIT Press, 1983, 1995), p. 172.

23 James Thomson, "Cozy Corners and Ingle Nooks," *Ladies' Home Journal* 10, no. 12 (November 1893), p. 27; Halttunen, "From Parlor to Living Room," pp. 164–165.

24 Henry L. Wilson, *Bungalow Book* (1910), quoted in Robert Winter, *The California Bungalow* (Los Angeles: Hennessey and Ingalls, 1980), p. 48.

25 Frank Alvah Parsons, *Interior Decoration: Its Principles and Practice* (1915; Garden City, NY: Doubleday, Doran, 1931), p. 6; Halttunen, "From Parlor to Living Room," p. 171; Elsie De Wolfe, *The House in Good Taste* (New York: Century, 1914), p. 148; Emily Post, *The Personality of a House* (New York: Funk & Wagnalls, 1930), p. 336, 341.

26 Wright, *Building the Dream*, p. 112.

27 Ibid., p. 255.

28 Judith Martin, "The Living Room: All Show, But No Go," *Boston Globe,* May 31, 1998, p. D8.

29 Post, *Personality of a House,* p. 403.

30 Patrick Dennis, *Auntie Mame* (New York: Vanguard, 1955), pp. 29–30.

31 Ad for Tulikivi, *Home,* October 1998, p. 72.

32 Mary Gilliatt, *English Country Style* (Boston: Little, Brown, 1986), pp. 129–130.

33 *House & Garden,* May 1998.

34 Jane Smiley, "The Bathroom," in Sharon Sloan Fiffer and Steve Fiffer, *Home: American Writers Remember Rooms of Their Own* (New York: Vintage, 1996), pp. 107–109.

35 Jerry Adler, "Feeling Flush," *Newsweek,* June 22, 1998, pp. 66–67.

36 Paul Deffenbaugh, quoted in Patricia Leigh Brown, "Public Eye: The Fridge Flees the Kitchen," *New York Times,* July 9, 1998, p. F1.

37 Brown, "Public Eye: The Fridge Flees the Kitchen," p. F1.

38 Mark Girouard, *Life in the English Country House* (New Haven: Yale University Press, 1978), pp. 205, 230, 287. Girouard's invaluable study is the source of much of the information in this paragraph.

39 William H. Pivar and Bradley A. Pivar, *The Big Book of Real Estate Ads,* rev. ed. (Chicago: Real Estate Education Company, 1997), p. 268.

40 Mary Davis Gillies, *What Women Want in Their Dining Rooms of Tomorrow* (New York: McCall, 1944), p. 3.

41 Ernest Jones, *The Life and Work of Sigmund Freud,* ed. Lionel Trilling and Steven Marcus (New York: Basic Books, 1961), p. 377.

42 Mary Davis Gillies, *What Women Want in Their Bedrooms of Tomorrow* (New York: McCall, 1944), pp. 28–29.

43 Alecia Beldegreen, *The Bed* (New York: Stewart, Tabori & Chang, 1991), p. 36.

44 *Pillow Talk* (1959). A film called *Twin Beds,* a comedy about a neighbor constantly interrupting a married couple, appeared in 1942. The proportion of twin beds relative to all beds purchased in the United States in the prewar period was 25 percent; by 1950—according to a number of studies—it had risen to 68 percent.

45 Paul Popenoe, quoted in Reginald Reynolds, *Beds* (London: Andre Deutsch, 1952), p. 139.

46 Parker Tyler, *A Pictorial History of Sex in Films* (Secaucus, NJ: Citadel Press, 1974), p. 61.

47 "Choosing Your Favorite House Style: What Our Readers Want in a Home," *Colonial Homes*, July 1998, p. 96.

48 Lynne Forti, "The Family Bed," *Parenting*, a *Boston Globe* Advertising Supplement, Fall 1998, p. 13.

49 Quentin Crisp, "An Evening with Quentin Crisp," quoted in Anita Gates, "Crisp, So Stylishly 89, Gets to the Point, Well, Crisply," *New York Times*, June 26, 1998, p. B4.

50 Post, *Personality of a House*, pp. 201, 274.

51 Richard Ellmann, *Oscar Wilde* (New York: Alfred A. Knopf, 1988), pp. 193–194.

52 Ellmann, 581. Cited in Douglas Mao, "From Wallpaper, Crime: Aesthetic Education, Discipline, and *Dorian Gray*" (forthcoming).

53 Halttunen, "From Parlor to Living Room," p. 158.

54 De Wolfe, *House in Good Taste*, p. 22.

55 Ibid., p. 170.

56 Halttunen, "From Parlor to Living Room," p. 158.

57 Wright, *Building the Dream*, pp. 208–209.

58 Patricia Poore, "Bathrooms As They Were," *Old House Interiors*, Fall 1998, p. 53.

59 Post, *Personality of a House*, p. 197.

60 Ibid., p. 199.

61 Halttunen, "From Parlor to Living Room," pp. 157–158; M. H. Harmon, *Psycho-Decorating: What Homes Reveal About People* (New York: Wyden Books, 1977); Virginia Frankel, *What Your House Tells About You* (New York: Trident, 1972); Catherine C. Crane, *What Do You Say to a Naked Room?* (New York: Dial, 1979).

62 Cited in Halttunen, "From Parlor to Living Room," p. 158.

63 Jean-Christophe Agnew, "A House of Fiction: Domestic Interiors and the Commodity Aesthetic," in *Consuming Visions: Accumulation and Display of Goods in America, 1880–1920*, ed. Simon J. Bronner (New York: Norton, 1989), pp. 133–135.

64 Christa Worthington, "What is Glamour?," *Elle Décor*, October 1998, p. 58.

65 Advertisement in *House Beautiful*, October 1998, following p. 32.

66 Advertisement for Workbench, *Boston Globe Magazine*, August 30, 1998, p. 23.

67 Brooke Stoddard, "The Joy of Sexy," *House & Garden*, April 1998, p. 140.

68 Jackson Lears, *Fables of Abundance: A Cultural History of Advertising in America* (New York: Basic Books, 1994), p. 47.

FOUR   *The Dream House*

1 C. G. Jung, *Memories, Dreams, Reflections,* ed. Aniela Jaffé, trans. Richard and Clara Winston (New York: Vintage, 1989), p. 159.

2 Ibid., pp. 160–161.

3 As Richard Noll points out, it would be more accurate to call this a theory of a "phylogenetic" rather than a "collective" unconscious. Noll, *The Jung Cult: Origins of a Charismatic Movement* (Princeton: Princeton University Press, 1994), p. 6.

4 C. G. Jung, *The Psychology of the Unconscious: A Study in the Transformations and Symbolisms of the Libido,* in *Collected Works of C. G. Jung,* ed. Herbert Read, Michael Fordham, and Gerhard Adler, trans. Beatrice M. Hinkle (Princeton: Princeton University Press, 1991), para. 36.

5 Jung, *Memories, Dreams, Reflections,* p. 225.

6 Clare Cooper Marcus, *House as a Mirror of Self* (Berkeley, CA: Conari Press, 1995), pp. 40–41. Her book is introduced by a foreword from the former president of the C. G. Jung Institute of San Francisco.

7 Olivier Marc, *Psychology of the House,* trans. Jessie Wood (London: Thames and Hudson, 1977), pp. 13, 14, 118.

8 Gaston Bachelard, *The Poetics of Space,* trans. Maria Jolas (1958; New York: Beacon, 1994) p. 222.

9 Homer, *Odyssey,* 19:560; Virgil, *Aeneid,* 6:893. "There are two gates of sleep, one said to be/Of horn, whereby the true shades pass with ease,/The other all white ivory gleam/Without a flaw, and yet false dreams are sent/Through this one by the ghosts to the upper world." *The Aeneid,* trans. Robert Fitzgerald (New York: Random House, 1983), pp. 191–192.

10 George Ferguson, *Signs and Symbols in Christian Art* (London: Oxford University Press, 1971), pp. 42, 174.

11 Shakespeare, *Romeo and Juliet,* 2.2.63, 65–66.

12 Edmund Spenser, *The Faerie Queene,* Book II, Canto xii, stanza 43.

13 *Bestiaire Divin de Guillaume, Clerc de Normandie.* In some renditions of the story the animal lays his head, with its single horn, in the lady's lap, enacting the complex ritual of sexual aggression and submission in unmistakably emblematic terms.

14 Paul Fussell, *Class* (New York: Ballantine, 1983), p. 81.

15 Edith Wharton, "The Fullness of Life" (1891); Theresa Craig, *Edith Wharton: A House Full of Rooms* (New York: Monacelli, 1996), pp. 80–81.

16 John Keats, Letter to John Hamilton Reynolds, May 3, 1818.

17 Bachelard, *Poetics of Space*, p. 6.

18 *OED*, 2nd edition, "day-dreamer"; William Makepeace Thackeray, *Pendennis* (London: Brodbury and Evans, 1849–50), p. 272; John Addington Symonds, *Greek Poets* (London: Smith, Elder, 1873), p. 376.

19 Leslie Bennetts, "A Film That Sings Renovation Blues," *New York Times*, March 27, 1986, p. C1.

20 Freud, *Interpretation of Dreams*, 5:292.

21 Rainer Maria Rilke, letter to Witold von Hulewicz, November 13, 1925, in *Duino Elegies*, trans. J. B. Leishman and Stephen Spender (New York: 1963), p. 129, cited in Jackson Lears, *Fables of Abundance* (New York: Basic Books, 1994), p. 398.

22 "Artists Show There's No Place Like Home," *Boston Globe*, May 19, 1996, pp. 1, 5.

23 From a letter soliciting subscriptions to *Renovation Style*.

24 *The National Trust Handbook for Members and Visitors, 1998*, ed. James Parry (Bromley, Kent: National Trust, 1998).

25 "A House Filled with Ideas," *New York Times*, September 26, 1996, p. C14.

26 Christine Pittel, "Showhouse Winners 1997," *House Beautiful*, October 1997, pp. 161, 162, 159.

27 Christa Worthington, "What Is Glamour?," *Elle Décor*, October 1998, p. 58.

28 Quoted in Worthington, "What Is Glamour?," p. 56.

29 Bachelard, *Poetics of Space*, p. 62.

FIVE   *The Trophy House*

1 Julie Connelly, "The CEO's Second Wife," *Fortune*, August 28, 1989, p. 53.

2 William Safire, "On Language," *New York Times Magazine*, May 1, 1994, sec. 6, p. 26.

3 Olivia Goldsmith, *The First Wives Club* (New York: Poseidon, 1992), p. 224.

4 Margo Miller, "The Old, the New," *Boston Globe,* December 11, 1997, p. E4.

5 Thorstein Veblen, *The Theory of the Leisure Class* (1899; New York: Modern Library, 1931), pp. 28–29.

6 Robert D. McFadden with Rachelle Garbarine, "A Haven for the Super-Rich With Room for the Servants," *New York Times,* April 25, 1998, pp. A1, A12.

7 Carl Swanson and Kate Kelly, "Manhattan Transfers," *New York Observer,* July 27, 1998, p. 23.

8 Tracie Rozhon, "Now, the Six-Figure Rent (Yes, Rent)," *New York Times,* January 8, 1998, p. C1.

9 Alex Kuczynski, "Sorry, Wrong Conversation," *New York Times,* December 21, 1997, sec. 9, p. 1.

10 Amanda Loose, "Millionaire Trophies," *Times* (London), August 27, 1997, Features section, np.

11 Tracie Rozhon, "Condos Take a Cruise," *New York Times,* December 4, 1997, p. C13.

12 Carl Swanson, "Just Lookin'! Phony Big Spenders Bluff Their Way Into Dream Homes," *New York Observer,* July 27, 1998, pp. 1, 19.

13 Veblen, *Theory of the Leisure Class,* p. 31.

14 Froma Harrop, "Trophy Houses Rarely Reward the Neighborhood," *Sacramento Bee,* September 8, 1997, p. B8.

15 Peter Passell, "Vicarious Consumption," *New York Times,* February 8, 1998, sec. 3, p. 10.

16 Quoted in Tina Cassidy, "Old Money—New Money," *Boston Globe,* June 9, 1996, Real Estate sec., p. A1.

17 Alex Kuczynski, "How the Glitz Stole Greenwich," *New York Times,* May 3, 1998, p. 2.

18 Emanuel Tobier, quoted in ibid.

19 Tom Kligerman and Robert A. M. Stern, quoted in Julie V. Iovine, "When What You See Is All You Get," *New York Times,* January 23, 1997, p. C6.

20 Spencer Goliger, quoted in Iovine, "When What You See Is All You Get."

21 Arlene C. Travis, quoted in Debra West, "Mass-Market Mansions for the Suburbs," *New York Times,* March 18, 1998, p. A21.

22 "As Tastes Grow Lavish, Profits Rise," *New York Times,* September 14, 1997, p. 34.

23 Bob Ardren, "Versailles Model a Royal Treat in Cory Lake Isles," *Tampa Tribune*, June 20, 1998, p. 8.

24 Letters to the Editor from Audrey Salderelli and Joseph Salderelli and from Kathleen Anderson, *New York Times*, March 24, 1998, p. A26.

25 Philip Fisher, "Appearing and Disappearing in Public," in *Reconstructing American Literary History*, ed. Sacvan Bercovitch (Cambridge, MA: Harvard University Press, 1986), p. 174.

26 William Dean Howells, *The Rise of Silas Lapham*, ed. Don L. Cook (1885; New York: Norton, 1982), p. 48.

27 Ibid., pp. 36–37.

28 Larzer Ziff, "Literary Hospitality: William Dean Howells," in Howells, *Rise of Silas Lapham*, p. 502.

29 F. Scott Fitzgerald, *The Great Gatsby* (1925; New York: Scribner, 1995), p. 9.

30 Ibid., p. 93.

31 Ibid., p. 54.

32 Ibid., p. 103.

33 Ibid., pp. 155–156.

34 Ibid., p. 11.

35 Tracie Rozhon, "The Agent as Hot Property," *New York Times*, April 9, 1998, p. C1.

36 Daniel J. Boorstin, *The Image: A Guide to Pseudo-Events in America* (New York: Atheneum, 1968, 1987), p. 57.

37 "Star Gazing: Hollywood Homes Have Allure for Buyers," *Phoenix Gazette*, August 23, 1996, p. A2.

38 Mark Edmonds, "Pounds 17m for the House that Rocky Built," *Daily Telegraph* (London), February 17, 1998, p. 12.

39 Felicia Paik, article reprinted as "When Stars Move In, It Gives Rest of Neighborhood a Boost," *Minneapolis Star Tribune*, March 8, 1997, p. 6H.

40 "Star Gazing," p. A2.

41 Advertised in *Unique Homes*, February–March 1996, p. 179.

42 Michael Kaplan, "If These Walls Could Talk: Buying a Celebrity Home," *In Style*, November 1996, p. 61.

43 Joseph Giovannini, "When It's Time For Filming, a House Can Be a Star," *New York Times*, February 3, 1998, p. B1.

44 Russell Smith, "Movie Houses That Steal the Show," *Orlando Sentinel Tribune*, August 15, 1992, p. G1.

45 "1966 saw Castle Howard tackling the demanding role of Moscow's Kremlin . . . in *The Spy with a Cold Nose*"; "1978 and it was time for Vanbrugh's creation to have a go at some Shakespeare." In short, "along with actors, directors, writers and producers, movies houses—given a meaty role and eye-catching design—can attain star status. Some become icons." Ibid.

46 C. [Mrs. James F. Cox], *Home Thoughts* (New York: Barnes, 1901), pp. 72–73.

47 Ibid., p. 73.

48 Mary Douglas, "The Idea of a Home: A Kind of Space," *Social Research* 58, no. 1 (Spring 1991): *Home: A Place in the World*, pp. 304–305, 301.

49 Jean Nathan, "Up to the New York Minute," *Travel & Leisure*, June 1998, pp. 156–157.

50 Heather Smith MacIsaac, "Seek and Hide," *Travel & Leisure*, June 1998, p. 121.

51 Quoted in Lloyd Chrein, "Living at Home in a Hotel," *Newsday*, May 14, 1994, p. C2.

52 Fran Lebowitz, in Ruth Rosenthal and Maggie Toy, *Building Sights* (London: Academy Editions, 1995).

53 Cynthia Robins, "Hammer Sells Mansion that Rap Built," *Tampa Tribune*, May 11, 1997, p. 3.

54 Joan Duncan Oliver, "Heading Home," *New York Times Home Design Magazine*, October 2, 1994, p. 34.

55 "Botanico, a subtle beige marble with delicate veining, on the Lobby and Reception area walls"; "the dramatic Red Verona for the floors of the Lobby"; "Michelangelo White, quarried from the same place that Michelangelo selected marble for his statue of David, used to border the Red Verona," and "the bolder-grained beige Napolean [*sic*] marble for the Reception counter." Photocopied handout at Donatello Hotel.

56 Lettice Stuart, "A Rare Breed of Speculators Who Build Mansions," *New York Times*, May 19, 1991, sec. 8, p. 1.

57 Christa Worthington, "What Is Glamour?," *Elle Décor*, October 1998, p. 58.

58 Brochure for Cuddledown of Maine (312 Casco Road, Portland, ME 04103), Autumn 1996, pp. 16–17.

59 Ibid., 16.

60 Theodor Adorno, "Gold Assay," in *Minima Moralia: Reflections*

from Damaged Life, trans. E. P. H. Jephcott (1951; London: Verso, 1974), pp. 152–155.

61 Jackson Lears, *Fables of Abundance: A Cultural History of Advertising in America*. (New York: Basic Books, 1994), pp. 346–347.

62 Sinclair Lewis, *Babbitt* (1922; New York: Signet, 1992), pp. 81–82.

63 Lewis, *Babbitt*, p. 133.

64 Veblen, *Theory of the Leisure Class*, p. 128; Adam Gopnik, "Display Cases," *New Yorker*, April 26 and May 3, 1999, p. 179.

SIX   *The House as History*

1 Walter Benjamin, "The Work of Art in the Age of Mechanical Reproduction" and "On Some Motifs in Baudelaire," in *Illuminations*, trans. Harry Zohn (New York: Schocken Books, 1968), pp. 221–223, 186.

2 Real estate advertisement in Luxury Homes and Estates section, *New York Times Magazine*, March 22, 1998, p. 65.

3 Some examples: Rheinbeck Castle, Burg Rheinbeck, Bad Breisig, Germany; Palazzo Mangilli Valmarana, Venice (both offered in *Unique Homes*, February–March 1996); Castello Di Reschio, Perugia, Italy (offered by *Christie's Great Estates*, Fall 1996).

4 Todd S. Purdum, "Once Again, Tinseltown Brings Down the House," *New York Times*, July 31, 1998, p. A8.

5 Cartoon by Liza Donnelly, *New Yorker* (1989).

6 Thorstein Veblen, *The Theory of the Leisure Class* (1899; New York: Modern Library, 1931), p. 156.

7 Kathleen Howley, " 'This Old House' Star to be Spun Off," *Boston Globe*, March 1, 1998, pp. G1, G6.

8 Timothy Jack Ward, "Renovation Style, Now Just a Click Away," *New York Times*, April 2, 1998, p. C10.

9 Leon Edel, *Henry James* (New York: Harper & Row, 1985), p. 243.

10 Quoted in Ken Murray, *The Golden Days of San Simeon* (Garden City, NY: Doubleday, 1971), p. 36.

11 "Hearst at Home," *Fortune*, May 1931, pp. 56–68, 130.

12 Douglass Shand-Tucci, *The Art of Scandal: The Life and Times of Isabella Stewart Gardner* (New York: HarperCollins, 1997), p. 166.

13 Edel, *James*, p. 258.

14 Morris Carter, *Isabella Stewart Gardner and Fenway Court* (Boston: Houghton Mifflin, 1925), p. 183.

15 Lady Gregory quoted in Susan Sinclair, "Lady Gregory and Mrs. Gardner," *Fenway Court* (1972), p. 61; De Wolfe and Mrs. Frederick Winslow, from Gardner Museum Archives, quoted in Shand-Tucci, *Art of Scandal*, p. 232.

16 Shand-Tucci, *Art of Scandal*, p. 236, quoting from Barbara Strachey and Jayne Samuels, *Mary Berenson* (New York: Norton, 1983), p. 237.

17 Emily Post, *The Personality of a House* (New York: Funk & Wagnalls, 1930), pp. 232–233.

18 George Gordon, Lord Byron, "English Bards and Scotch Reviewers," lines 1029–1032, in *Lord Byron: Don Juan and Other Satirical Poems*, ed. Louis I. Bredvold (New York: Odyssey Press, 1935), p. 41.

19 Information provided by Patrick Pilkington, a dealer in fine architectural and decorative antiques, to Salvo, "the Site for Antique & Reclaimed Materials for Buildings & Gardens" (http:www.salvo.co.uk).

20 Monique P. Yazigi, "Where Those Who Would Be Gatsby Go," *New York Times*, August 23, 1998, sec. 9, p. 4.

21 Julie V. Iovine, "Making the Imperfect Picture Perfect," *New York Times*, July 17, 1997, pp. C1, C.7.

22 Molly Milligan, "Printers Row Units Get an 'Urban Country' Kick," *Chicago Sun-Times*, November 8, 1996, p. 10.

23 All listed in the catalogue for Ballard Designs, Atlanta, GA.

24 *OED*, 2d ed, "distressed," citing J. Judson, *What Every Woman Should Know About Furniture*, p. 33.

25 *OED*, 2d ed., "distressed," citing *Daily Telegraph*, October 4, 1966, 13/5.

26 Further citations for "distressed" from the *OED*, 2d ed., the last from Lilian Jackson Braun, *The Cat Who Ate Danish Modern* (1967).

27 Milligan, "Printers Row Unit Gets an 'Urban Country' Kick," p. 10.

28 Elizabeth Navas Finley, "Furniture That Looks Older than Its Years," *San Francisco Chronicle*, January 25, 1990, p. B4.

29 Christopher Petkanas, "An Essential Guide to Shopping in Provence," *Travel & Leisure*, May 1998, p. 172.

30 Patricia Leigh Brown, "A Hardware Store With a Big Ego," *New York Times*, February 20, 1997, p. C4.

31 Stephen Gordon, quoted in Brown, "Hardware Store," p. C4.

32 Patrick Dennis, *Auntie Mame* (New York: Vanguard, 1995), pp. 190, 193.

33 Robert J. Stoller, M.D., *Observing the Erotic Imagination* (New Haven: Yale University Press, 1985), p. 155.

34 Carol Stocker, "From $25 to a Cool Half Million," *Boston Globe,* February 26, 1998, p. F5.

35 Mark Verkennis, quoted in Tom Pelton, "Shades of Gray," *Boston Globe,* September 29, 1996, p. B3.

36 David Fennema, "The Great Beige Reversal," *Design Times,* February/March 1998, p. 84.

37 Adrian Dobinson, "The Colour Lottery: Conservation Police Dictate Colour Choice," *Salvo Magazine,* no. 31 (February/March 1996) (http:www.salvo.co.uk).

38 Jane Clifford, *Laura Ashley Decorates a London House* (Birmingham, England: Studio Press, 1985), p. 28.

39 Clifford, *Laura Ashley* p. 56.

40 *OED,* 2d ed., "nostalgia," citing J. Banks, *Journal* (1770) in J. Cook, *Journals* (1955).

41 Gwendolyn Wright, *Building the Dream: A Social History of Housing in America* (Cambridge, MA: MIT Press, 1981), p. 86.

42 Harold R. Shurtleff, *The Log Cabin Myth* (Cambridge, MA: Harvard University Press, 1939), p. 6; Daniel Webster, *Works* (1851 ed.), II, 30.

43 *Southern Literary Messenger* 24, p. 462, quoted in Lyon G. Tyler, *Cradle of the Republic* (Richmond, 1900), pp. 21–22, and in Shurtleff, *Log Cabin Myth,* p. 191.

44 Shurtleff, *Log Cabin Myth,* p. 194.

45 Julie V. Iovine, "Little House on the Brownstone," *New York Times,* January 4, 1996, p. C1.

46 Quoted in David Silverman, "Builders Just a Bunch of Romantics," *Chicago Tribune,* February 3, 1990, Home Guide section, p. 2.

47 Philip Langdon, "A Good Place to Live," *Atlantic,* March 1988, p. 39.

48 Phil Patton, "In Seaside, Florida, the Forward Thing Is to Look Backward," *Smithsonian,* January 1991, pp. 82ff.; Jeff Giles, "This Is Your Life," *Newsweek,* June 1, 1998, p. 62; Janet Maslin, "So What's Wrong With This Picture?" *New York Times,* June 5, 1998, p. B18.

49 Paul Goldberger, "Land of Make-Believe," *New Yorker,* June 22 & 29, 1998, p. 42.

50 Andrew Phillips, "The Disney Dream," *Maclean's*, July 21, 1997, p. 24; Wendy McNally, quoted in "Celebrating Southern Style," *Country Living*, May 1997, p. 58; John Henry, Orlando architect, quoted in Phillips, "Disney Dream," p. 24.

51 Warren Hoge, "One Prince's Cause is Another Man's Castle," *New York Times*, June 11, 1998, p. C1.

SEVEN *The Summer House*

1 Russell Baker, "Life Among the Swells," *New York Times*, May 15, 1998, p. A25.

2 Carolyn Klemm of Klemm Real Estate, quoted in Tracie Rozhon, "Still for Rent: Hamptons Summer," *New York Times*, May 21, 1998, p. C14.

3 Monique P. Yazigi, "Where Those Who Would Be Gatsby Go," *New York Times*, August 23, 1998, sec. 9, p. 4.

4 Mary S. Ludwig, *Your Dream Vacation Home* (Blue Ridge Summit, PA: Liberty Hall Press, 1991), p. ix.

5 Elisabeth Bumiller, "It's a Summer Thing," *New York Times*, May 16, 1996, p. 27.

6 Anna Mingione, quoted in David W. Chen, "Lower East Side on the Jersey Shore," *New York Times*, September 3, 1998, p. A26.

7 Judy Huggins Balfe, quoted in Jay Akasie, "Passing on the Summer House Is a Family Affair," *Inquirer and Mirror*, Nantucket, July 11, 1996, pp. 1C, 7C.

8 Bruce Mohl, "History Loses on Cape, Islands," *Boston Globe*, August 24, 1998, p. B6. James S. Gould, quoted in Mohl, "History Loses," p. B6.

9 Lou Sagar, *Zona Home: Essential Designs for Living* (New York: HarperStyle, 1996); "The Rise and Fall of Santa Fe Chic," *House & Garden*, October 1996, pp. 46–47.

10 Diane Saatchi, of Dayton-Halstead Real Estate in East Hampton, quoted in Tracie Rozhon, "In the Hamptons, Prices Are Soaring, but Not All," *New York Times*, October 11, 1996, p. A32.

11 Marianne Rohrlich, "In Mini-Storage, All the Comforts of Home," *New York Times*, February 26, 1998, p. C1.

12 Tracie Rozhon, "Even in Winter, Summer Rental Market's Hot," *New York Times*, February 23, 1997, p. 30.

13 *Builder's Guide to the Second Home Market* (Tacoma, WA: Douglas Fir Plywood Association, 1963), ch. 6, p. 6.

14 *OED*, 2d ed., "nostalgia," citing *The Listener*, October 3, 1957, 512/1.

15 *OED*, 2d ed., "cottage."

16 Mark Girouard, *Life in the English Country House* (New Haven: Yale University Press, 1978), p. 228.

17 Jane Austen, *Sense and Sensibility* (1811; London: Penguin, 1995), pp. 211–212.

18 Cited in Anthony D. King, *The Bungalow* (New York: Oxford University Press, 1995), p. 129.

19 Quoted in King, *Bungalow*, p. 135.

20 Robert Court, "Vacation Homes in the Woods," quoted in King, *Bungalow*, p. 135.

21 Henry Saylor, *Bungalows, Their Design, Construction and Furnishing (with Suggestions also for Camps, Summer Homes, and Cottages)* (New York: Grant Richards, 1911, 1912), p. 1.

22 King, *Bungalow*, p. 136.

23 Richard D. Lyons, "View Tax Outrages a Connecticut Town," *New York Times*, August 9, 1987, sec. 8, p. 9.

24 "A Surcharge for Blissful Vistas" (editorial), *Tampa Tribune*, August 8, 1996, p. 14.

25 Tom Kelly, "Putting a Price on a View: Another Tax on Homeowners?," *Seattle Times*, September 1, 1991, p. G1.

26 Carol Vogel, "In the Dunes," *New York Times Magazine*, May 31, 1987, p. 74.

27 Phil Patton, "In Seaside, Florida, the Forward Thing Is to Look Backward," *Smithsonian*, January 1991, pp. 82ff.

28 Ibid.

29 All from the Nantucket Association of Real Estate Brokers Supplement, *Inquirer and Mirror*, June 11 & June 18, 1998.

30 "Nantucket Real Estate Review," advertising supplement to the *Inquirer and Mirror*, June 6, 1996, pp. 10–11.

31 Robin Young, "The Cottage Is Top When Buyers Have Dunchoosin," *Times* (London), February 25, 1998, Home News section, p. 35. The Halifax surveyed over ten million homes.

32 Agatha Christie, *The Body in the Library* (1942; New York: Pocket Books, 1971), p. 24.

33 Gillian Gill, *Agatha Christie: The Woman and Her Mysteries* (New York: Free Press, 1990), p. x.

34 Jane Austen, *Sanditon,* in *Lady Susan, The Watsons, Sanditon,* ed. Margaret Drabble (Harmondsworth, England: Penguin, 1974), p. 159.

35 Austen, *Sanditon,* pp. 169–170.

EPILOGUE   *Why We Love Houses*

1 Cathleen Medwick, "Reading Room," *House & Garden,* September 1996, p. 242.

2 Jean-François de Bastide, *The Little House: An Architectural Seduction,* trans. Rodolphe el-Khoury (1879; New York: Princeton Architectural Press, 1996), p. 67.

3 Ibid., p. 80.

4 Ibid., p. 83.

Index